Native American Communities in Wisconsin, 1600–1960

Native American Communities in Wisconsin, 1600–1960

A Study of Tradition and Change

Robert E. Bieder

The University of Wisconsin Press

A North Coast Book

The University of Wisconsin Press
114 North Murray Street
Madison, Wisconsin 53715

3 Henrietta Street
London WC2E 8LU, England

All illustrations are courtesy of the State Historical Society of Wisconsin.
Negative numbers are as follows:
p. 107, WHi(X3)27564; p. 108, WHi(X3)27563; p. 109, WHi(X3)31270;
p. 110, WHi(X3)49405; p. 111, WHi(X3)45432; p. 112, WHi(X3)18849;
p. 113, WHi(X3)32486; p. 114, WHi(X3)49401; p. 115, WHi(X3)18850;
p. 116, WHi(X3)49409; p. 117, WHi (X3)18851; p. 118, WHi(X3)49410;
p. 119, WHi(X3)24965; p. 120, WHi(X3)23295; p. 121, WHi(W63)2943;
p. 122, WHi(X3)49407; p. 123, WHi(X3)9633; p. 178, WHi(X3)49402;
p. 179, WHi(W63)6107; p. 180, WHi(X3)49406; p. 181, WHi(X3)32710;
p. 182, WHi(X3)32712; p. 183, WHi(X3)12224; p. 184, WHi(X3)19009;
p. 185, WHi(X3)49403; p. 186, WHi(X3)49404; p. 187, WHi(X3)49411;
p. 188, WHi(X3)37329; p. 189, WHi(X3)23186; p. 190, WHi(X3)18963;
p. 191, WHi(X3)23184; p. 192, WHi(X3)26255; p. 193, WHi(X3)49408;
p. 194, WHi(X3)35353.

Library of Congress Cataloging-in-Publication Data
Bieder, Robert E. (Robert Eugene)
    Native American communities in Wisconsin, 1600–1960 /
Robert E. Bieder.
    302 p.   cm.
    "A North Coast book."
    Includes bibliographical references and index.
    ISBN 0-299-14520-4   ISBN 0-299-14524-7 (pbk.)
    1. Indians of North America—Wisconsin—History.
    2. Indians of North America—Wisconsin—Social life and customs.
    3. Indians of North America—Government relations.   I. Title.
    E78.W8B54   1995
    977.5'00497—dc20   94-24314

To Nancy O. Lurie,
long a supporter of Wisconsin Indians,
and to Leo Schelbert

Contents

Illustrations

Illustrations

Maps

Acknowledgments

Two grants, a travel grant from the National Endowment for the Humanities and a short-term grant from The Newberry Library, made possible the first of several short trips to Wisconsin and Chicago for research. The writing, however, proved more difficult. Although a draft of the book was written in Indiana, where I drew upon the facilities of Indiana University's American Indian Studies Research Institute and the Ohio Valley–Great Lakes Ethnohistorical Archives, the later reworking of the chapters was carried out in Malaysia; Germany; Washington, D.C.; Greece; and Hungary. Meanwhile, at the University of Wisconsin Press, Ezra "Sam" Diman—generously tolerant—grew accustomed to receiving cards with exotic stamps from all over Asia and Europe with cryptic messages on the book's progress. Then one day shortly after he had despaired of ever seeing a completed manuscript or ever hearing from me again, I called and told him the book was done.

This epic has many heros. Parts of the book were tried out before audiences at the University of Wisconsin–La Crosse; Indiana University; the John F. Kennedy Institute at the Free University–Berlin; Humboldt University, Berlin; the University of Basel; Massy University, New Zealand; Lajos Kossuth University, Hungary; University Paul Valéry, France; the University of Genoa; Joensuu University, and Tampere University, Finland. The comments and discussion generated on such occasions proved very helpful. I also wish to thank the National Endowment for the Humanities and The Newberry Library for the above-mentioned grants that were vital in the early stages of the work and the staffs of the State Historical Society of Wisconsin, Indiana University Library, The Newberry Library, and the Chicago Historical Society.

In any work of this kind, one owes much to those ethnographers and historians who previously explored the terrain, leaving signs for others to follow. One who deserves particular notice is Nancy Oestreich Lurie, whose works, notes, and ideas on the Winnebago and Menominee and whose ideas about community were indispensible for this study. Lurie, who has spent a lifetime writing about and championing the cause of Wisconsin's native peoples, is also one of the best sources on contemporary Wisconsin Indian affairs. Others who deserve mention for their encouragement and advice at critical junctions include: Maryellen Bieder, Martin Zanger, Raymond DeMallie, Douglas Parks, Leo Schelbert, Gerhart Baer, Walter Bieder, Renate Bader, Roy Goldblatt, Éva Becsei, John Aubrey, Meg Meneghel, Matthias Dietz-Lenssen, and Sandra Herzog, who died before the book went to press. I would also like to acknowledge the invaluable aid of those who read chapters or the whole book and made suggestions for its improvement. They helped to make the book better, contributed generously from their own research notes, and instructed me on aspects of Wisconsin tribal histories that had escaped my notice. Here I wish to thank again Martin Zanger, Nancy Oestreich Lurie, George and Louise Spindler, Peter Nabokov, Robert Hall, Ronald N. Satz, and Helen Hornbeck Tanner. Not the least is Sam Diman, Associate Director of the University of Wisconsin Press, who with unflinching good humor extended support and encouragement. Jeff C. Kaufmann constructed maps based on maps in the *Atlas of Great Lakes Indian History*, edited by Helen Hornbeck Tanner. Others at the press, editors Elizabeth Steinberg, Robin Whitaker, Carol Olsen, and Raphael Kadushin, who kept the fax lines hot between Wisconsin and Hungary and labored diligently over my text, contributed to giving form and precision to what started out years earlier as random thoughts, suppositions, and scratches on paper.

Native American Communities
in Wisconsin, 1600–1960

Introduction:
Songs from the Powwow

In the early 1970s, when I attended the powwows at the YMCA in St. Paul, Minnesota, the Indian world was exploding. At the powwow, listening to the singers who were seated in a circle and hunched over their drums with left hands cupping their ears, one could hear the explosion in the throbbing of the drums. When the leader started the song, singing high and clear and then like an eagle diving, pulling the other singers into the song, one could hear the reservation voices. They were singing both the past and the future. Dancers—men, women and children—swayed in step and song. Dancing the 49 dances, the round dances, the contest dances, their bodies listened carefully to the song that guided their steps. They were dancing both the past and the future. They came from Mille Lacs, White Earth, Red Lake, but also from Lac Courte Oreilles, St. Croix and Lac du Flambeau. They came from Tomah, from Black River Falls, from Oneida. The dancing, drumming, and talking could also be heard in Milwaukee and Chicago. The voices were saying: for too long they had been hungry; for too long they had been poor; for too long they had been sick; and for too long they had received inadequate education. But why were they speaking out now? Why were they singing? The songs subverted what the dominant culture said they had to be; it was a symbolic act of both incorporation and defiance, a rhetoric that could not be debased.

Perhaps it grew out of their experiences during the years when John Collier was commissioner of Indian affairs (1933–1945) and inspired in them a new hope, a new assertiveness, a sense that once again they could manage their affairs. Perhaps the crisis introduced into Indian Country and especially Wisconsin, by the threat of termination of reservation status and, to a lesser extent, by the relocation program, gripped Indians with a sense of urgency that spurred a will to resist the further destruction of their communities and loss of other reservations. Perhaps the 1961 American Indian Chicago Conference gave a certain resonance to Indian fears and concerns, fears that treaty rights would be ignored or nullified, fears that echoed all the way to the highest echelons of government. Perhaps Indians had acquired a new sophistication in learning how to manipulate television and the press for their own advantage. Perhaps the voices had always been saying these things, but non-Indian Americans had preferred not to hear. Whatever the reason, the winds of protest that gathered in the West—at Alcatraz, at Frank's Landing, at Wounded Knee—began to blow across Wisconsin.

Termination, relocation, and unemployment sent many Wisconsin Indians to Minneapolis, St. Paul, Madison, Milwaukee, and Chicago. At Lac du Flambeau, the Ojibwa saw brochures produced by the Bureau of Indian Affairs (BIA) depicting the wonderful world of opportunities that awaited Indians in Chicago. The pictures implied that all they saw could be theirs if they were to move to the city. Ojibwa youth, eager to improve their condition and enter the glamorous life the city seemed to offer, said goodbye to the reservation and headed south.

They did not find the city as exciting and glamorous as its depiction in the BIA literature. Instead they found dirty, cockroach-infested lodgings in the "crash area" of north Chicago, an area where poor newcomers and transients find accommodations; an area of cheap boarding houses, bars, dirt, drugs, and crime. Some who ventured to Chicago became involved in the activities of the Chicago Indian Center. Others, with the impatience and impetuousness of youth, joined more radical organizations like the Chicago Indian Village. Still others, not so adventurous, settled down passively to "getting urbanized."[1] Some escaped back to the reservation, but most stayed.

Urban areas did provide some opportunity and comforts not found on the reservations. Indian run organizations helped to make transition to city life easier. Still, life on the reservation beckoned, and Indians returned for visits, for family affairs, for powwows and ceremonials, or when unemployed. They would pile into cars and head north or east into the night, happy to be headed home even if only for a short while. Invigorated, they would head back and launch another attack on the city.

Among the Wisconsin tribes, only the reservation status of the Menominee was terminated, and their fight to restore reservation status to Menominee land must be seen in the threatening context of loss of

4

community and tribal identity. Included in the termination plan was the setting up of Menominee Enterprises, Inc. (MEI), an organization devised to oversee Menominee resources and tribal assets when the old reservation received county status. Although all Menominee were shareholders in MEI, they had little control over the board of directors of the new organization, which included both Menominee and non-Menominee, with the latter in the majority. Despite the fact that many Menominee objected to handing over control of their resources to non-Menominee, they were outmaneuvered by arguments that such a board would more efficiently oversee Menominee resources and "convince the state that the corporation had a stable management basis."[2] As set up, MEI strengthened a Menominee elite who, while sharing power with a non-Menominee majority, "could expand their control over Menominee affairs."[3] No longer would they have to win approval from the Menominee General Council for land leases or sales and other major decisions, but could now move unencumbered in their negotiations and sales of Menominee resources.[4]

When the MEI sought to construct a lake and then sell off lakefront plots for tourist homes in order to offset a mounting tax burden, scattered resentment over the corporation's handling of Menominee land and resources crystalized in the tribe. But the anger among the Menominee ran even deeper. The changes brought about through the termination of reservation status were destroying tribal self-determination, and many Menominee resented being excluded "from participating in corporate business and hence tribal affairs." When repeated MEI failures brought staggering poverty to the Menominee, they believed less and less in the corporation's promise of better times ahead and the claims of a light at the end of the tunnel. To the Menominee, the tunnel seemed awfully long and the light kept going out. What they saw was not a light but "discrimination in the Shawano school system." Along with being "disinherited from their share of tribal wealth by closure of tribal rolls," they saw "young Menominee children dropping out of school at alarming rates and abandoning hope in any future for themselves or the tribe."[5]

Rallies to protest this and the actions of MEI led to the creation in 1970 of DRUMS (Determination of Rights and Unity for Menominee Shareholders), which both harassed MEI with litigation, eventually taking over the corporation, and began lobbying in Washington, D.C., for the return of reservation status. Although Congress now disavowed termination, few thought the government would return already terminated tribal land to reservation status. To the surprise of many, in 1973 the lobbying efforts paid off when the Menominee Restoration Bill passed Congress and was signed by President Richard M. Nixon.[6]

The scar of termination, however, did not heal quickly. The Menominee Restoration Committee, set up to oversee the restoration process, found itself, on the one hand, resisting the efforts of the government to reassert itself as arbiter of tribal destiny and, on the other hand, appeasing disgruntled Menominee who feared government involvement in Menominee affairs. Furthermore, the Menominee Restoration Committee, headed by Ada Deer, began to make decisions without tribal input. Incensed by being snubbed, many Menominee protested the actions of the restoration committee. The protest spilled over into violence when a group calling itself the Menominee Warrior Society took over the Alexian Brothers novitiate in the nearby town of Gresham. The action proved misguided, but it gave vent to frustrations building within the community and had symbolic value in that it highlighted grass-rooters' anger over being ignored.[7]

While the Menominee moved forward into a new tribal future, there were other disruptions that derailed community efforts to promote economic reform. Factionalism again beset the tribe, and there was a series of violent deaths.[8] Slowly, however, the Menominee moved on to better times with both reservation and spirit intact.

The Menominee were more fortunate than other terminated tribes in that they not only regained and preserved their homeland, but in the process also reignited a sense of community pride and tribal identity. For the Menominee, the reservation homeland served as an important link to tribal identity. Such is also the case with other Wisconsin Indians. To promote reservation life and combat the drift to urban areas and the erosion of tribal communities, Wisconsin tribes and the Great Lakes Intertribal Council (GLITC), founded in 1961, initiated programs for reservation economic development.

The Ojibwa were stressing this importance when in 1971 they, along with some 25 American Indian Movement (AIM) members, took over the Winter Dam near the Lac Courte Oreilles reservation. "We have to do something to show the white people we will no longer tolerate being kicked around. We must do these things to preserve our culture and to instill some pride in our people."[9] The dam, built in 1921 by Northern States Power Company, flooded large sections of the reservation and destroyed rice beds and waterfowl habitat. In 1973, despite the nearby power project, many Ojibwa still did not have electricity.[10]

Shortly after the Winter Dam take over, members of the Milwaukee chapter of AIM occupied the vacant Milwaukee Coast Guard station, later releasing it for use to an Indian school that had outgrown its old quarters in a church basement. In Milwaukee, as in Chicago, discrimination against Indians in the city school system led to alternative Indian-run schools. After a year of using the Coast Guard station as a school, the Indians agreed to a new educational program for native peoples, WE Indian program, to take place in neighborhood schools, so the station was given up.[11]

All these events, the restoration of the Menominee reservation, the occupation of Winter Dam, Alexian Brothers novitiate and the Coast Guard station, in conjunction with national Indian unrest, focused public attention in Wisconsin on local Indian concerns. A series of newspaper articles drew further notice to the plight of Indians on Wisconsin reservations.[12] Added to these were articles on the Trail of Broken Treaties, which passed through Wisconsin on its way to Washington, D.C., in 1972, further articulating the callousness of American society toward the land's original people.

But by the late 1970s, the public's patience and concern with Indian problems turned to apathy. Indians protesting in colorful regalia drew little response, and newspapers turned to other news. Growing economic problems in American society brought a cool response to Indian demands that Americans recognize the legal rights of Native Americans. Indeed, such demands began to engender open hostility in some American communities.

Many Americans believed that the Indians in their legal pursuit of treaty rights had gone too far. In northern Wisconsin, where Indians had won legal battles upholding their fishing rights, sportsmen, resort owners, and others dependent on tourism grew hostile, attacking Indians both verbally and physically. The anger increased when Indians objected to non-Indians' destruction of their wild rice areas. In turn, many Americans objected to Indian hunting rights and demanded that Indians be forced to obey state hunting laws.[13]

The facts that the Ojibwa fish hatchery at Lac du Flambeau introduced thousands of fish into the waterways of northern Wisconsin and that tribes enforced their own hunting restrictions on their members were ignored by organizations opposed to tribal rights, such as the Interstate Congress on Equal Rights and Responsibilities and the Citizens League for Equal Rights. What these groups wanted was not only to overturn court decisions that were in favor of treaty rights but also to terminate reservations and all treaty rights, which they interpreted as special minority privileges.[14] What these groups were advocating, in essence, was the destruction of Wisconsin Indian communities. In promoting such views, these groups were calling for the forced acculturation policy that the federal government has implicitly and explicitly promoted for over 200 years.

Books often have curious inceptions, and this one is not an exception. When coming of age in the 1950s in upstate New York, I had the opportunity to associate with Seneca and Mohawk youths. At this time, I also began to learn from them their songs and dances and acquired an interest in Iroquois history and an awareness of contemporary concerns that beset Indians in the region. But while these incidents acted as early conditioning influences on my development and led me, upon entering college, to explore further the histories of American Indian cultures, they were only indirectly responsible for my writing this book. More immediate causes were a law case and informal discussions at a meeting of the American Historical Association.

In 1978, while serving as acting director of the Native American Studies Program at the University of Illinois, Chicago, the U.S. Department of Justice approached me and asked if I would help them as a researcher and expert witness for a case involving the Sault Ste. Marie Chippewa (Ojibwa). The Department of the Interior had granted the Sault Ste. Marie Chippewa tribal status. This was contested by the city of Sault Ste. Marie and resulted in a lawsuit brought by the city against the Department of the Interior. The Department of Justice was brought in to defend the Department of the Interior and its tribal-status decision. My task was to research and compile data supporting that department and the tribal status of the Sault Ste. Marie Chippewa.

After three and a half years, the case was decided in favor of the Department of the Interior and Chippewas. With the data I had accumulated on this case, I decided to expand my investigation and explore more deeply the underlying conflict between the Sault Ste. Marie Chippewa and the city of Sault Ste. Marie as well as the nature of the Chippewa community and its ability to continue over time. I had in mind a comment made by anthropologist Nancy Oestreich Lurie that both historians and anthropologists had generally ignored the sense and importance of community to Indian people.[15] By this, I understood her to mean that community had been studied as a context in which social, economic, political, and religious activities were conceived and carried out, but had never been examined in its own right. What mechanisms were used to redefine and preserve community over time? This, I thought, I would investigate with my Sault Ste. Marie Chippewa data.

While in the process of organizing my data into not so neat piles on my office floor, I attended an American Historical Association meeting and met Sam Diman of the University of Wisconsin Press. By way of conversation, I sounded out the possible interest the press might have in my Sault Ste. Marie study. There was none, but he did ask me if I knew anyone who could take on a study of Wisconsin Indians. I mentioned several names including, the most obvious, Nancy Oestreich Lurie of the Milwaukee Public Museum. A day later, taking the same bus to the airport, Sam and I met again, and he asked me if I would be interested in writing such a book. Still thinking of my Sault Ste. Marie project, I declined, but I did say that I thought such a work ought to focus on the sense of community and how this sense was transmitted over time.

Two weeks later, Sam called reporting that the press was interested in my idea for such a book and asked again if I would consider writing it. Extremely flattered by his call but mindful of the piles of Sault Ste. Marie data scattered over my floor, I again declined. My rejection was also based on a practicality. Employed as I then was as book review editor for the *American Historical Review,* I had little opportunity to engage in the kind of research that such a project entailed. Sam, however, was persistent and said he was putting a contract in the mail and hoped that I would reconsider.

I did eventually reconsider. I envisioned a book for a general audience and not for the specialist, and because of the sheer scope of the project and the data involved, I decided to eschew an elaborate anthropological-sociological interpretation of community and opted instead for a narrative approach. While this approach downplayed a structural reading of community, I hoped that it would make the resulting text more congenial to the general reader.

When conceptualizing the book, I rejected the idea of writing a series of tribal histories. Excellent histories and ethnographies of Wisconsin tribes already exist. Book-length studies on individual groups include the works of George and Louise Spindler, Felix Keesing, and Patricia K. Ourada on the Menominee; the studies of Paul Radin and Nancy Oestreich Lurie on the Winnebago; of Harold Hickerson, Ronald N. Satz, Edmund J. Danziger, Thomas Vennum, and Christopher Vecsey on the Ojibwa (Chippewa); of James Clifton on the Potawatomi; and of Ruth Landes on the Santee Sioux. These remain the best accounts for students pursuing the study of a particular tribe.[16] I saw my work as expanding upon the excellent short account *Wisconsin Indians* written by Nancy Oestreich Lurie and covering a longer period than Carol Mason's *Introduction to Wisconsin Indians: Prehistory to Statehood*. I also sought to produce a more unified interpretation of Wisconsin Indian history than that provided by John Boatman's *Wisconsin American Indian History and Culture: A Survey of Selected Aspects;* or his *My Elders Taught Me: Aspects of Western Great Lakes American Indian Philosophy* and Donald L. Fixico's *An Anthology of Western Great Lakes Indian History,* which employ topical approaches.[17]

The present study, I decided, should be a general work, synthesizing other accounts, and presenting an interpretation of the historical evolution of and resistance by Wisconsin Indian groups to the destruction of their communities beginning in the 1600s, the period when French and Iroquois policies in the East sent shock waves through Indian communities in the Midwest, to the mid-twentieth century when the United States government embarked upon a policy of termination of government support to tribal groups. In exploring this resistance, I attempt to situate it in the changing natural and manmade environments of the region.

I begin the book with a chapter on the Wisconsin environment. In this I am not suggesting environmental determinism but presenting the environment as a limiting framework within which Indian people constructed their cultures and communities. Seeing the environment in this way does not negate, of course, the fact that Indian people manipulated their environment. They did. How they did is the focus of my second chapter, where I offer an interpretation of Wisconsin Indian cultures at the time of contact. This interpretation, although to a degree hypothetical, is built upon archaeological findings and early French accounts. In the third chapter, I explore the years of the French among the Wisconsin Indians, the beginnings of the fur trade, and the French effect on Wisconsin Indian communities. Chapter four focuses on the British in Wisconsin and how Indian communities were affected by contact with the British and the growing economic importance of the fur trade in their communities. Neither the French nor the British were interested in extensive land acquisition and concentrated instead on the fur trade. This situation changed with the arrival of the Americans in Wisconsin. The loss of land, the creation of reservations, and the stresses and strains on Wisconsin Indian communities resulting from the growing American presence in Wisconsin are the subjects of the next three chapters.

Although I would have liked to bring the book up to the present, my decision not to was based on the lack of opportunity to do the local research and intensive interviews that I felt necessary for such an account. I concur with others that a history of the last 30 years would be valuable, but I leave that task to others.

The narrative I present here on Wisconsin Indians underscores their tragic situation. Tragic not in the inevitability of cultural change, for all cultures change, but in the increasing frustration that tribal people experienced in trying to control the rate and direction of change. Lacking political and economic power, they often were forced to expend tremendous energy just to secure the few gains they made. But it was tragic also in another sense. For cultures that "were touched into being by words," as Ojibwa author Gerald Vizenor claims, words in the contact situation lost their value and became debased.[18] Rhetoric no longer clarified but now masked meanings; words were contested and discourse was obfuscated. Wisconsin Indian people, who valued words, had put their faith and trust in the words of a government whose honor was too often compromised by social, economic, and political interests at the local as well as at the national level. In time, words became a casualty of contact, and the faith and trust in them turned to cynicism. Discourse became strained or broke down altogether. By the mid-twentieth century, nonviolent and militant protest seemed for many the only rhetoric possible in the field of political (power) discourse.

1

The Land That Winter Made

A long time ago, according to Winnebago legend, Earthmaker sent
Trickster to earth to make it habitable for humans. Trickster's many adventures and scrapes in carrying out his assignment made amusing and
instructive tales for the Winnebago. Trickster possessed power that allowed him to talk to animals, to plants, rocks, and wind, and to the creatures of the spirit world. He could turn himself into an animal, a plant,
or a woman, and then back into a man. He possessed power and cun-
ning, and his name, Trickster, well describes his personality. But despite
all his abilities and talents, he could not keep out of trouble. It was this
aspect of Trickster's life that provided both farce and instruction to the
Winnebago.[1]

Other Wisconsin tribes also had culture heroes like Trickster. Among
the Ojibwa, Manabozho (sometimes spelled Nanabozho) possessed similar powers, and also had similar adventures and misadventures. Through
the tales of Trickster or Manabozho, Indians learned that their world
consisted of more than just themselves and what they could see and feel;
it consisted of more than just humans, animals, plants, earth, water, air,
and stars. Spirits that could help or hurt humans roamed the world. The
world was alive with spiritual forces that humans could not overpower
but could learn to manipulate and draw upon for assistance. This required humans not only to learn about the physical world but also to recognize its spiritual dimension. It is this physical world of the Wisconsin
Indians that it is necessary to learn about before proceeding further.

A long glacial winter of ice, water, and frigid winds blasting out of
the North across mountains of frozen waste is what shaped Wisconsin.
About 15,000 B.C., or 17,000 years ago, the mountains of ice known as

12

the Wisconsin glacier began their slow retreat. They left in their wake a scarred landscape. Like a giant grinder, the glaciers moved boulders and ground rock to sand, leveled hills in some places, and in other places raised up hills of earth and rock. As the glaciers melted, the water tumbled down and swept across the land carving out rivers and streams, or lay in depressions forming lakes and swamps. A long spring of 10,000 years followed the glacial winter. Not until about 3000 B.C. did plants and animals in Wisconsin evolve into their modern forms. The empires of Greece and Rome were still waiting to make their appearance on the stage of world history, and Columbus still had to wait 4,500 years to sail to what he thought was the fabulous world of India. As humans in Europe, Africa, and Asia groped toward forms of civilization, men and women in the Western Hemisphere also sorted through their world and discovered ways to make life easier in a hard and, at times, very hostile environment.

Nature is unstable; what today is considered normal will probably not be normal 1,000 years hence, nor was it normal 1,000 years ago. Climatic variation over the centuries has affected the growing season and determined which plants have survived. The flora in turn determined which animals would inhabit a particular area. Heavy snows and rains or droughts can change riverbeds or lake levels, affecting not only aquatic plants but also fish and animal populations. Periodic disease epidemics among animal populations have seriously reduced their numbers and had ramifications for human populations as well.

It is no wonder that the Winnebago Indians of Wisconsin appreciate Trickster's efforts to make their world a better place in which to live. What are the features of this land that, according to Trickster, people would eventually inhabit? Scarred by glaciers and softened by the long postglacial spring, the land exhibits a varied habitat.

THE GEOGRAPHICAL PROVINCES OF WISCONSIN

The Wisconsin land mass is usually divided into five zones according to soil and biotic community. The parameters of these zones are often blurred when one section blends into another, so biotic communities characteristic of one zone may appear in another. It is best to remember that biotic zone descriptions are based on a frequency distribution of species.

In the far north of Wisconsin on either side of the Bayfield Peninsula and forming a narrow shelf along the Lake Superior coast is the Lake Superior Lowland. Although the first documented French explorer, Jean

Nicolet, who in 1634 visited the land mass that is now the state of Wisconsin, did not mention what he thought of the land he saw,[2] another Frenchman, Pierre Esprit Radisson, who came shortly after, did record his impressions of the country. Although the accounts of his wanderings were written years later and so must be used with care, Radisson's memories of the area around Chequamegon Bay were quite effusive. Here, in the Lake Superior Lowland, he found a land wooded and with abundant game, fish, and waterfowl. He mentioned killing moose, deer, caribou, bear, and buffalo. Despite this favorable report, however, the winter that he spent in this region with its deep snow and periodic lack of game proved a time of extreme hardship.[3]

When the Jesuit missionary Father Claude Allouez visited the Chequamegon area in 1665 and established his mission of Saint Esprit at La Pointe, where the Huron and Ottawa had taken refuge from Iroquois attacks, he found fields of Indian corn. But despite the warming effects of Lake Superior, the growing season was still too brief for extensive agriculture.[4]

South and east of the Lake Superior Lowland in an area of low rolling hills are the remains of mountains worn down by glacial action. These hills sweeping across the northern third of Wisconsin, interspersed with small lakes, swamps, and crossed by streams, are known as the Northern Highland. Here, in this sandy, stony land, an extensive boreal forest of mixed hardwood, pines, and spruce predominated, but along the streams and in the swamps or in areas where fires had swept through the hardwoods or pine forests, white birch and aspen grew. The lakes and streams of the Northern Highland proved an attractive environment for many fur-bearing animals such as snowshoe hare, red fox, wolf, martin, lynx, mink, muskrat, beaver, fisher, and otter. In the mixed hardwood forests of the interior, where the understory growth of bushes could not survive in dim light, deer and other browsing and grazing animals that depended on such for food were absent. Some moose, woodland caribou, and black bear existed, but in small numbers.

Game was extremely scarce the winter Radisson spent in this region near the headwaters of the Chippewa River. Deep snow in the region made hunting difficult, and Radisson, like the Indians he stayed with, was forced to eat powdered tree bark, ground up bones, shoe leather, and old animal skins in order to survive. Even the dogs went into the pot in order "to fill our bellies."[5] The dense forest and heavy boughs created a depressing atmosphere that Radisson found "as dark as in a cellar."[6]

In 1766, Jonathan Carver, an Englishman traveling in the region of the upper Chippewa River, complained as Radisson had of "a most dreary wilderness of trees or timber of all sorts, but principally birch and uneven land."[7] Only along the stream beds where birch and aspen grew were any animals to be found. The area still struck travelers as dismal in 1834, as when Henry Rowe Schoolcraft and Douglass Houghton, two Americans returning down the Bois Brule River from an exploring expedition to the source of the Mississippi River, recorded seeing from the riverbank immense tamarack swamps, scanty deciduous undergrowth, and beyond them the river hills covered with pine.[8]

The Central Plain that sweeps southward like a giant crescent from the St. Croix River in the west to Green Bay in the east and extends below the Northern Highland appealed more to the browsing needs of the white-tailed deer. This region supported a varied environment of plants and animals. Leaving Lake Pepin on the Mississippi and traveling up the lower Chippewa River, Carver was impressed with the land. Here were great meadows. "I found excellent good land and very pleasant country. One might travel all day and only see now and then a small pleasant groves [sic] of oak and walnut. This country is covered with grass which affords excellent pasturage for the buffeloe which are very plenty [sic]. Could see them at a distance under the shady oaks like cattle in a pasture and sometimes a drove of an hundred or more shading themselves in these groves at noon day which [afforded] a very pleasant prospect for an uninhabited country." Carver found the region also populated with elk so tame that a hunter could approach them quite closely before they would move.[9] In this mixed coniferous-decidous forest of sugar maple, basswood, beech, hemlock, and yellow birch were vast areas of open savannas where prairie grass, as Carver noted along the Fox River, grew as high as a man's head and so thick that it was difficult to walk through.[10] Situated throughout these savannas were oak groves and pine barrens that afforded protection to both browsing and grazing animals. Here too were buttes and mesas, massive land formations, and in the low areas conifer swamps and marshes that drew waterfowl and provided fertile ground for the growth of white cedar, tamarack, and black spruce.

South and west of the Central Plain and stretching to the Mississippi River lay the Western Upland. This area, unaffected directly by glacial action and hence known as the driftless area, contains deep valleys where rivers of melted ice rushing from the glaciers sliced through the hills on their way to the Mississippi. The Wisconsin River cut through the center of the Western Upland and watered the rich soil and luxurious prairie grasses that supported large numbers of buffalo, elk, and deer. Here along the river, stands of oak, maple, and elm could also be found. In the rich alluvial soil along the Wisconsin River, Carver found villages of the Sauk and Fox Indians with extensive fields of corn, melons, squash, beans, and tobacco.[11]

By 1820, when Schoolcraft passed through the Wisconsin River valley, the flora and fauna were much the same as described by the earlier French and English travelers, but with two exceptions: "The largest animals now found along its banks, are the deer, the bear, and the fox. The elk and the buffalo, have been driven off many years ago."[12]

The last geographical area is the Eastern Ridges and Lowlands stretching north and south from just west of Green Bay and the Fox River to Lake Michigan. Evidence of glacial action on the land is seen in the low ridge of hills, also running north and south, from southern Wisconsin to the Door Peninsula. Known as moraines, these ridges mark the extent of the Wisconsin glacier. The vast Horicon Marsh and Lake Winnebago, sustaining large numbers of waterfowl, are situated in this region, and the Fox River, its source near Portage, Wisconsin, flows north and slices through prime glacial soil before emptying into Green Bay. Historically, mixed hardwood and evergreen forests interspersed with swamp conifers predominated around Green Bay and stretched out to the end of Door Peninsula and extended almost to Lake Winnebago. From Lake Winnebago southward, open prairie grasslands spotted with groves of oaks and other hardwoods prevailed.

In this region and near Green Bay the Menominee Indians lived; it was here that their culture hero, Me'napus, the Great Hare, and all the game animals were born. According to Menominee legend, Me'napus was born soon after the creation of the world. "He who created all things, having completed this island [earth], then created man. When he had completed him, he gave him Indian-corn and squash and beans; these things he doled out to his creatures." Here near Green Bay in the mixed hardwood and evergreen forests the creator placed an old woman and a girl child. This girl child would give birth to Me'napus and all the game animals. As the Menominee relate, "Oh, truly it was beautiful, as the game-animals were born; all of them even then started away in single file."[13]

The region around Green Bay and south to the tip of Lake Michigan was very productive in the mid-1600s. Radisson left a glowing account of its productivity. "I can assure you," he wrote, "I like no country as I have there wherein we wintered, for whatever a man could desire was to be had in great plenty, viz., stags, fishes in abundance, and all sorts of meat, [and] corn enough."[14] Heading south along the Lake Michigan coast, Radisson proved equally enthusiastic. Noticing the Indian towns and countryside, he was struck with the beauty and fruitfulness of the land.[15] Perhaps Radisson can be excused for his hyperbole regarding the plenitude of eastern Wisconsin, because he wrote this description years later and memory often twists reality into strange shapes. Although he found the winters near Green Bay less severe than those up on the Lake Superior shore at Chequamegon, Radisson would still have experienced excruciatingly cold winters in the Green Bay area, with the fear of starvation real.

Certainly in 1669 when Father Allouez began his missionary work in the area of Green Bay, he found little cause for enthusiasm regarding the abundance of the country. Rather than finding "all sorts of meat," during the winter, as Radisson had, Allouez fed on Indian corn, acorns, and a few fish. He informed his readers, however, that during the summer the tribes in the vicinity grew fields of corn, squash, beans, and tobacco.[16] This observation is substantiated today by archaeological and palynological findings of village sites in this same area. Because of the moderating influence of Lake Michigan on the climate in the Green Bay area, the growing season was longer than in comparable areas of Wisconsin at this latitude.

Heading south from Green Bay along the Fox River to Lake Winnebago and then through the Fox River passage to the Wisconsin River and the Mississippi River beyond, both French and later English travelers found a delightful country. Along the Fox River and at Lakes Winnebago, Butte des Morts, and Poygan, the water teemed with fish and wildfowl, the latter drawn by the profusion of wild rice, which at times obscured the shores of the lakes and so blocked the rivers as to hinder canoe travel. The land around the Fox River was not heavily timbered, and the few groves that did dot the rolling prairie consisted primarily of oak and hickory, with some pine.

Wisconsin's waters are a vital resource. Lake Superior and Lake Michigan were water highways facilitating the migrations of eastern tribes into the Wisconsin region. In time the French used these same waterways seeking furs and empire. The river systems were also part of this great communication system. In a day when canoes were the most practical method of travel, waterways served as highways for both Indians and Euro-Americans for hundreds of years. From Green Bay both Indians and Euro-Americans traveled south down the Fox River, portaging to the Wisconsin River near the present-day city of Portage and then down the Wisconsin to the Mississippi River. The Mississippi served as a river road going north and, when combined with the Chippewa River, the St. Croix, and the Bois Brule rivers, trips could be made all the way to Lake Superior. Numerous lakes, like Lake Winnebago, and smaller streams allowed access into the interior.[17]

More important than providing access for travel, the water system nurtured an ecosystem from which Indian people obtained most of their food.[18] Fish, vital to their diet, included lake trout, whitefish, sturgeon, and siskowet. Allouez mentions weirs erected across the lower Fox River early in the spring to catch migrating sturgeon. Deep pools at the mouths of the northern rivers were prime fishing sites. The Mississippi River and other slow-moving rivers in southern Wisconsin were home to channel catfish and shovelnose sturgeon. Mussels were another primary source of protein for Indian people.

Aquatic plants in the waterways attracted waterfowl such as geese, ducks, and swans, but perhaps no plant was more attractive to them than the wild rice that grew in dense stands in the shallow lake margins and slow-moving waters of the Fox and St. Croix drainage areas. Harvested from canoes primarily by the Menominee, Ojibwa, and perhaps the Winnebago in August and September, wild rice when dried and stored sustained Indian communities throughout the winter and spring, when game and other sources of food were scarce.[19] Unfortunately, wild rice yields fluctuate over three-year cycles, with only one year in three providing abundant yields.

Humans Shape Their Environments

The waterways also hosted an ecosystem with trees and plants that Indians utilized to make life more comfortable. Bark from the white birch trees was used to construct their canoes, their houses, and numerous household utensils such as food containers, storage boxes, and writing scrolls. Many aquatic plants were also used for medicinal purposes. The sand cherry growing along the Lake Michigan shore yielded edible fruit, and the inner bark substituted for tobacco.

Environments place certain limitations on lifestyle choices available to a people. Obviously, a short growing season or poor soil will inhibit the extensive development of agriculture. Likewise, where fish are more plentiful than large game, people will expend more energy developing techniques for catching fish. The cultural adjustments of Wisconsin Indians to their environment, or what one environmental historian has

18

termed "ethno-ecological technique,"[20] involved making use of different environmental options throughout the year. Knowledge of their environment led Wisconsin Indians to utilize seasonally those foods that offered the greatest energy for effort expended: for example, fish and maple sugar in the early spring; fish, berries, corn, beans, and squash in the summer; wild rice, waterfowl, and large game animals in the fall.[21]

Wisconsin Indians, however, did more than merely adjust to their environments; they took active roles in shaping their environments and forcing concessions from them. In essence they continued the process where Trickster left off. In harvesting wild rice, Wisconsin Indians would knowingly or unknowingly scatter the rice and thus take a hand in planting new beds; in clearing the land for garden plots or fields in which to grow corn, they would kill trees by girdling them and burn off smaller trees and understory providing both garden spaces and grazing areas for deer. Other times man's alteration of the environment produced devastating results, as when Indians overhunted or, during the years of the fur trade, overtrapped and depleted the fur-bearing animal population, which in turn forced villages to remove to new areas in a search for more furs. This often introduced cultural changes. So humans not only adjust to their environment but also respond to it creatively and strive to mold it to their needs. A continuous cycle of adjustment and change is ensured.

This is one of the issues this book seeks to explore. It will consider how Indian communities were affected by their environments and how in creating and reshaping their social worlds they also reshaped their environments, both natural and manmade. But the more important question for exploration is how changes produced by either nature or humans affected Indian communities.

2

How They Lived in the Old Time

There are problems in learning about Wisconsin Indians in what they refer to as the Old Time, that time before Europeans arrived on the scene. To be sure, there are artifacts and bones, but what do they tell about the people who are known as the Menominee, the Winnebago, the Ojibwa? They tell little of their human qualities and nothing of their personalities. At best they provide only a blurred profile of a people. We know nothing of their feelings, hopes, dreams, or fears.

Forest, farm field, and asphalt now cover their village sites, and in the night that has descended upon their history, there are only a few lights to guide us. So what do we look for? Here, as in non-Indian history, interpreting the past presents certain cultural problems. Contemporary culture and personal perspective distort interpretations of the past and permit the historian to see only certain things, and then not necessarily as they actually were but as he or she expects them to have been. So one must be careful in writing history, especially the history of another culture, since the so-called historical facts are filtered through lenses of our own making.

Despite cultural differences, there are certain needs that all humans have in common. Everyone needs to sleep and eat, enjoy social contact with family and others, and possess shelter and clothing. In meeting these requirements Wisconsin Indians demonstrated similarities. Family structure varied and included nuclear families, that is, two parents and children, and extended families consisting of a nuclear family and one or more close relatives. Food items among Wisconsin Indians varied with the locale, but preparation of food generally remained similar from place to place. Before acquiring metal pots from the French, food was roasted, steamed in pits, or boiled in pottery jars or by adding hot stones to clay, bark, or wood containers filled with water. Clothing consisted primarily of leather and fur robes. And shelters were made of bark, skins, or woven reeds.

The Menominee were the first Algonquian-speaking people[1] in Wisconsin. In time, other Algonquian-speaking people took up residence there, including the Illinois, Sauk, Fox, Mascouten, Miami, Kickapoo, and Ottawa peoples, but only the Algonquian-speaking Ojibwa (also known as Chippewa) and the Potawatomi moved to Wisconsin and remained. Also in Wisconsin were Siouan-speaking peoples,[2] including the Winnebago and the Santee, or the Mystic Lake Sioux (Mdewakanton), and, in the early 1600s, perhaps the Iowa, a Chiwere-Siouan-speaking people distantly related to the Winnebago.

In the early nineteenth century three other Indian groups also came to Wisconsin, having been moved there by the United States government: the Iroquian-speaking Oneida from New York, and the Algonquian-speaking Stockbridge-Munsee and Brothertown. Originally from Massachusetts, the Stockbridge in the 1780s accepted an offer from the Oneida to reside among them in New York. Later a group of Mahican, Mohegan, Pequot, Narragansett, Montauk, and other Algonquians moved near the Oneida and became known as the Brothertown Indians. This group of Brothertown Indians was later joined by a group of Delaware Indians known as the Brotherton Indians because of a reservation given to them at Brotherton, New Jersey, in 1758. Eventually these combined groups joined the Oneida in Wisconsin.[3]

Unfortunately, historical information on Wisconsin Indians for the 1600s is rather sparse. Furthermore, the disruptive social changes produced after contact with Euro-Americans complicate and prevent any accurate description of precontact social structures. The French left few records regarding Indian society for this region, and archaeologists, who have provided information on Wisconsin Indians for the prehistoric period, have not investigated the late 1600s, the postcontact period, with equal success.[4] Despite these constraints, ethnohistorians have drawn upon archaeological and other sources to construct hypothetical models of Wisconsin Indian cultures for the early and mid-1600s.

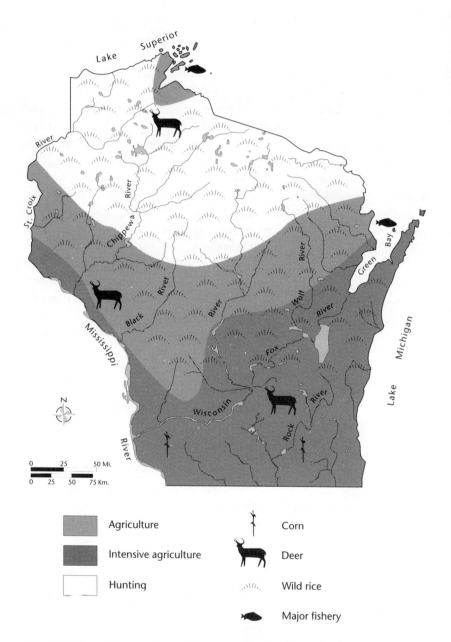

Map 1. Subsistence Patterns. Drawn from a portion of map 4 in the *Atlas of Great Lakes Indian History*, edited by Helen Hornbeck Tanner, University of Oklahoma Press, 1987.

ALGONQUIAN CULTURES

The Central Algonquian Pattern

In Wisconsin the Algonquian cultures can be divided into two basic patterns, or what anthropologist Bruce Trigger describes as the Central Algonquian Pattern and the Eastern Collecting Pattern.[5] The first pattern includes the cultures of the Menominee, Sauk, Fox, Illinois, Potawatomi, Kickapoo, Shawnee, Miami, and Mascouten peoples, who inhabited the woodlands and prairie regions.[6] Although there were differences among these groups, they generally shared in a subsistence pattern that emphasized maize horticulture and seasonal hunting and gathering. In summer and winter they were sedentary and lived in large villages of multifamily dwellings made of bark or woven mats of reeds or cattails. In the fall and spring they would split into small groups or camps for hunting and, after acquiring metal pots, for sugaring. Whether these small camps would be composed of extended families or whether such families would split up remains a question.[7]

Village society was organized around lineages and patrilineal or sometimes matrilineal clans. Lineages were composed of people descended from a known individual, and thus members of a lineage were all related. Lineages declined after Euro-American contact, but there is some evidence to indicate that when they existed they had political functions. Clans were exogamous and composed of lineages. They traced their ancestry to a spiritual source, generally an animal or landscape figure. Although clans did not control productive property such as land, they (at least individuals according to their particular lineage) did have certain duties to perform, as the Winnebago did, and they possessed rights to certain religious rituals and perhaps to medicine bundles or sacred packs.[8] It was also through the agency of the clan that strangers were incorporated into the community. Clans regulated marriages of their members, and when community members married outsiders, clan acceptance marked their successful entrance into the community. When the new member was a male, in some instances he brought a new clan with him to the community; in other instances the community assigned him individually to a clan membership on the basis of his name.[9]

The clan also was important in politics. Some communities, like the Menominee,[10] Winnebago, and Miami, were divided into two groups, or moieties, with each group consisting of two or more clans. These divisions were identified with either the earth or the sky, and each division supplied a chief to the community.[11] Among the Menominee, for example, the head of the Bear clan, a member of the earth division because the bear is an earth animal, became the peace, or head, chief. The head of the Thunder, or Eagle, clan, a member of the sky division, became the war chief. In the Menominee origin legend, when the Bear chief suggested to the Thunderer, the eagle, that he should be chief, the Thunderer replied, "Nay! it is you yourself are the chief. But as for me: in the course of time a certain nation will assail you; and it is I shall then strike them for you."[12]

Thus the dual roles of peace and war chiefs are set forth in the origin legend, the important peace chief coming from the Bear clan and the powerful war chief coming from the Thunder clan. The peace chief governed during times of peace, but when war broke out he and his advisors retired and handed over authority to the war chief. When the war ended, governing authority reverted to the peace chief. Both chiefs had advisors drawn from their own division of earth and sky. Among some Indian groups, the political divisions were reversed; that is, as among the Winnebago, the head of the Bear clan is the war chief, and the head of the Thunder clan is the peace chief. Other groups like the Sauk, Fox, and Prairie Potawatomi also maintained dual divisions, but—unlike those of the Menominee, Winnebago, and Miami—the divisions were not made according to descent or kin groups, but cut across clan lines.[13]

As seen above, leadership in the community was hereditary, with leaders drawn from certain clans or, as anthropologist Charles Callender points out, really from lineages. Politics was highly ritualized. Political leadership almost certainly involved ceremonial leadership. The position of chief inherited respect, but the man who held that position had to live up to it. Chiefs not only had to be generous with their property, but also had to remain above the petty squabbles of the community. Their power lay not in the control they maintained over their people but in their reputation and in the examples they set in their daily life. Rule was not one of force but of reputation and respect. A chief's role was not to lead through innovation, although innovation undoubtedly existed, but to govern through consensual politics.[14]

It is entirely possible that chiefs had other duties, and perhaps there was more than one set of chiefs, but if so this information has been lost in time. We do not even know whether chiefs governed only when the people were gathered together in their large community, or if they continued to govern in the spring and fall, when some communities dispersed into smaller encampments.

There were lesser chiefs and village or multiple village councils, but their political roles, as well as how they were appointed, are still unclear.[15] Evidence indicates that there was a system of ranking among the warriors, but again little is known regarding how the ranking functioned in the community. Each village had warrior organizations that served as police or enforcing agents within the community and especially at times of communal buffalo hunts or to prevent separations of individuals and families during periods of village relocation. They also carried out the council's orders and assumed control of a community when it was under attack. To resist their orders meant loss of property or whipping, expulsion, or death.[16] Some groups like the Ojibwa and perhaps the Menominee elected special chiefs known as rice chiefs, who, along with a rice council, would oversee and regulate the harvesting of wild rice.[17]

The Menominee

Perhaps by examining particular groups like the Menominee and the Ojibwa in more detail, a clearer understanding of the Central Algonquian Pattern and the Eastern Collecting Pattern would result. Beginning with the Menominee, what was their community like in precontact time? Keep in mind that without more archaeological data, it is possible only to approximate community life by projecting back in time early French descriptions of Menominee culture.[18] It appears that the Menominee lived in one or perhaps two sedentary villages on the Menominee River near the western shore of Green Bay.[19]

Physically, the community appeared as a cluster of rectangular-shaped bark lodges in the summer and circular dome-shaped lodges of either bark or reed mats in the winter. Especially adapted to the forest environment and the needs of the Menominee community, these bark and reed lodges changed little until the late nineteenth century.[20]

Menominee subsistence patterns made possible the sedentary village life. Anthropologists have noted that the degree of community life is directly related to the economics of the community. In general, hunting and fishing people tended to have less stable communities than those people who relied on agriculture.[21] If a sedentary community, however, had access to large amounts of fish, like the Indian cultures of the Northwest coast or the Menominee, then the stability of the community was enhanced.[22] The Menominee made communal hunts for bear and sometimes for buffalo west of the Mississippi River. These buffalo hunts were often made with the Winnebago. But the vast quantity of migrating fish in the spring and autumn in the rivers that flowed near or into Green Bay, the abundance of large game and waterfowl in the vicinity of Menominee villages, the wild rice and, to a lesser extent, crops of corn, beans, squash, and wild plant food in the Green Bay locale, all allowed the Menominee a full range of foods that supported the existence of community life and enabled them to maintain their villages all year long. This plentiful supply of fish and wild rice, wood and stone crafts, and their location astride the water route from Mackinac Island to the interior of Wisconsin placed the Menominee in an excellent position to trade with other Indian groups.

Village life entailed cooperation among its members. Extended families shared the work, property, and economic benefits. Certainly bows, arrows, spears, fish nets, and birch bark or dugout canoes were necessary for their existence, but so too were the songs, rituals, and charms that, according to members of the household, were employed to catch fish or kill large game and waterfowl. These items were owned by individuals, but they were shared for the survival of the family. Although wild rice harvesting was undoubtedly a communal effort, individual families may have possessed rights to certain rice beds.

The extended family was the basic economic unit in the Menominee community, but it was also part of a larger unit, the totemic descent group, or clan. Each individual belonged to a clan, and each family counted descent from one of the estimated 22 clans. Because both individuals and families owned certain kinds of property, each family contributed to the larger wealth and prestige of its respective clan.

Menominee political structure at the time of contact is vague and sometimes, in the French accounts, contradictory. From Menominee legends it appears that both the town and the government were organized around a dual system. As seen above, the village, really the clans, divided into two large groups, or moieties. On one side were those clans related to the Bear clan, and they provided the civil, or peace, chief for the village; on the other side were those clans related to the Thunder clan, which provided the village war chief and police. The office of war chief went to that person of the Thunder clan who had acquired military honors or who had achieved power through his dreams and visions. Besides being the military leader, the war chief served also as the keeper of the community's war medicine and as the public spokesman on official occasions. The civil chief's measure of power had little to do with accomplishments in war and rested, not on his might or wisdom, as with some tribes, but on his generosity and his ability to moderate village disputes.[23]

There were other leaders besides the civil and war chiefs. Each clan elected or appointed a chief of the clan who, in turn, sat as a member on the village council and contributed to constructing community policy.

The real force, however, for social control in the community lay in gossip and public opinion: ". . . the force of public opinion, and the benefits to be gained by adherence to the rules surrounding economic, social, ceremonial and like activities, these backed in many cases of course by supernatural sanctions, made for relatively harmonious community living."[24] Looking at a hypothetical year cycle of Menominee activities, it is possible to glimpse not only this harmony but also how Menominee life interrelated with their environment.

A visitor to the Menominee in June, "the Strawberry Moon," or in July, "the Blueberry Moon," would find them in their rectangular summer lodges of bark and the community busy with seasonally appropriate activities. Gender roles were fairly well defined. Men hunted, fished, made canoes, tools, and weapons, defended the community from attack, and performed the ceremonies that assured continual blessings from the powers. Women cooked, kept the household in order, reared the children, planted and tended the crops, made the mats necessary for the lodge, the baskets and bags necessary for storage of food, and collected berries, wild foods, and firewood.

At that time of the year, the fish that the Menominee depended on were easy to catch in nets, to spear from canoe or from the bank, or to catch in weirs placed across streams. Hunting, another activity in the warm days of early summer, occurred only as the need for meat and hides arose. Not only individuals but also families or groups of friends would leave camp for a few days to hunt deer and moose. Sometimes in early summer the village would organize a communal hunt for deer or buffalo. Then hunting charms and "hunting bundles" would be employed to assure a successful hunt. Canoes would be loaded, and the Menominee would pass down the Fox and Wisconsin rivers to the open prairie of southern Wisconsin, or they might join their neighbors, the Winnebago, and cross the Mississippi and hunt in Iowa or even farther west.

Not everyone, however, would leave the village to hunt. Many, including the elderly and the very young, would stay behind. Although the Menominee did not plant large fields of corn, beans, and squash, they did plant some gardens, which had to be watched. Of equal importance were gathering reeds for making mats, searching for fibers for making or mending nets, and collecting birch bark for lodge coverings and canoes. From early spring to early autumn women and children picked berries that would be eaten fresh or dried for later use in soup.

In late summer, or the "Turning Leaves Moon," the Menominee

would set off to gather wild rice. Because the Menominee were known as the wild rice people, legends held that, "whenever the Menominee enter a region, the wild rice spreads ahead, whenever they leave it the wild rice passes."[25] Unfortunately, when the rice harvest failed every three or four years, the Menominee were sorely affected. In good harvest years, there was plenty of rice for the community, and some was traded to other Indian groups.

After they gathered the rice in canoes, a pit would be dug and a deer skin or mat would be laid in the pit and the rice placed on top. Then women and children would pound or dance on the rice to separate it from the chaff. Next it would all be spread out so that breezes would blow away the husks, leaving only the grain. Another way to separate rice from the chaff was to toss the rice in shallow baskets, allowing the chaff to blow off. Once dried, grain would be taken back to the village in woven sacks or in birch bark containers and stored in pits for winter use.

In the cool days of October, or the "Falling Leaves Moon," the season when deer and moose are their fattest, the men would hunt for them again or gather together for a communal bear hunt. Bears are also nice and fat just before winter hibernation. Since September, fishing was also an important activity in the village. Women and children gathered nuts and acorns for winter food and rushes for mats to be placed on the outside of their round dome-shaped winter lodges. Women were also busy drying the fish, meat, and wildfowl that the men brought home and preparing the skins that in winter would be made into clothing.

With the coming of snow, the life of the village slowed down. Now the lodges were tight against the winter wind. The men would still hunt, but everyone was more dependent on fish caught or speared through holes in the ice. Evenings were spent mending nets or weapons, telling tales of exciting hunts or war adventures or stories of Me'napus, and other sacred stories. Such sacred stories could not be told on summer evenings because then the spirits were awake and roaming the earth and would get angry. During the winter, the Menominee spent most of their lives in their lodges, but this does not mean that the community ceased to operate as a community during the cold months. Visiting other lodges and sharing songs and stories made passing the winter nights enjoyable.

February, the "Sucker Moon," and March, the "Snow-crust Moon," roused the Menominee village to increased activity. Now the suckers were running in the streams to spawn, and soon the large sturgeon would follow. Men would be out spearing, and an abundant supply of fresh fish would be welcomed in the village. Other men might set out over the hard snow crust to hunt. In groups, the men would track deer and moose. The hard crust that sometimes cut the animals' legs and prevented them from fleeing made them easy to kill. Maple sap was also collected at this time by making a V-shaped cut in the maple trees, but the sweet sap that flowed was not that important as a dietary supplement until after the Menominee acquired metal pots from the French, in which they could boil down the sap into sugar.

With the return of the fish and migrating wildfowl, with the return of the warm days of spring, life in the Menominee village took on a new appearance. Women gathered bark and set up summer lodges. They also prepared garden plots and collected berries and wild roots. Summer's approach promised dances and bundle ceremonies that would ensure Menominee health for another year.

Religion was integral to Menominee community life and essential to its well being. Both animate and inanimate objects in their world possessed spirits that had to be propitiated and manipulated through proper ritual procedures. Each animal had a spirit that had to be treated with proper respect. Failure to do so would prevent successful hunts. Even tools, like weapons and pots, possessed spirits that demanded proper attention in order to perform in useful ways. Luck in hunting or fishing did not exist. Humans were successful only if they had power or the proper medicine to control the numerous elements in their world. Humans survived only if the spirits helped them.

Me'napus, the Great Hare and culture hero of the Menominee, left instructions for religious observances that the Menominee must always follow. When the various deities, "the powers," took pity on the Menominee, they instructed Me'napus to give to the Menominee certain songs, rituals, and prayers that would ensure their success or power over the environment. Fast-induced visions and dreams could grant even more power to the Menominee. This power was incremental and could be increased through additional visions and also through the purchase or inheritance of songs, rituals, or sacred objects from another person. Power also came through knowledge. The knowledge possessed by shamans and priests, who knew how to communicate with the spirit world, and knowledge of medicinal plants or procedures for curing the sick were extremely valuable and guarded with great care. All these powers, or "medicines," were real to the Menominee and constituted their most important property. Without such power an individual or a community was helpless and could not survive. Before any major undertaking, such as going to war, hunting, traveling, planting, or harvesting, the spirits were consulted and their blessing sought. If the Menominee believed the blessing was denied, they would not venture the undertaking. Life was too full of risks to attempt projects which met with spiritual disapproval.

Fears of unappeased spirits were central to Menominee lives and community. So far only the actions of beneficial spirits have been mentioned. The Menominee sought blessings from good spirits through gifts of tobacco, which, according to legend, the spirits craved. The Menominee also were careful to appease evil spirits, like the water panther and the horned snake, with gifts of various kinds. Evils could befall either an individual or a community upon failure to observe the proper customs or to conduct the proper ceremonies.

It is obvious that the Menominee community, like any community, is more than a collection of people living in one place. Seemingly for the Menominee, as for many other Indian peoples, the individual was less important than the community. For the Menominee, the community represented both an organism, a living entity in which individuals merely represented parts of a collective whole, and a way of life, a culturally prescribed pattern for correct behavior despite the fact that its members did not always act according to the ideal. If someone departed too far from the Menominee way, that person suffered intense criticism. That this criticism came from relatives made it all the more effective as an expression of disapproval and a form of social control. To depart from the proper way of doing things could not only disrupt the community but also call down upon oneself the anger of the village police. More important, such departures from community norms could anger the spirits and cause them to deny blessings to the community. The world was a dangerous place for humans without the help of the spirits. Similar views of community and human relationships with the spirit world were held, possibly through diffusion, by other Wisconsin Indians.

The Eastern Collecting Pattern

The Ojibwa

The second pattern, the Eastern Collecting Pattern, predominated in the northern forest of the upper Great Lakes. This pattern included two cultural groups important in early Wisconsin history, the Ojibwa and the Ottawa.[26] When first encountered by Europeans, both groups resided in the area that drained into northern Lake Huron and Lake Superior. It is most likely that small nonlocalized Ojibwa groups extended from the Georgian Bay west along Lake Huron and north to Lake Superior and the Upper Peninsula of Michigan. Not much is known of these early

Ojibwa settlements, and even less is known about the Ottawa. Given the severely limiting conditions that the environment imposed, Ojibwa and Ottowa society was fragmented and organized in patrilineal bands rather than clans. Living in small groups, from a few families to several hundred people, the Ojibwa totaled perhaps 3,000–4,000 in all, although some scholars have placed the total as high as 25,000.[27] Community size depended on the environment and on the severity of the winters.[28] In most of the area short, cool summers prohibited extensive horticulture. Through trade with other groups, both the Ojibwa and the Ottawa probably acquired some corn and other vegetable produce, but fish, game, wild rice, berries, nuts, and other wild plants probably constituted the bulk of their diet.[29]

To acquire these foods, both groups were forced to move seasonally. In the summer several Ojibwa groups would gather at a known fishing site and erect a village of round dome-shaped lodges of birch bark. They would fish and enjoy a social gathering that included dancing, gambling, courting, picking berries, trading, forming new alliances or renewing old ones, and visiting or raiding other groups. Where soil and climate permitted, some corn and beans would be planted, but they were less important to the diet than fish, which were caught with bone hooks, or speared from canoes with harpoonlike devices, or scooped out of the water into canoes with nets.[30] If fields were planted with corn, the villagers sometimes departed after planting and went on a summer hunt or visited other villages. In late summer they would return to their fields and harvest the corn and other crops.

Although fish proved so abundant at some sites that some villages existed there year round, the usual pattern was the dispersal of the Ojibwa into small bands in the autumn, after gathering wild rice. Birch bark canoes facilitated moving their summer store of fish, wild rice, traded articles, and birch bark lodges.

Despite summer fishing and hunting, there was seldom enough food to last through the year, and so the autumn, winter, and spring were given over to hunting large game, such as deer, moose, and bear, along with smaller mammals and fowl. Because game was scarce, especially in the early spring, each family, in order to survive, required a vast hunting territory, which for a band of about 600 might necessitate an area of at least "1,200 square miles and probably much more."[31] A severe winter that depleted the animal population or reduced its nutrient value sometimes resulted in starvation for whole family units. Thus, the large sedentary villages characteristic of the Central Algonquians could not exist in the hardwood forests surrounding Lake Superior; there would not be enough game in the village locale to feed the population.

Given the nomadic nature of Ojibwa and Ottawa society, their social and political organizations were not as complex as those of the Central Algonquians. It is quite probable that neither the Ojibwa nor the Ottawa possessed clans before the late seventeenth century, although there does appear to be some question about this. Some ethnologists have suggested that clans, a more complex sociopolitical organization than bands, may have arisen among the Ojibwa and Ottawa about the time that Europeans made contact. Clans also arose perhaps out of changing ecological, demographic, and cultural factors. As the Ojibwa moved west and south, they discovered more abundant and diverse natural resources, they seized the opportunity to engage in agriculture, and they developed semi-sedentary communities with clans, which, in turn, gave rise to a more complex social and religious organization than had existed previously.[32] Regardless of whether clans existed in the early 1600s or came into existence later, they served to designate eligible marriage partners, and because the totemic clans[33] cut across village lines, they provided the Ojibwa with friendship and support from clan members in other villages. For example, a member of the Crane clan could travel to other communities and expect to receive lodging and comfort from other members of the Crane clan. Small patrilineal bands seemed to be the rule among both the Ottawa and the Ojibwa and the leadership of the band passed from father to eldest son as long as the rest of the band approved.[34]

If the early seventeenth-century Ojibwa possessed elaborate group ceremonials like some of the Central Algonquians, it is now unknown. They did celebrate the Feast of the Dead, a ceremony perhaps borrowed from the Ottawa, who in turn, may have borrowed it from the Huron, an Iroquoian-speaking people living near the Georgian Bay.[35] Also, unlike the Central Algonquians, the Ojibwa and Ottawa bands seem not to have possessed special medicine bundles or rituals. Shamans, sometimes called conjurers or jugglers by European observers, were important in both societies.[36] Because both peoples were predominately nomadic, emphasis was placed on individualized religious practices rather than on group ceremony.[37] The Midewiwin, or Medicine Lodge, ceremony, practiced extensively by the Ojibwa in the nineteenth century and once thought to be a ceremony that came about after European contact because of what appear to be Christian elements incorporated into the rites, is now believed to have earlier origins.[38]

The Ojibwa village at Sault Ste. Marie, although not a typical Ojibwa summer village, was probably the largest of the seventeenth-century villages. Here at the rapids on the St. Mary's River, where the waters of Lake Superior tumbled forth on their way to Lake Huron, the Ojibwa gathered each year to catch thousands of whitefish, weighing between 6 and 15 pounds each, to perform ceremonials like the Feast of the Dead, to seek marriage partners, and to trade. Although the Ojibwa were the dominant group at Sault Ste. Marie, the Ottawa, Potawatomi, and others also came to fish, trade, and renew political and military alliances. Indeed, as with most Indian groups at this time, agreements to engage in trade were also agreements of political and military support. Trade in corn, wild rice, shells, tobacco, and other items led to alliances that bound the different groups. Once secured, the alliances were often tested when war parties set out to raid traditional enemies.

The abundance of fish at Sault Ste Marie enabled some Ojibwa to remain at this site through the winter, subsisting primarily on the whitefish they had caught during the summer.[39] Ojibwa summer villages were primarily collections of bands, and with the arrival of autumn the more typical villages fragmented along band lines and departed to their winter hunting grounds to spend the season on a favorite stream. Among the few Ojibwa bands that remained at the Sault, and among other Ojibwa who lived where environments allowed the development of large semi-sedentary populations, clans probably evolved.[40] Again it must be emphasized that year-round villages for the Ojibwa were unusual.

When it was October, the "Falling Leaves Moon," and there was a film of morning ice on pools of standing water and the aspen were a yellow blaze against the sky, the Ojibwa bands prepared to remove to their winter camps. The corn, beans, and squash, if they had been planted, were now harvested and dried, and some that were set aside for later use were placed in deep pits covered over with birch bark and earth. The wild rice had also been gathered, dried, and stored in pits to be used in the spring, or it was placed in *mukuks* (birch bark containers) for travel. The summer lodges were taken down, and the birch bark covering was carefully rolled up, as were the floor mats of bulrushes and wall mats of cattails, and all were placed in the canoes along with the containers of corn, wild rice, and dried fish. Objects received in trade for furs and hides were also placed in the canoe: tobacco; catlinite, or red pipe stone, from Minnesota or western Wisconsin; shells; and paints. These would be useful in communication with the spirit world. The pipestone would be made into pipes during the cold winter evenings, and the tobacco would be smoked or placed in the fire. Either way the burned tobacco would summon the spirits and cause them to listen to Ojibwa prayers. Even the paints were sometimes offered to the spirits in hopes of blessings.

Once on their way it would take several days for each of the small groups of about 20 to reach their first camps. The trip along the Lake Superior or Lake Michigan shore would be made at a leisurely pace, with stops along the route for fishing and hunting. Upon reaching the mouth of the river that would take them into their interior camps, they sometimes stopped and hunted for a couple of weeks before traveling farther. Moves into the interior were accomplished in stages. If the river was large enough and free of ice, the trip was sometimes continued in canoes as far as possible. If not, then the canoes were cached and the trip continued on foot.

Transporting supplies into the interior often required several trips. The women would divide the meat and supplies into bundles that could be carried as backpacks. Leaving early in the morning the party would travel up the river. About midafternoon, they would stop to build a scaffold on which to store the meat to keep it away from wolves and other animals, and then they would return to the first camp on the river for another load, arriving there by evening. This would continue until they had transported all the supplies to the first camp up the river. At that place they would perhaps spend another week before moving on. If they were fortunate enough to kill a couple bears and some deer, they would cut the meat into strips and dry it by the fire. The bear fat they would render into oil and pour into porcupine skins. Into this oil was placed some of the fire-dried meat, where it would be preserved until spring.

Similar camps were made at about 20-mile intervals until the group reached its final destination. That spot would not be an arbitrary one, for the band had claimed use of the area for a number of years. Here in December, or "the Little Spirits Moon," they would erect their winter lodges of birch bark on which they piled cedar boughs and snow. With the mats laid out inside and a fire started, they were ready for winter. The lodges were small and smoky, but they were warm. The leader of the band would assign hunting territories to the men, and days would be spent hunting or, when the snow prevented them from that, mending their weapons and snowshoes. Women would be busy skinning any game the men brought home, working with the hides, cooking the meals perhaps from the large fire in the middle of the camp circle, making or mending clothes and finger-woven bags, making fish nets from nettle stalk fiber, and collecting firewood and water.

Darkness came early, and with the darkness came a glowing fire, singing, and tales of Manabozho, who could turn himself from man to woman to animal and back to man. He had great powers, but he could not avoid mischief. There were also tales of the various spirits, tales that could be told only in the winter. Most frightening were the tales of cannibal giants, or Windigos, who lived in the woods. Perhaps there were rumors of some being seen in the neighborhood, and this would send fear through the camp, for Windigos were difficult to kill. At night when the wind moved through the ice-covered trees and there were cracking sounds outside the lodge, one wondered if the Windigos were about.

At such times there was comfort in numbers. Other band members might stop by the lodge, and they were always welcomed and offered food even if there was little to give. Custom would not allow conversation to begin until the guest was made comfortable, given food, and had his moccasins dried. Not to offer these courtesies was an insult; not to accept them was also an insult. To insult another could be very dangerous and could disrupt the harmony of the camp. Insults could lead to witchcraft, and spells might be cast against the injuring party, resulting in either illness or death. Shamans would perhaps be used to cast the spell, and they would have to be paid. Likewise those who had spells cast against them would also have to pay a shaman to have the spell removed. It was much wiser to behave according to custom and refrain from giving offense.

By the end of February, or the "Sucker Moon," finding game grew increasingly difficult. Sometimes a "bear tree" could be found, and the bear forced out of hibernation and killed, but the meat did not go far because it was split among the several families. When the snow turned hard, men found hunting easier, but if there was little game, then they ate food dried the previous summer. When that was gone, soup was made of tree bark, scraps of leather, and roots dug from the frozen earth. Each family knew tales of members of other bands, or even whole bands, that had starved to death during a particularly bad winter. These days of cold and starvation filled people with yet another fear—the fear of roaming Windigos, the cannibal giants who reputedly possessed hearts of ice and roamed the snowy woods searching for victims to appease their hunger.

In late winter when the land seemed mysteriously barren of animals, the streams, where the ice was nearly gone and the water black and cold, suddenly filled with suckers swimming upstream to spawn. The annual run of suckers brought relief to the hungry band. Fish would now constitute the bulk of the diet. Some men strung nets across the stream, always careful to rub medicine on the nets to attract the fish. Others fished with bone hooks, and still others used spears.

Many of the fish were eaten immediately, either boiled or roasted. The boiled heads of suckers were especially liked. Some fish were dried on racks over a low fire and packed tightly in deerskin; this dried fish constituted much of the people's diet until they arrived back at the summer village. The trip back to the summer village would be made in easy stages.

By May, the "Flowering Moon," or June, the "Strawberry Moon," most bands had arrived at their summer villages. They unearthed the food they had cached the previous summer, and this would sustain them until their new gardens began producing. Before planting their gardens, the men would help in clearing new areas and breaking up the ground. After the crops were planted, many would leave the village to gather sheets of bark for canoes and lodges, rushes for mats, and berries. Roots and the flowers of the milkweed plant were also collected for food. At this time men hunted deer, moose, and elk, sometimes by trapping them and sometimes by driving them into large enclosures, where they could be killed with bows and arrows. Pigeons and waterfowl were also killed for food.

This was a time for ceremonies, renewing alliances, and going to war. In the Feast of the Dead, the dead were remembered with songs, dances, and games. Other ceremonies occurring in the summer, such as puberty vision fasts, were more individual. These ceremonies put youth in direct relationship with the spirits, or *manitos,* who gave the youth knowledge that they would need in order to live a long life.

The ceremonies and an active social life in the Ojibwa village continued until September, or the "Wild Rice Moon." Then the Ojibwa bands traveled to the ricing areas in groups, set up camps, and carried out the harvesting as a community activity. They took care to begin the rice harvest at just the right moment. Beginning too soon would only break down the fragile rice stalks that grew in the rivers or near the shore in the muddy lake bottom. Some from each family gathered the rice in canoes. Harvesting required one to paddle or pole the canoe and another to bend the rice stalks over the canoe and with a stick beat the rice heads into the canoe. Others remained on shore and carefully spread and dried the rice. With the dried rice packed in mukuks for winter, the bands would return to the village and harvest whatever crops the short growing season allowed. Winter would come soon to the Ojibwa country, and by late September the early morning chill seemed to linger longer in the morning air. A new cycle was about to begin.

THE CHIWERE-SIOUAN CULTURES

The Winnebago

Not all the Indian groups in Wisconsin were Algonquian. The Winnebago, as already pointed out, were Siouan speakers and related to the Chiwere-Siouan Iowa, Oto, and Missouri peoples. All these groups probably emerged out of what archaeologists call the Oneota tradition, that is, a prehistoric culture complex that flourished from A.D. 1000 to A.D. 1600 in the upper Mississippi Valley. Although there are numerous theories regarding the early history of the Chiwere-Siouan people, the absence of good archaeological data for critical periods and confusing ethnohistorical accounts leave many questions unanswered. Just when the Oneota tradition broke down, giving rise to the Chiwere-Siouan, remains a subject of archaeological debate.[41] Unknown also is when, why, and how the Winnebago, Iowa, Oto, and Missouri emerged as individually defined entities.

Probably environmental pressures acting over long periods of time on isolated groups of the Chiwere-Siouan led to separate cultural adjustments. Conflicts also undoubtedly played a role and resulted in altered settlement patterns, military and hunting practices, and social organizations. The warm prairie country of Iowa and southern Wisconsin also contributed to shaping the cultures of the Winnebago, Iowa, and Santee Sioux who inhabited this region. This, according to one archaeologist, led them to emphasize "mixed horticulture, communal hunts, and a dependence on local resources."[42] Whether the Winnebago and Santee were in Wisconsin before the Menominee (Algonquians) or arrived later cannot be answered. It is certain that both groups, but especially the Winnebago, were influenced by the Central Algonquian peoples.[43]

The subsistence pattern of the Winnebago and Santee, like that of the Central Algonquians, depended on corn, beans, squash, and pumpkins. These were supplemented by wild rice, wild prairie turnips, berries, and nuts. Tobacco was also an important crop. Both the Winnebago and Santee organized communal buffalo and deer hunts. Besides bear, waterfowl and fish were also important staples in the Winnebago and Santee diets. Among the Santee and other Siouan groups whose hunting range included northwest Wisconsin, moose were another welcomed source of protein.

Unlike the Ojibwa, who generally were forced to break up their summer village each autumn, both the Winnebago and Santee lived in semi-permanent villages. In the summer the Santee lived in large gable-roofed bark houses called *tipi-tanka,* meaning "big house," and in winter they constructed smaller, conical lodges of elm bark, cattail mats, or hides.[44] If a cold winter were expected, the lodge might be banked with earth. The Winnebago built several different kinds of lodges including some made of grass, reed mats, and bark. Grass and reed lodges were built for summer living, but the bark lodges were utilized year round.

Among the Winnebago and the Santee, clans played an important role in village life. In both groups, clans were exogamous (i.e., mates were found outside of one's clan) and patrilineal. With the Santee, the lodges of each clan had particular places in the large camp circle or village. Similarly among the Winnebago, villages were divided, but evidence indicates that they could be divided in two different ways: either by a line that ran through the village or by concentric circles. In either case, the lodges of the various clans were always grouped the same way; certain clans were always opposite others across the line or, in the case of concentric circles, always in one particular circle.

Given the similarities between the Winnebago and the Santee, it might be expected that they had similar kinds of government. In both cases chiefs were selected from particular clans, and the office was generally passed down from father to son.[45] Both groups had governing councils, drawn from clan leaders, and village police, who enforced the rules of the chief and council. Among the Santee the police were appointed by the chief and council. With the Winnebago, police functions were assumed by the Bear clan.[46] As with the Algonquians, the police worked to maintain order both in the village and on the hunt. To disobey the police when on the communal buffalo or deer hunt generally led to whippings and the destruction of the offender's property. If the offender attempted to resist the police, he was sometimes killed.[47] Punishment was severe and with good reason. Individuals who dared to sneak out of camp and begin the hunt early could frighten the herd in the case of buffalo, causing them to flee from the area. This placed in jeopardy the food supply of the whole community.

The ancient villages of the Santee were composed of kin groups that through common need and obligation unified community life and promoted individual identification with the group. Helping to foster this common village identity was the sharp rivalry that existed between villages, despite the fact that spouses were acquired from rival villages. Individuality, both at the personal. and family level, was suppressed in favor of community interests. Both individuals and households were "responsible to the whole [village], and derived status only from full cooperation with village requirements."[48] Village activities, according to anthropologist Ruth Landes, were "rigorously organized" and announced by village criers both morning and evening.[49] No one was above village judgment, and everyone accepted as village duty the task of inquiring into a neighbor's business. Except for the matter of exogamy, or acquiring mates from outside the village, the Winnebago probably followed quite similar patterns to achieve village cohesion.

When the Winnebago or Santee conducted summer buffalo hunts, their respective villages combined into a single village. According to Landes, for the Santee "the buffalo-hunting group was the village; the personnel was continuous; and the groups acted together throughout the year."[50] If Landes is correct, then the village was organized as an effective hunting machine.

The Winnebago claim that their original home was Red Banks on the Door County Peninsula. It is not known just when the people we now know as the Winnebago moved to Red Banks from the south (or east),[51] but it is here that the earliest French explorers appear to have first encountered the Winnebago.[52] It is at Red Banks that the Winnebago identity probably crystalized when they came into contact with the Algonquian-speaking Menominee. Despite different languages, the Menominee and Winnebago seem to have enjoyed a relatively harmonious relationship, and, indeed, the Winnebago over time accepted many Algonquian practices from their Menominee neighbors.[53] Both utilized their environment in similar ways. Although the Winnebago practiced extensive horticulture, both they and the Menominee hunted, fished, and gathered wild rice. Both employed medicine bundles to assure success in hunting and war, and sometimes there was joint participation on large communal hunts that extended into what is now Iowa and Nebraska.

The Winnebago did not extend their cordial relationship with the Menominee to other Indian groups. According to Winnebago legends and early French accounts, the Winnebago were a very militant people. Even the Menominee acknowledged the Winnebago as the superior military force. Winnebago war parties ranged south to Illinois and west into Minnesota, Iowa, Nebraska, and Missouri. Trading parties of Winnebago traveled east to Michigan, but it is not known whether war parties roamed that far east. The latter generally ventured forth in the summer, for in the winter the Winnebago, like most Wisconsin Indians, devoted their time to hunting. Winter for the Winnebago was also a time for ceremonial feasting.

Again, to gain a better understanding of Winnebago culture, it is useful to follow them for a year, beginning with their ceremonies for the new year. In January, when the sun disappeared early over the western horizon and the snow covered the earth and wind swirled around their elm or birch bark lodges, the Winnebago watched for the new moon, the "First Bear Moon," that marked the beginning of the year and the holding of the Bear clan feast. This feast to honor the founders of the Bear clan and to appeal to the spirits for a good year began at dusk. Members of the Bear and Wolf clans along with invited guests filed into the lodge and took their places around the perimeter. When all were seated the Bear clan host would rise and address the assemblage, making offerings to the ancestors for safety and a good life and reminding the guests, "We are praying now not only for our own, but for all the clans."[54]

On warm days during the "Raccoon-breeding Moon," or March, Winnebago men would hunt near their village. Before going on a hunt, they were careful to hold a ceremony in which the spirit of the animal to be hunted was sought and sacrifices were made to it. Special hunting medicines purchased by the hunter or learned of in a vision fast were rubbed on the arrows to assure their efficacy. At this time, smaller animals were preferred to deer because the Winnebago considered deer meat unwholesome in late winter. In the "Fish Become Visible Moon," or April, when the fish swam upstream to spawn, men fished at night using torches of pine pitch and spears, or they killed the fish with arrows specially made for this purpose.

In late spring, or May, the "Drying of the Earth Moon," groups of hunters searched for deer that were known to frequent streams at this time. The hunter who killed a deer received only part of it. Factors such as who was near when the deer was killed, the size of the hunting party, the age and social rank of the members, all determined how the meat was divided. Such customs assured that the community, not just the skillful hunter, benefited from the hunt. In this season, hunts did not take the men far afield, for it was necessary for them to be in the village come the "Digging Moon," or June, the month when corn, beans, and squash were planted.

Although planting and tending crops were considered women's tasks, men probably helped, particularly if land needed clearing of brush. Family groups controlled certain fields near the village, and they placed an earthen replica of their clan totem in the center of the field or garden area. Some small fields were set aside for the men to grow ceremonial tobacco and sacred gourds. Besides working long hours planting, tending, and watching their crops, women had other duties: Berries had to be picked and dried, meals prepared, meat dried, deer hides tanned, children watched, and clothes made. Men did little garden work; they were busy at other tasks. Hunting trips could be long, tedious, and dangerous, and when not hunting men spent hours repairing their weapons. A killed animal had to be skinned, cut up, and carried back to the village. Those men who were members of the Bear clan also had village police functions, and on the summer communal hunts they were responsible for maintaining order among the villagers engaged in the hunt and for guarding against enemy attacks.

After the crops were planted and their growth assured, the village prepared for the communal buffalo hunt. These were the warm days of early summer. As soon as the village chief decided to hold a hunt, he gave a feast inviting everyone. The feast finished, the chief called a hunting council and appointed criers to inform the village of when the hunt would begin. At this point the village gathered at the lodge of the Bear clan chief. Here ten of the village's best warriors were chosen to scout ahead and locate the buffalo and check for enemies. On the scouts' return, they informed the Bear clan chief of both the location of the buffalo and the possible presence of enemies. Before leaving for the hunt, the Winnebago performed ceremonies and dances, like the buffalo dance, to ensure hunting success.

The trip to the hunt area was carefully organized. Not everyone went on the hunt: the elderly, those crippled from arthritis or accidents, the very young, and those needed to protect the village remained behind. Those who did go traveled by canoes in a large group down the Rock and Wisconsin rivers. Upon reaching the Mississippi, the Winnebago concealed their canoes or left them with allied villages.

Before setting out across the plains the Winnebago reorganized. The Bear clan soldiers took the lead carrying the lodge poles for the tepees that provided shelter during the hunt.[55] Next followed the women and finally the old warriors to protect the rear. Each night, the Bear police placed their staffs in the ground at the head of the line of march. No one was allowed to move beyond these staffs, for to do so would incur punishment at the hands of the police. When they came upon buffalo the hunt would begin. Amidst heat, dust, and noise, there was always a careful watch maintained for enemies. The flesh of the buffalo was cut up and dried on the grass. When enough buffalo were taken, the hunt would end and the Winnebago would return in the same order they had taken to the buffalo grounds. They considered it improper to kill more animals than needed. On the hunting party's return to the village, the Winnebago gave dances and feasts thanking the spirits for a successful hunt and safe return. Such thanks were necessary because animals possessed souls and stood in the same relationship to the spirits as humans did. Their lives were not to be taken without cause, and when taken apologies were made and thanks given.

When the warm days of summer faded and a sharp morning chill greeted the Winnebago as they left their lodges to begin the day, they knew that the "Tasseling Moon," or August, was nearly over and the "Elk-whistling Moon," or September, was about to begin. Harvesting now took up the people's time. Beans and squash were gathered and dried, the latter cut and placed on poles for this purpose. Holes in the earth were dug for the storage of corn to protect it from insects and rodents. After lining the pit with leaves, the corn was placed in the center and then covered with more leaves and earth. In another method, the pit was lined with rocks on which a large fire was built. When the rocks were hot, corn husks were laid on them and ears of corn were placed on top. The corn was covered with more husks, water was poured over them, and the pit was then covered with earth. After about 12 hours, the Winnebago removed the corn and cut off the kernels to dry for winter.

Once the crops were harvested and stored for winter, the Winnebago might have begun a wild rice harvest. After the rice was gathered it was dried, winnowed, and placed in woven bags for transport back to the village and for storage. This activity took several weeks.

As the days grew colder, the Winnebago left their villages in large parties to hunt for deer and bear. Ceremonies were held to assure success. Youth who had successfully completed their vision fast during the summer sometimes went to test the strength of their newly acquired "medicine." Deer were often driven past concealed hunters or were caught in traps. Hunting bear required different methods. When the acorns fell and bears were feeding on them, the Winnebago made large clearings under oak trees. Here the bears congregated having less trouble finding acorns. Careful to keep out of sight and downwind from the bears, the Winnebago were able to kill many of them without wandering far through the woods. The meat of both bear and deer was preserved, generally by hanging strips of it in the sun to dry. Another way was to hollow out a log, place partly cooked meat in the cavity, and pour melted tallow over the opening. Once the tallow hardened the meat could be preserved until needed. A Winnebago coming across meat preserved in this way never disturbed it, but always respected the rights of the person to whom it belonged.

Falling snow in December, "When the Deer Shed Their Horns Moon," generally induced the Winnebago to return to their village. Now as the cold winter set in, the Winnebago enjoyed the fruits of their summer and autumn harvests. The cold outside seldom penetrated their warm bark lodges. Tales of summer hunts and war adventures were told over the fires. There were tales of Trickster, Wak'djunk'aga, who was sent by Earthmaker, and also tales of another culture hero, Hare.

SUMMARY

By now it is evident that both similarities and differences exist among the Menominee, Ojibwa, and Winnebago peoples. Looking at the differences first, since they are the most obvious, it is clear that the various cultures considered are affected by different environments and historical traditions. The rolling open prairies crossed by rivers and dotted with lakes and stands of hardwood timber characteristic of southern Wisconsin enabled the Winnebago Indians to support an extensive population in multiple villages, some possibly quite large, with a patrilineal clan structure, a political organization, and a complex religious system. This was all made possible through a subsistence pattern based on horticulture, large game hunting, wild rice, and fish. North of the Winnebago, the Menominee lived in the mixed hardwood forest near Green Bay. Although deer and bear were hunted, the Menominee also made communal hunts with the Winnebago for buffalo. Their greatest reliance, however, proved to be on wild rice and fish. Some corn, beans, and pumpkins were grown, but it was rice and fish that made possible the large sedentary village near Green Bay. Unlike the Menominee and the Winnebago with their large sedentary villages, the Ojibwa were generally nomadic. Whereas both the Winnebago and the Menominee often went out on winter hunts in small groups, hunting in the winter for the Ojibwa was an imperative; not to hunt meant starvation. Only those few Ojibwa at places like Sault Ste Marie with a plentiful supply of fish were able to maintain a village year round. Because the environment forced most Ojibwa to lead a nomadic life, there was little possibility of their creating complex social and political organizations.

It would, however, be a mistake to think that the environment solely determined the cultures of the above groups. Each group adapted technologically to their environment in order to exert more effective control over it and to preserve their community and enable it to prosper. In the thick boreal forest filled with swamps and muskegs and dotted with lakes, the Ojibwa raised to high art the manufacture of the birch bark canoe. For travel in winter, they utilized sleds and snowshoes. The Ojibwa became skilled in the use of canoe, harpoon, and net for fishing in rapids. The Menominee, not faced with having to fish in rapids, developed both weirs to catch fish and a proficiency in spearing sturgeon from canoes when the fish made their spring run or in spearing them through the ice after attracting them with lures. The Winnebago devised sophisticated methods for hunting and dressing buffalo that involved both technology and social organization. Their practice of burning off the prairie kept it open, providing both grazing areas for deer, elk, and buffalo and land for extensive gardens.

Evolving systems of social organization by the various culture groups certainly were as important as technological innovations. Regardless of size, each community had to shape a system of rules and regulations, a way of doing things, that would allow it to cope with outside and inside threats. Effective leadership channels had to be devised to enable the community to unite in times of danger, be it from another community or from natural disasters. Social policies also had to evolve to allow a community to preserve itself and prosper or, if ruptured because of internal discord or environmental demands, to separate in the least disruptive way. Rival villages, or bands, that were once united generally would join again in temporary support when faced with a common enemy. Each Wisconsin Indian community recognized the need to organize community life and so developed different patterns of social control and governing institutions.

Similarities among some of the groups so far examined may have come about through like responses to environment; they may also have arisen from an acquaintance with other communities' methods of handling certain common problems. Wisconsin Indian communities were not isolated from each other. When marriage took place between different culture communities, new ways and ideas were also exchanged. Trade and defense alliances were common. The Winnebago traded with the Menominee for stone and wooden tools and may have also acquired legends, songs, and rituals.[56] The Ojibwa may have learned the Feast of the Dead from the Ottawa and Huron. Some cultural similarities are undoubtedly due to independent invention, but many more are probably the result of diffusion of information from one community to another.

These last similarities, or cultural traits, are sometimes possible to trace from one community to another. More difficult to trace, however, are those similarities related to cosmology, or world view. These are lost in time. Yet it should be stressed that Winnebago, Menominee, and Ojibwa cosmologies did more than affect how each group interpreted its world; the cosmological similarities of these groups also help to explain some of their common responses to events.

Among all the Wisconsin Indian communities, the perception of community was greater than the physical location of both lodges and people who were circumscribed by imaginary boundaries or state of mind. Spiritual communities existed on both horizontal and vertical planes. Totemic identification with animal or inanimate objects related Wisconsin Indians to spirits beyond the limits of their physical community. On the vertical plane, Wisconsin Indians believed that the universe existed on several levels; that is, there were worlds both above and below this one. The Menominee origin legend, for example, relates how they emerged from the underworld.[57] The strong attachment that Indian peoples often exhibited in regard to a particular location may derive from more than the mere fact that kin are buried nearby or that community history is located in a certain geography. It may also grow out of the belief that their homes, their communities, are situated both horizontally and vertically in spiritual space.

This chapter depicts the physical, social, and spiritual world of Wisconsin Indian communities as they perhaps existed before contact with Europeans. Drawing on scanty historical sources and projecting them backward in time, without the luxury of extensive archaeological findings, makes it possible only to approximate the changing conditions of Wisconsin Indian life and society at the time of contact with Europeans. The intent is not exactness. Rather, it is to convey a sense of what the communities were probably like at a certain moment in their history. It would be a gross mistake, however, to think that this description—or any other—represents an unchanging situation. During their existence, all cultures, including prehistoric ones, are in a constant state of change and should not be considered as stable or timeless. The French, along with the English and later the Americans, affected Wisconsin Indian communities and influenced—intentionally and unintentionally—directions of change, but change had always been present. The French, perhaps, merely altered or accelerated the rate of change. More immediate, however, were the changes initiated by the influx of eastern Indian communities into Wisconsin just before French contact. These groups profoundly affected Wisconsin Indian communities, causing both chaos and death. This invasion from the East, both native and French, is the subject of the next chapter.

3

The Years of the French

The world as the Winnebago and Menominee knew it, indeed as the Huron and Central Algonquian knew it, collapsed between 1634 and 1760. During those years, the impacts of multiple Iroquoian attacks and the French presence combined to reshape the Indian world of the western Great Lakes. Their new world would be vastly different. The degree of change would surpass anything in the peoples' memory.

The communities briefly sketched in the previous chapter, although hypothetical, nevertheless approximate the social and ecological situations at which the several Indian cultures had arrived just before contact with Europeans. Each of the various Indian groups over a long period of time had adjusted its culture to the demands of its environment and through ritual and skill attempted to induce parts of its environment to conform to its culture. Although trade and alliances between groups existed, the communities were largely self-contained entities. Food, shelter, and clothing were acquired through horticulture, hunting, fishing, and gathering. Rituals were considered necessary to assure the ripening of crops, the fertility of women, and success in hunting and military engagements. Rituals, gifts, and intermarriages were necessary to maintain alliances of friendship, protection, and support between groups. Although some groups had village chiefs for war and peace, other groups living in scattered bands relied on clan chiefs or elders.

Over a period of approximately 40 years, from 1640 to about 1680, this self-sufficient Indian world crumbled. Yet despite the forces of disintegration, communities worked to keep their old world from completely falling apart. Change proved rapid, and although it did not completely alter communities, it often moved them in directions that neither the In-

47

dians nor the French could control. Wisconsin Indian groups absorbed and reworked cultural ideas and material items not only from the French but also from other Indian groups. Such innovations as guns, traps, foods, cloth, and religious ceremonies, among others, were acquired only if they could be fitted easily into the host cultures. In this selection process many ideas and items were rejected or ignored.

A period of rapid cultural decline for the Winnebago and Menominee Indians of Wisconsin came in the years just before extensive French contact. The main cause of this decline can be attributed to the dislocation of Michigan Indian groups and their entry into Wisconsin, which resulted from their wars with the Iroquois. This intrusion into Wisconsin precipitated a series of wars among the various Indian groups that proved destructive both to the environment and to the indigenous Winnebago and Menominee. The French followed the Michigan groups into Wisconsin and contributed to the process of cultural disintegration taking place among all the competing Wisconsin groups. The primary goal for the French was the control of the fur trade, which would establish their political claim to the upper Mississippi Valley. Saving Indian souls was an important, but secondary, consideration. The first move of the French into Wisconsin was, in the short run, not a significant one. It is this move and a brief account of French difficulties with the Iroquois, which prompted the diaspora of Michigan Indians to Wisconsin, that will be considered next.

INDIAN AND FRENCH ALLIANCES

In 1634 the French governor-general, Samuel de Champlain, sent Sieur Jean Nicolet to Green Bay to negotiate a peace between the Winnebago, reputed masters of the bay area, and the Ottawa. The Ottawa, who had sent trade envoys to the Winnebago, claimed their envoys were killed and eaten, and they appealed to the French for help.[1] The Ottawa and probably the Huron were moving as middlemen into the Green Bay area and trading French goods for beaver skins. In involving the French as mediators in this dispute with the Winnebago, an involvement that could open French entry into the western regions, the Ottawa were probably taking a calculated risk but one they had decided to take.[2]

Nicolet's appearance in Wisconsin was brief, and little is learned from his visit, either about the Indian people there or about the environment. If the French entertained plans to return immediately to the region, they were thwarted and kept occupied by difficulties in the East with epidemics and with the Iroquois. The Mohawk, one group in the Iroquois

Confederacy, had in 1632 negotiated a peace treaty with the Algonquian in the St. Lawrence Valley, who were under the protection of the French. The Mohawk broke this treaty in 1635. During the 1630s the groups that made up the Iroquois Confederacy (the Mohawk, Oneida, Onondaga, Cayuga, and Seneca), whose villages were south and east of Lake Ontario, grew increasingly militant. After 1640 when they had exhausted the beaver in their own territory—beaver whose skins were needed to acquire European goods—they grew desirous of the beaver-hunting grounds of their neighbors, the Huron, Erie, and Neutral, to the north and the west. Although these last groups were also Iroquois-speaking Indians, they were not members of the Iroquois Confederacy. What the confederacy did not know, however, was that these groups had already exhausted their beaver-hunting grounds by the 1630s.

The Huron, more skillful in trading than in fighting, used their alliance with the French to good advantage. While prohibiting Indians from the north and west to travel through their territory to trade with the French at Montreal, the Huron also kept the French from penetrating the area beyond Lake Huron. The Huron assumed the role of middlemen, buying furs from the western Indians in return for French goods and corn. Eventually the Ottawa, who were both neighbors of the Huron and disdained by them, also worked their way into this broker position.[3]

The Erie and Neutral, because their beaver grounds were exhausted and they were perhaps feeling unable to compete with the Huron in trade, decided to usurp the beaver grounds of Algonquian Indians in southern Michigan. This move in the 1630s sent the Michigan Algonquian groups—the Potawatomi, Miami, and others—westward.

Throughout the 1640s, the Iroquois turned their faces and their guns, acquired from the Dutch and the English, against the Huron, who were politically and economically allied with the French, and then against other Iroquois-speaking groups—the Petun, Erie, and Neutral. Although warfare had simmered long between the Huron and the Iroquois Confederacy south of Lake Ontario, the latter's destruction of the Huron villages in the 1640s was primarily an economic move. Many of the defeated Huron, and later many of the defeated Petun,[4] Erie, and Neutral peoples, were taken to Iroquois villages and adopted. The Iroquois, in moving against these groups, were interested not only in picking up the recently conquered beaver areas from the Erie and Neutral and the rich beaver grounds north of the Petun, but also in the western trade of the Huron.

By the 1650s the Iroquois maintained a supremacy over the eastern

Great Lakes. The Huron, Ottawa, Petun, Erie, and Neutral were dead, adopted into Iroquois villages, or driven west. The French trade empire was shattered and the French forced back to the confines of the St. Lawrence Valley. Success, however, had a price for the Iroquois. Large numbers of prisoners were held in their villages and, in the process of being absorbed into Iroquois society, proved a possible security problem, especially since Iroquois men were often away from the villages for long periods of time on raiding trips. Success also created factionalism within the Iroquois Confederacy, and a split developed between the Mohawk in the east and the Seneca in the west over what the confederacy's policy should be toward the French. Finally, the Iroquois, who excelled in diplomacy, never seemed able to translate this particular ability into trade negotiations and sought to accomplish through force what the Huron were able to do through peaceful means. Despite decreased resistance from both the French and their Indian allies, the Iroquois control over the western trade was sporadic at best. Their attempts to control the trade ended in failure and sometimes in costly defeat.[5]

If events in the West seemed to be spinning out of control for the Iroquois, in the East events detrimental to their interests were also taking shape. In 1664, the British began a naval blockade of the Dutch port of New Amsterdam, which eventually led to the Dutch surrender of their North American colony. For the Iroquois, the blockade made goods more expensive at the Dutch trading center, Fort Orange. Seeking cheaper prices, the Iroquois made peace with the French but did so on Iroquois terms. The peace, however, did not last long. It allowed the Ottawa and Huron, who had fled west, to continue as middlemen in the fur trade, and soon flotillas of canoes arrived in Montreal bringing furs from the West. While the Iroquois squabbled regarding what course to take with the French, the French, buoyed economically by shipments of western furs, began to explore trade possibilities in the western Great Lakes. This made it more difficult for the Iroquois to maintain any semblance of economic control in that region. In 1657, the French colony—again on a sound economic footing—pushed their Algonquian allies to renew their war with the Iroquois.[6]

Two Frenchmen, Pierre Esprit Radisson and his brother-in-law, Medard Chouart Des Groseilliers, at this time were eager to explore economic opportunities in the West. Sometime in the 1650s, they traveled with a group of Huron to Wisconsin.[7] Other Frenchmen soon followed. Upon assuming the post of intendent general, Jean Talon sent Nicolas Perrot to Green Bay in the hope of opening up Wisconsin and the western country to French penetration. The next governor of New France, Count Louis de Frontenac, anxious to expand French domination in the West sent Robert Cavelier, Sieur de La Salle, Father Louis Joliet, and Father Jacques Marquette into Wisconsin and beyond. Frontenac hoped to stretch French influence and power from the Great Lakes down the Mississippi River to the Gulf of Mexico. In Europe, however, the Glorious Revolution, or King William's War (1689–1697), intervened in those plans. War broke out between England and France, and in New France funds were diverted from exploration and expansion.[8]

What proved to be more disruptive for the area of Wisconsin was the French government's policy regarding Indian treatment and trade. Missionaries complained of the abuses that French traders and *coureurs de bois* inflicted on the Indians. As a result, in 1696, the fur trade was curbed and the number of trading places reduced.[9] New locations for trade were designated; a series of posts located at Detroit, Chicago, St. Louis, and New Orleans were set up, and Indians were required to trade only at these places. In truth, it was also an attempt to collect Indians around those posts and "teach," or acculturate them to, French ways. The plan proved not entirely altruistic. With the fur market in Europe glutted and an increasing number of furs pouring into France, reducing prices even further, something had to be done. Limiting the fur trade in America seemed the logical answer. Unfortunately, regardless of the fur market condition in Europe, many Indian people by the late seventeenth century had become dependent on the goods the fur trade made available to them. The fur trade forced gradual cultural adjustments on Indian people, and limiting the trade or altering trading patterns caused extensive hardships. With the French fur trade reduced, Wisconsin Indians began to turn more to the Iroquois and English goods. Discontent among those Indians that the French were able to gather at places like Detroit soon spilled over into war. The French blamed the Fox at Detroit and set out to chastise them with the result that the French again became embroiled in an extensive though sporadic frontier war that split their influence and caused further erosion of French power in the West.[10]

In the early 1700s, the French were able to retrieve some of their lost influence. They abandoned the policy of collecting Indians at designated posts. French traders and *coureurs de bois* continued in more or less legal fashion a trade they had previously carried out illegally. The French government tended to ignore such activity because the existence of fur traders in the West constituted a legitimate claim by France to the western territory. But despite some military success in the East against the

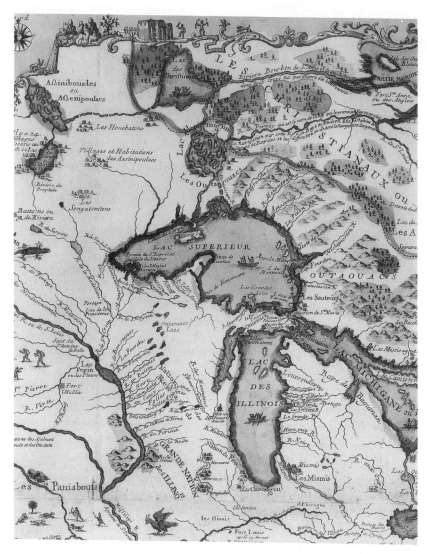

Map 2. A section of the map *Le Cours du Missisipi* drawn by Nicolas de Fer for the Compagnie d'Occident detailing the area of Wisconsin and the western Great Lakes. The map was published in Paris by J.F. Benard in 1718. Courtesy of the Edward E. Ayer Collection, The Newberry Library.

Iroquois, the power of New France was ebbing compared with that of the English colonies. New France was no match for the rapidly growing population and economic influence of the English colonies. With the end of the French and Indian War in America (1754–1760) the official French presence came to an end. In the French administrators' departure from America, they traveled for the last time the Fox, Wisconsin, and Mississippi rivers to New Orleans on their return to France. Their Indian allies, along with many of French and Indian blood, who had fought with the French in the East, returned to Wisconsin and Green Bay to await the English and a new era.

FRENCH INFLUENCE ON THE INDIANS

What influence did the creation of New France have on the history of Indian people and communities of Wisconsin? Early French accounts indicate that the fur trade, along with the wars in the East and the movement of other Indian peoples into Wisconsin, introduced strains into Wisconsin Indian communities. How these factors affected these communities and shaped their goals and what strategies Wisconsin Indians took for community preservation are now important to consider.

Between 1640 and 1680 the territory of Wisconsin filled up with Indian groups fleeing Iroquois thrusts into the areas west and south of Lake Huron and Lake Erie. These groups included Algonquian-speaking Ottawa, Sauk, Fox, Potawatomi, Miami, Mascouten, and Kickapoo, and Iroquoian-speaking Huron, Petun (Tobacco), and Neutral. The influx of these peoples, in combination with the Winnebago and Menominee peoples already in Wisconsin, produced strains both on the environment to provide food and on human adjustment. This was a tense time for all these groups. While fear of the Iroquois continued unabated, a new fear loomed in the West. The Sioux, a people the French sometimes chose to call the Iroquois of the West, thwarted further Algonquian expansion. Insecurity and the need for weapons, along with the greater competition for food, contributed to the growing Algonquian involvement in the fur trade. This raised questions regarding not only which Indian groups would control the trade—or even *if* any Indian group would control the trade—but also, and more important, how the fur trade would fit into and affect community life.

The Winnebago

As seen above, the first hint of growing tension in Wisconsin was the Ottawa complaint against the Winnebago that resulted in Nicolet's trip to

Green Bay.[11] The Winnebago-Ottawa conflict perhaps ensued because the Ottawa were trading with the Sioux or other groups living beyond the Winnebago. Rather than a Winnebago rejection of French trade goods, as some have contended,[12] the conflict probably erupted in order to prevent the Ottawa from trading directly with people that the Winnebago considered either enemies or within their own trading sphere.[13] It is unknown whether all the Winnebago or just one village or even a few individuals took this action against the Ottawa. According to later French accounts, the vociferous arguments among the Winnebago at the time regarding the wisdom of the attack on the Ottawa seem to indicate that the action did not enjoy total Winnebago support.[14]

Regardless of why it was committed or by whom, the Ottawa incident had unfortunate repercussions for both the Winnebago and the Menominee. The Ottawa not only enlisted the French in their cause against the Winnebago, but also prevailed upon other Algonquian—whom the Ottawa supplied with French goods—to join the attack. If Nicolet negotiated a peace in 1634, it broke down in 1635, plunging eastern Wisconsin into war. The Winnebago and their Menominee allies were pitted against an array of Algonquian peoples then moving into Wisconsin. Under repeated attacks the Winnebago, who lived in a single, large, possibly fortified village of several thousand people, perhaps at a spot called Red Banks on Green Bay or perhaps on Lake Winnebago, suffered heavily. Some archaeological evidence supports this contention.[15] The Winnebago battles with the Fox, who entered the region from Upper Michigan around 1634,[16] and perhaps with the Sauk, were especially fierce, and Winnebago defeats proved costly. According to one French account, the wars that raged in eastern Wisconsin at this time scattered the game, thus jeopardizing subsistence. Fishing also most likely proved dangerous. Along with war came even greater scourges: famine and disease.[17]

In 1634 epidemics broke out among the Iroquois and Huron peoples and by the 1640s had spread to Wisconsin. Nicolet may even unknowingly have brought disease on his visit to the Winnebago in 1634.[18] At the large Winnebago village the concentration of population would prove favorable for the rapid spread of disease.

According to Winnebago legend, it was here that disease and internal dissension, compounded by the debilitating effect of constant war, led to community depression. Constant attacks undoubtedly stretched village social, economic, and political resources to their limits and probably served to exacerbate an already bad situation.[19] But it was disease that caused the greatest misfortune. In the words of La Potherie, "Maladies wrought among them more devastation than even war did, and exhalations from the rotting corpses caused great mortality."[20]

Some Winnebago may have attributed the epidemic to their deity Disease-giver and believed it punishment due to their own iniquity in killing a delegation of Illinois Indians who had come to offer the Winnebago aid probably sometime between 1630 and 1650. Anthropologist Paul Radin records Winnebago legends that may refer to this time. The legends record how, at one time when the Winnebago were at war and had suffered great losses, some Indians paid them a visit. So upset were the Winnebago over the losses they had incurred in battle that they plotted the death of the visitors, who were in the chief's lodge. Calling their chief from his lodge, the Winnebago proceeded to kill the visitors despite his protests. This violation of the chief's lodge, a sanctuary or sacred space where all life was protected, other Winnebago saw as a heinous crime from which they as a people could expect retribution from the spirits.[21] The stress and tension produced by war and disease probably contributed to the decline in Winnebago fertility. Even the children born during this period were probably weaker and made more so by ritual fasting and poor diet.[22]

Unfortunately, the French sources are inadequate, and the Winnebago legends are sometimes too vague regarding this early period. It is apparent, though, that "some great upheaval affected the tribe after 1634, [and left] the Winnebago disorganized and greatly reduced in population."[23] Obviously, the cycle of activities that defined society was in disarray, and those kinship ties and institutions that gave meaning and bound society together faced severe strain. By the 1650s, these tensions proved too much, and Winnebago society began to fragment.[24] Any attempt to reorganize along traditional lines was precluded by the continuing influx of the refugee Algonquian from the East.[25] The Winnebago by 1650, forced to reevaluate their situation, moved toward alliances and the exchange of spouses with the invading Algonquian—to establish kinship ties with them and hence, in effect, make permanent hostages of them—and toward a rapprochement with the French. While such intermarriages did not obliterate Winnebago culture (indeed, there were attempts to protect and maintain it), they did introduce significant Algonquian cultural elements into Winnebago society. The French alliance also seemed particularly advantageous.[26]

According to La Potherie (writing many years after 1650), the Winnebago were still "subtle and crafty in war." He claimed they were "very fond of the French, who always protect them; without that support, they would have been long ago utterly destroyed, for none of their neighbors could endure them on account of their behavior and their insupportable haughtiness."[27]

La Potherie is perhaps too severe in his judgment of the Winnebago, but it is true that little is heard of them again as a major fighting force until the 1700s. They appear to have become a scattered population in the process of recuperating from their early devastating wars. Some took up residence at Mechingan, a Potawatomi village built sometime in the early 1650s near Green Bay.[28] This may be the village where the French Jesuit Father Allouez found them in 1660. He also found some with the Sauk, Fox, and Potawatomi at the mouth of the Oconto River on the west side of Green Bay.[29] Some may have taken refuge with other Algonquian groups in the area or resided at a smaller Winnebago village. By the 1670s, with the crowding of their domain, intermarriage with the French and other Indian groups, and the collapse of much of their traditional society, the Winnebago were compelled to rely on the French and the fur trade for survival. Unfortunately, there is little precise information on the Winnebago for this period.

French missionary accounts contain scant references to the Winnebago during the late 1600s. The only references to them are to their living in mixed villages, or villages composed of more than one people. By the late 1600s, however, the Winnebago population seems to have regained sufficient numbers for them to set up villages apart from other groups. It is probable that at this time the Winnebago became fully committed to the fur trade, which perhaps led to an acceptance of patriliny that was reinforced by the "shifting economic emphasis from gardening to male pursuits of the hunt and trapping."[30] This does not mean that the Winnebago gave up gardening, for they did not. Indeed it was their gardens and large stores of corn that cushioned bad years in the fur trade, bad years that caused suffering among other northern groups who relied primarily on the hunt.[31]

In the early 1680s, when the Iroquois seemed less of a threat and La Salle urged Wisconsin Indians to move to Illinois, some of the Algonquian began to leave Wisconsin. Some took up residence in Illinois, and others returned to Michigan and Indiana.[32] When this migration took place, the Winnebago probably expanded into the areas vacated. By 1700, the Winnebago appear to have concentrated their population on the north and west side of Lake Winnebago and were in the process of consolidating their control over the Rock River. When some Algonquian groups moved to the Detroit area in 1710 on French urging, the Winnebago chose to remain in Wisconsin. In 1718 the Winnebago were again near Green Bay and are reputed to have had about 80–100 warriors. By 1721 they were in the vicinity of Lake Winnebago, and for that time the number of warriors is put at 600. Although this population increase is probably inflated, it is possible that it reflects their regrouping from other villages or settlements in eastern Wisconsin. But this was not to last.[33]

When the Fox Wars broke out in Detroit in 1712 and quickly spread to Wisconsin, the Winnebago supported the Fox. In this move they incurred the wrath of the French, who attacked and burned their village on the lower Fox River in 1728. The Winnebago, warned of the approaching French, had deserted their village, but its destruction was a serious blow. The incident caused a rift in the Winnebago community. Some fled to the French, then at the Menominee village, to plead for mercy and forgiveness, and others joined the fleeing Fox, who headed west to the Mississippi River and settled at Lake Pepin.[34] What caused this social rupture into pro-French and pro-Fox groups is unknown. Most likely kinship ties were a factor. The Winnebago had intermarried with both the Fox and the French, and the schism may have split along ethnic lines. Then too, those more acculturated may have opted to seek a future with French protection, whereas those less acculturated perhaps threw in their lot with the Fox. The large Winnebago village also may have suffered the political factionalism that had beset their earlier village at Red Banks or Lake Winnebago. Even without having been destroyed by the French, the village perhaps would have broken up of its own accord. Trade obligations, combined with the loss of their winter food supply when the village was burned, would undoubtedly have been a major factor, driving half of the village back to the French at Green Bay. But all this is supposition about what may never be known.

From 1728 to the 1750s, the schism seemed to continue, whether as an expression of political factionalism or merely the exploitation of a wider hunting-trapping area is unclear. Perhaps Green Bay was less attractive as an environment able to sustain an increased population. In 1739, when the French requested that the Sauk return to Green Bay, the Sauk replied, "The majority would not like to go there, as they say that the Puants [Winnebago], who passed the summer there, Had great difficulty in subsisting, and that there are no longer any Crops, fishing, or hunting to be had there, because it is a soil that can no longer produce anything, Being Stained with French blood and with our own."[35] Although the Sauk believed the area of Green Bay to be cursed, the statement may also indicate a period of poor harvests and a decline in both fish and game animals. It does appear that buffalo and elk were gone from the Green Bay area, but other factors were probably more important in keeping the Winnebago apart.[36]

Changes in the fur trade and in subsistence patterns were most likely the reason the Sauk chose not to return. Since the early 1700s, French traders had followed Indians to their hunting areas, making it no longer imperative for Indians to take their peltry to Green Bay. As the beaver declined near the Indian villages close to Green Bay, Indians began to drift westward in search of more productive beaver grounds. Less time was devoted to fishing in the fall and more time to the winter hunt. The southern Winnebago found the area along the Wisconsin River both fertile for corn and a good area for beaver. They may have begun to acquire horses by this time and had easier access to large game in oak openings in southern Wisconsin and in Iowa.[37] Hence the changing fur trade and the necessity for beaver likely caused the extension of Winnebago settlements from Lake Winnebago to the Wisconsin River.

By the close of the French period in Wisconsin, the Winnebago were still divided into two groups. Those who had fled to Green Bay were still in the area of Lake Winnebago, and those who had fled to Lake Pepin had relocated to the Rock River.[38] Heavily engaged in the fur trade, the Winnebago seem to have trapped throughout southwest and west-central Wisconsin and made hunting forays into Iowa for buffalo.[39]

In a little over 100 years, the Winnebago moved from their large village to small villages to social reorganization to social collapse. During the years following the fragmentation of their society, the Winnebago intermarried with both the Algonquian and the French and in the process slowly absorbed new customs. By the time the Winnebago population recovered at the beginning of the eighteenth century from its precipitous decline in the 1640s, they were firmly entrenched in the fur trade. The demands of the trade had social costs. A greater emphasis on the hunt increased Winnebago mobility, and agriculture suffered. It is believed that at this time the Winnebago moved from matrilineal to patrilineal descent. As noted, their alliance with the Fox in the 1720s led to more destruction and social fragmentation. By the 1750s, Winnebago society was still divided, whether by politics, by the exigencies of the fur trade, or by both, is not known.

The Menominee

The Menominee, long-time allies of the Winnebago, shared in their defeats and misfortunes. Obviously, there is little known about Menominee culture before contact, but the changes introduced first by the refugee Algonquian and later by the French greatly altered Menominee culture.[40] Unfortunately, even the French records throw little light on the early history of the Menominee. Like the Winnebago, they were a sedentary people, but unlike the Winnebago, who depended heavily on agriculture, the Menominee relied on fish and wild rice. In the mid-1600s, their world was shaken by invading refugee Algonquian. Although linguistically related to the invaders, the Menominee resisted these incursions into their territory. This resistance brought, as it did for the Winnebago, death and disease.

In 1667, when the trader Perrot visited them, the Menominee lived in a small village on the Menominee River. Perrot noted that they were "no more than forty in number" but did not indicate whether he was counting families, lodges, or warriors.[41] In 1669 Father Allouez observed that the Menominee had "been almost exterminated by the wars."[42] As with the Winnebago, confrontations with the refugee Algonquian left the Menominee in a weakened state. The smallpox epidemic of the mid-1600s that ravaged other Indian communities in the area probably hit the Menominee. If it did, this combined with war losses would have caused the Menominee to suffer population decline. Smallpox was even more distressful than deaths from warfare because the strange disease, which attacked primarily the young and the old, defied traditional curing practices. With the death of the young, the Menominee future was suddenly cast into doubt, and with the death of the elderly, leadership in the present became a matter of momentous concern.

Yet despite their small population, Perrot found them in 1667 engaged in a war with the vastly more numerous refugee Potawatomi, then living at the southern end of Green Bay. Perrot, fearful that the conflict would disrupt the French trade with the Potawatomi, offered to mediate. When the Menominee learned that a Frenchman was approaching their village, they met him in the customary way. "All the youths came at once to meet him, bearing their weapons and their warlike adornments, all marching in file, with frightful contortions and yells; this was the most honorable reception that they thought it possible to give him." Such an impressive greeting possessed symbolic functions; not only did it indicate the high regard which they extended to their approaching guest, but it also fully apprised him of the martial strength of the village. To show further respect the Menominee attempted to carry Perrot to their village, but he refused. In the village the men assembled at the cabin of the head of the Thunder clan, the war chief. Before conducting business, the Menominee smoked the calumet and danced again in honor of their guest.[43]

Whether the Menominee met and heard Nicolet in 1634 when he visited Green Bay is uncertain, but by 1665 they certainly knew of the French and their trade goods. Perrot's admonitions not to go to war with the Potawatomi, and perhaps the Mascouten, probably made less of an impression on the Menominee than his offer of trade and an alliance. "I come to make the discovery of [new] tribes, only to return here with my brothers, who will come with me among those people who are willing to unite themselves to us. Could you hunt in peace if we give [weapons of] iron to those who furnish us beaver-skins?"[44]

The Menominee believed they could, and they accepted the offer that Perrot held out to them, perhaps hoping also to circumvent Potawatomi traders. The Menominee man whose son's death had precipitated the conflict with the Potawatomi accepted Perrot's gift and proclaimed that he "attached himself wholly to the French" and that "all his tribe had the same sentiments; and that they asked only the protection [that is, an alliance with implied reciprocity] of the French, from whom they hoped for life and for obtaining all that is necessary to man."[45] The welcomed alliance with the French in 1667 offered some security from attacks by the refugee Algonquian and had the added benefit of bestowing French goods.

The Menominee did take some furs to Montreal, but later the more usual pattern was to trade them to the Ottawa, and later still the Potawatomi. The Ottawa would convey the furs in large flotillas to Montreal or Fort Michilimackinac and return with French goods. These canoes loaded with prime furs from west of Lake Michigan riveted French attention, and traders hurried to the region. Although flotillas controlled by the Ottawa and Potawatomi would continue until 1700, by 1680 they were becoming less frequent, being replaced by Frenchmen, who now brought trade goods into Indian country. The introduction of Frenchmen, especially the *coureurs de bois,* into the Menominee village and their growing preoccupation with hunting beaver for the fur trade led eventually to other problems.[46]

The Menominee displayed little resistance to early missionary activity. The Jesuits were received cordially. Their black robes, beads, crosses, and Bibles were replete with spiritual semiotic power. In 1669 Father Allouez began the mission of St. Francis Xavier on the Oconto River near the Menominee and a mixed village of Sauk, Fox, Potawatomi, and Winnebago. In 1670 Father Louis Andre, who replaced Father Claude Jean Allouez, taught the village children religious songs and hoped that in this way he might spread Christian ideas to the adults. But it was his use of the cross seemingly to induce fish into the streams that won over the majority of the Menominee. That act impressed the Menominee of the practical application of the new religion's power.[47]

Their enthusiastic reception of both the Jesuit and the religion he brought declined after 1680. Sharp Jesuit attacks on traditional native religious practices and polygamy alienated many Menominee. The Menominee also increasingly fell under the influence of French traders, who saw the Jesuits' attempt to keep the Indians in villages for missionizing as hostile to trade interests. The Jesuits in turn accused the traders of exercising an immoral influence on Indian society in supplying brandy, abusing Indian women, and obstructing the church's mission. Calling for reforms in the trade and the removal of traders from Indian country, the Jesuits made a bad situation worse.[48]

The growing Menominee antagonism toward the Jesuits erupted in the 1680s when a smallpox epidemic swept through the Green Bay area. The priests' inability to halt the disease, which some Menominee suspected them of having caused, led the Menominee to violence. According to French sources, the epidemic "caused great mortality," and those who survived were left in an extremely weakened state.[49] Although traders could have brought the smallpox, the Menominee and other Green Bay groups blamed the Jesuits, whom they believed had cursed them with the disease.[50] "In the midst of this affliction, our Missionaries found themselves in great danger; for, since the Savages are extremely superstitious, they imagined that the Fathers had cast upon them some spell of witchcraft." The Menominee, although not the only Indian group involved, attacked and burned Jesuit lodgings and the church at St. Xavier Mission. The missionaries narrowly escaped with their lives; their servants, however, were killed. Their deaths were attributed to the Menominee.[51]

This attack took place about 1684. The effectiveness of the missions in the area of Green Bay had apparently declined by then. According to Felix Keesing, the peak of Jesuit activity was during the years 1679–80. "From then on, the number of workers in the field dwindled, and the personnel declined in worth and fervor."[52] The dual French policy of trade and salvation was in conflict. The Jesuit "policy of keeping the Indians in 'their simplicity and ignorance, only to be taught to worship the true God' was doomed to failure in such an age of expansion; their [the Jesuits'] influence became increasingly negligible, except in Versailles politics."[53]

The needs engendered by the fur trade were of more significance to the Menominee than the rewards offered by the missionaries. The acceptance of trade items at first was probably slow and at a pace that allowed such things as knives, awls, needles, brass bells, and cloth to be accepted without much disruption to Menominee culture or to be easily transformed into objects more meaningful to their existence. But as the fur trade flourished, the Menominee grew increasingly dependent on French goods.[54] The Iroquois-French peace treaty of 1663 and the resulting exodus of some of the Algonquian from the area west of Lake Michigan had repercussions on the fur trade in Wisconsin. With the route from Green Bay to Montreal now safe from Iroquois attack, French traders were increasingly drawn to the Wisconsin country. The wars of the 1650s and 1660s had depleted the Indian male population, leaving many villages with a surplus of women, and epidemics in 1666, 1672, 1676, and 1683 reduced the population even further. The French and the mixed-blood children they produced found a welcome in these communities.[55]

With constant encouragement from the French traders and a growing dependency on trade goods the Menominee devoted more time to hunting and trapping and less to the traditional occupations of fishing and gathering wild rice. As the beaver, once plentiful near the Menominee village, began to decline under intensive hunting, the Menominee in their search for pelts began to roam farther afield. This undoubtedly led to strains within the community. It may well account for the demise of the traditional clan system and the creation of bands corresponding to evolving social and economic needs and altered environment.[56] But the new life that the Menominee charted for themselves, which included dependency on the fur trade, was rudely shaken in 1698 by a new French policy.

In France the glut of furs produced a decline in the market. That fact, and the king, who responded to cries in France that traders despoiled the Indians with liquor and sexual abuse, issued orders revoking trade licenses and withdrawing French officials and troops to a few designated areas. Trade could be continued only at such posts, and since Detroit was to be such a post, the Indians of Green Bay were urged to resettle there. Some of the remaining Miami, Mascouten, and Kickapoo, along with some Fox and Potawatomi, migrated to the Michigan center. The

Menominee, like the Winnebago, Sauk, and some Potawatomi and Fox, elected to remain in Wisconsin. The Menominee returned to fishing and gathering wild rice and, when necessity compelled them to seek French goods, trading with the illegal *coureurs de bois* living among them.[57]

The French experiment in Indian resettlement collapsed in a few years. Dissension among the Indians at Detroit and fears of losing both the fur trade and the western empire to the British forced the French to reopen the western fur trade and build new posts in Wisconsin and the Mississippi River valley. At Green Bay, the French in 1716 rebuilt their fort, which again brought abundant trade goods to the Menominee.[58] By 1746, however, the beaver were nearly depleted in eastern Wisconsin. The Menominee search for beaver had already led them to settle on the Fox River, where Charlevoix found some of them living in 1689. Although this may have been only a temporary trading village, since no other reports of it exist, the Menominee did erect another village on the Fox River near Green Bay sometime after 1740. Traders began urging Menominee to move to western lands. Some Menominee had already moved their hunting camps there, but the Fox Wars of the 1720s and 1730s and the chronic hostilities between the Sioux and the Ojibwa forestalled any large migration.[59]

By the mid-eighteenth century, the Menominee had changed dramatically since their first contact with the French in the seventeenth century. Their population had increased and their economy had changed. About 1740 the old village on the Menominee River split up, with part of the village heading south and setting up a new village on the Fox River close to Green Bay.[60] Several factors may have contributed to this development. Debts accumulated through the fur trade may have "destroyed the old pattern of village life."[61] Already noticed is the fact that the clan system had given way to the band system, a form of social organization much more appropriate for the mobility demanded by the fur trade. Then too, the traditional sociopolitical organization under which the Menominee had lived may have become inadequate to withstand the strains produced by the larger population. Intermarriage with the French and, by the 1750s, with the Ojibwa may have altered community leadership patterns, making traders and those connected with them the significant men in the community rather than native priests or clan leaders. This perhaps proved another factor for further instability.

Probably also changed was the role of women in Menominee society. As the community became more preoccupied with hunting and trapping than with fishing and gathering of wild rice, the role of the women most likely was redefined. Whether changes in Menominee economy enhanced or undermined women's position in society is difficult to say. Did the men's absence from the village on long winter hunts allow the women in residence to assume more power in village affairs? Finally, by 1760 trade goods were replacing goods of local manufacture.[62] The pursuit of furs produced not only a mobile population but also a drastically altered economy. Menominee community life had indeed changed.

INTRUSIONS FROM THE EAST:
THE INFLUENCE OF THE ALGONQUIAN
AND IROQUOIAN INFLUX ON
MIDWESTERN INDIAN GROUPS

As seen, a major force in disrupting Winnebago and Menominee society was the influx of Algonquian and Iroquoian peoples. In the 1640s and 1650s, the Iroquois were like a destructive wind blowing from the East across parts of Ontario and Michigan, scattering the people of those areas north and west. The balanced social order these refugees had known, the delicate ecological and ritual adaptations they had made in their old world, were jettisoned in their desperate flight to gain the protection of the Wisconsin woods. There were four escape routes into Wisconsin. The Sauk, Fox, and some Ottawa, Huron, and Potawatomi fled across the open waters of upper Lake Michigan and down into Green Bay. Other Potawatomi, along with Miami, Kickapoo, and Mascouten, fled around the southern tip of Lake Michigan and up the west side of the lake. Another group of Ottawa and Iroquoian-speaking Huron and Petun traveled across southern Wisconsin and northern Illinois to the Mississippi River and then up the river, arriving eventually at Chequamegon on Lake Superior. Still other Ottawa, Huron, and some Ojibwa traveled along the southern shore of Lake Superior to Chequamegon.[63] Along these paths flowed the Indian population from Michigan, Indiana, and parts of Canada near the Georgian Bay, but in this migration the refugees fled to a world more uncertain and perhaps more dangerous than the one they had left. Confronting new environments complete with new spiritual terrors, their ritual systems severely damaged or destroyed, their economies shattered, these refugee groups felt vulnerable. Under such conditions it became increasingly necessary for them to turn to the French for protection and to the fur trade for economic subsistence. These conditions also spurred experiments in social organization, religion, and economics.

The shock of accepting a new life perhaps fell hardest on the Huron and, to a lesser extent, on the Ottawa. For the Huron, whose elaborate social and political organization depended on kinship and conformity to tradition, their humiliating defeat and precipitative flight were a shattering ordeal. Consummate traders and agriculturalists, the Huron were now compelled to take up a life of hunting and gathering as they fled westward. With a population severely reduced and scattered, old ceremonies that served as props for society, friendship, solidarity, and goodwill were difficult, if not impossible, to perform. The Huron also, along with the Ottawa, antagonized the Sioux, formidable enemies who added to the terrors of the new land.[64]

Although the Huron and Ottawa located at one of the few spots on Lake Superior where corn could be grown and they could enjoy an abundance of fish and waterfowl, life at Chequamegon still proved difficult. With the refugees' political and social organizations in shambles, they were forced for survival into an alliance with the French and participation in the fur trade.[65] Capitalizing on their earlier experience as middlemen in the fur trade, both the Huron and the Ottawa assumed this position again, trading French goods for beaver pelts with the Fox, Sauk, Illinois, and Potawatomi. These last groups, who came from southern Wisconsin and northern Illinois, still had no contact with the French, so they were eager for the trade opportunity the Huron and Ottawa offered.[66]

Trade alliances continued to be linked to political and defense alliances. As noted earlier, the exchange of goods between groups constituted in symbolic terms an act of friendship and a promise to participate in a common defense. Each summer the population at Chequamegon swelled when Indian groups from the south came to trade, and each summer the rituals of alliance and trade, the renewing of friendship and support, were performed.[67]

It was at such times that the Ottawa, Huron, and Petun seemed to resent the interference of the Jesuit priests. The Jesuits, who had followed the refugees to Chequamegon and founded the mission of St. Esprit to minister to their needs, railed against ceremonies of "indecencies, sacrifices, and jugglery" but to little avail. "Outaouaks [Ottawa], superstitious to an extraordinary degree in their feast and their juggleries, seem to harden themselves to the teachings that are given them"; they "turn Prayer to ridicule."[68] The priests seemed unaware that some of these "great revels" were probably ceremonies of solidarity between groups that made alliances, trade, and hence survival possible. Other rituals were performed as offerings to the spirits and to relieve anxiety in a hostile world. The Huron and Ottawa, like other Indians, did not strive to understand the world in an analytical way, only to coexist in a very dangerous environment with the spiritual forces of good and evil. They were willing to allow their children to learn hymns and be baptized, because such measures might be useful in confronting the world's dangers. Such willingness to comply with the priests' requests, however, did not exclude the practice of "proven" traditional rituals for survival.[69]

Chequamegon: Scene of Missions and Warfare

In 1666, because of Sioux attacks, life at Chequamegon became more precarious for the Indian groups gathering there. The Jesuits suffered more insults and insolence when anxiety and insecurity in the community increased. Father Allouez, who withdrew from the village when his church was destroyed and his few possessions were stolen, claimed that the "word of God was listened to only with scorn and mockery."[70] A couple years later, however, the Kishakonk band of Ottawa did find Allouez useful when they sought a closer alliance with the French. Whether they feared the departure of Allouez and with him French support or whether their conversion stemmed from a factional dispute with other Ottawa bands and a wish to gain greater influence with the French is unclear. For several years Allouez had preached to the Kishakonk, but they always told him that the time was not ripe for them to take up Christianity. Suddenly in the autumn of 1668, according to Allouez, the Kishakonk decided in council to accept Christianity. Allouez pointed out to the Kishakonk that "they should never be forsaken, but cherished [by the French] more warmly than all the other nations."[71] The Kishakonk undoubtedly welcomed Allouez's pronouncement, for they probably had such "cherishing" in mind when they chose to convert en masse. Apparently establishing closer ties with the French had benefits, because Allouez noted after their conversion, "They [the Kishakonk] have gained the upper hand over the other Nations and may be said to govern three others."[72]

This admission suggests discord among the Ottawa clans at Chequamegon. In accepting Christianity the Kishakonk anticipated stronger links with the French and a more favored position regarding French trade and protection. The statement of Allouez also suggests that some alliances with outsiders could lead to schisms between and within the Indian communities. Vying for better relations with the French spurred competition. If a strong alliance with the French could be achieved through becoming Christians, then some became Christians. This move was more often a political choice than a religious one. The decision for many Indian communities to accept Christianity, whatever the strength of commitment, remained in force only as long as they perceived practical results from their decision. In the very dangerous world of Chequamegon, always in jeopardy of sudden Sioux attack, a strong alliance with the French made sense. In the end though, despite French support, the Sioux attacks continued and, when the Iroquois threat lessened, the Ottawa and Huron in 1670 fled eastward to Upper Michigan and Green Bay.

The Ojibwa at Chequamegon

Chequamegon did not long remain uninhabited after the departure of the Huron and Ottawa. In 1680, many Ojibwa in search of furs left Sault Ste. Marie, perhaps on French urging, and located a village at Chequamegon. What precipitated this action was a peace between the Ojibwa and the Sioux engineered by the French official Daniel Greysolon du Lhut. According to La Potherie, "Because they [the Sioux] could obtain French merchandize only through the agency of the Sauteurs [*sic*] [Ojibwa], they made a treaty of peace with the latter by which they were mutually bound to give their daughters in marriage on both sides."[73] Such an exchange was a bond that helped guarantee peace. The Ojibwa, by 1680 not only were hunters and trappers but also, like the Huron and Ottawa, had assumed the role of middlemen in the fur trade. The alliance struck between the Ojibwa and the Sioux facilitated both economic and military interests.[74] During the 1680s and 1690s, another period of intense warfare in Wisconsin, Sioux and Ojibwa war parties joined against the Fox, Mascouten, and Miami Indians on the Sioux's southern frontier and against the Cree and Assiniboin on the Sioux's northern frontier.[75]

The peace achieved between the Ojibwa and Sioux in 1680 did not last. The rupture stemmed partly from French expansion westward in the 1720s. Only when the French extended direct trade to the Cree and the Assiniboin did these Indians allow the explorations of Pierre Gaultier de Varennes, Sieur de la Vérendrye west of Lake Superior. The French, fearing their trade with the Cree and Assiniboin would alienate the Sioux, opened a large trading station at Lake Pepin on the Mississippi River. Although prohibited from interfering with the Ojibwa-Sioux trade out of Chequamegon, the post drew many Sioux who had formerly traded with the Ojibwa and so eventually undercut Chequamegon trade.[76]

In 1736 the Sioux, in a campaign against the Cree, attacked and killed 20 Frenchmen. Most likely the Sioux suspected the Frenchmen of trading with the Cree. Some Ojibwa who were on this campaign were apparently angered at the Sioux action because they feared French retaliation and the ending of the trade upon which the Ojibwa depended. Because of this incident and perhaps because of other strains in the alliance, the Ojibwa broke with the Sioux. The war that now developed between the Ojibwa and the Sioux deprived the former of the rich hunting area south of Chequamegon and west to the Mississippi. Without access to these hunting grounds and without the Sioux trade, Ojibwa existence became perilous. The French commandant La Ronde at Chequamegon urged the Ojibwa in 1736 to make peace with the Sioux or face starvation.[77] During 1737–38, some Ojibwa wintered about 30 leagues from Chequamegon, but this is as far as they dared to locate. In 1738, La Ronde reported a Sioux attack on some Ojibwa hunting 15 leagues south of Chequamegon. Essentially the Ojibwa were confined to Chequamegon. Faced with the decision to retreat from this area on Lake Superior or attempt to wrest the land from the Sioux, the Ojibwa chose the latter. What had once been a rich hunting area south of Chequamegon now became a war road.[78]

Some ethnohistorians claim that during this time the weak leadership that characterized the small Ojibwa conjugal bands gave way to more powerful hereditary leaders. In her study of early Ojibwa leadership patterns, Ernestine Friedl finds early Ojibwa band chiefs weak and their authority limited to family and close relatives. A case in point is Chingouabe, a headman at Chequamegon in 1695, who told the French, "Father! it is not the same with us as with you. When you command, all the French obey you and go to war. But I shall not be heeded and obeyed by my nation in like manner. Therefore I cannot answer, except for myself and those immediately allied or related to me."[79] According to Friedl, the issue of Ojibwa leadership patterns is complex. It "was an achieved position of short duration and one which had to be acquired over and over again." Certain individuals successful as war leaders, elders, and *mide* priests possessed an advantage in persuading the community, but their arguments had to be pressed with "elaborate oratory and accompanied by gifts."[80]

By the 1730s, Ojibwa bands evolved stronger patrilineal leadership structures. What factors in Ojibwa society might account for this change? The Ojibwa's growing dependency on the fur trade throughout the seventeenth century dramatically altered their old hunting-gathering economy. By midcentury, Ojibwa as middlemen were trading French goods for furs with Indians far from Sault Ste. Marie. With the move westward after 1680 the old band system, with its major function in society of controlling marriage arrangements and hunting territories, probably gave way to a new band system that emphasized mobility for trapping, trading, and war. In an unknown territory, or one under contention, it would have been difficult for a band to designate hunting grounds for its members. Indeed, there is some evidence, although at a later date, that the French trader took over this task of assigning territories as well as urging bands to move to new areas.[81] It is also possible that the trader in *sotto voce* urged certain individuals to assume band leadership. This worked to the advantage of the trader, who "finding it more expedient to work through a band leader, strengthened the prestige and authority of the civil leader, who was traditionally weak in the almost apolitical system of pre-contact Chippewa-Ojibwa."[82] When helped along with presents or bribes, the urging might have proved irresistible. But other factors, such as the necessity to govern the large village at Chequamegon (a village that by 1696 already included about 1,000 Indians) and to provide for its protection during the prolonged war with the Sioux, were probably more important in bringing about an end to the ad hoc basis of band leadership and led to the concentration of power in the hands of the most capable individuals.[83]

By the 1750s, the Ojibwa were firmly entrenched at Chequamegon. They also achieved some success in pushing the Sioux south and west of the Mississippi, although Sioux war parties still posed a grave danger. Some Ojibwa began to move south of Chequamegon in an attempt to consolidate their hold on the area wrested from the Sioux. Other Ojibwa at Chequamegon were poised to move west beyond Lake Superior.[84] A few Ojibwa had also moved to the Green Bay area, where they had intermarried with the Menominee. While the Ojibwa spread across northern Wisconsin, other Algonquian Indians were leaving Wisconsin and moving to the prairies to the south and the west. These were the same Algonquian who had earlier poured into Wisconsin in the 1640s in their frantic escape from the Iroquois threat.

THE ADJUSTMENT OF THE ALGONQUIAN REFUGEES

The tide of the Algonquian who swept into eastern Wisconsin in the 1630s and 1640s, wreaking havoc in the Winnebago and Menominee worlds, included the Potawatomi, Sauk, Fox, Mascouten, Kickapoo, Miami, and Illinois. Today, known as the Central Algonquian, they share cultural traits that were developed in the open woodland prairie environment of southern Michigan, western Ohio, Indiana, and Illinois.

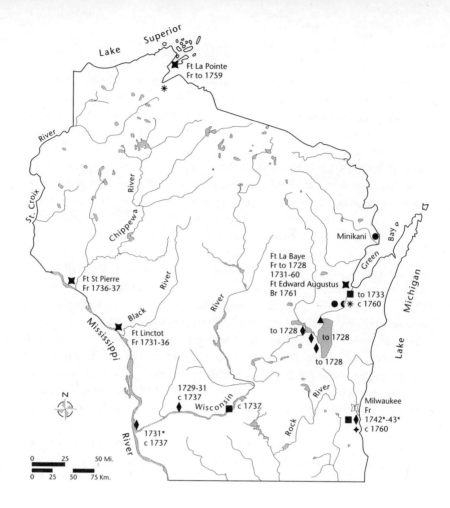

Map 3. The French Era, 1720–1761. Drawn from a portion of map 9 in the *Atlas of Great Lakes Indian History*, edited by Helen Hornbeck Tanner, University of Oklahoma Press, 1987.

70

Although they depended on horticulture, deer, bear, and buffalo were important supplements to their diet. During the summer they generally lived in large villages surrounded by gardens. All possessed patrilineal clans. Unlike the Ojibwa and Ottawa, the Central Algonquian, except for the Potawatomi and Menominee, did not have the birch bark canoe. They usually traveled by land or when by water, used the more cumbersome log vessel known as the dugout.[85]

The Wisconsin environment prompted experimentation and forced certain changes on the cultures of the Central Algonquian. Both the Potawatomi and the Sauk adjusted easily to the new conditions. Settling in the Green Bay area, they continued some farming but also took up collecting wild rice and fishing. It is not clear whether the Fox were as adept at adjusting to the Wisconsin environment as were the Potawatomi and Sauk, but it is apparent that the Miami, Mascouten, and Kickapoo never did.

The last three groups entered Wisconsin sometime around 1660 and set up a mixed village on the upper Fox River about 30 leagues from Green Bay. Not much is known about their Wisconsin sojourn, and it is doubted whether the mixed village comprised all the Miami, Mascouten, or Kickapoo. They remain shadowy figures in the historical records of these years.[86] Without canoes, they did not participate in wild rice gathering.[87] Although they engaged in the fur trade, trading most probably with the Potawatomi, they (at least the Mascouten and Kickapoo) resisted missionization.[88] Because the Miami, Mascouten, and Kickapoo were primarily horticulturalists and large game hunters, the cold northern woods little appealed to them. Even while located near Green Bay, they hunted the prairies of southern Wisconsin, Illinois, and Iowa for buffalo, deer, and elk, and during the winter, they hunted what large game they could find near the Fox River. After 1680, much of the large game in the vicinity of Green Bay disappeared, and so many of the Miami, Mascouten, and Kickapoo migrated to southern Wisconsin (near present-day Milwaukee), and to Illinois and Indiana.[89]

The Potawatomi made the most successful adaptation to the Wisconsin environment of any of the Central Algonquian group. The Potawatomi, who entered Wisconsin sometime in the 1640s, settled along the shore of Lake Michigan and erected the palisaded village Mechingan, a village which probably included some Sauk. Here several Indian groups gathered during the Iroquois seige of 1653. With at least half of the warriors supplied by the Potawatomi, the combined force successfully withstood the Iroquois assault. The Potawatomi, who astutely recognized their contribution in this event and were aware of their numerical superiority over the Indians of the Green Bay area, perhaps began to envision a new role for themselves. Probably aware that the role of middlemen between the French and the Green Bay Indians would bring increased status, the Potawatomi set out to wrest control of the fur trade from the Ottawa.[90]

During the early years of contact between the Indians of Wisconsin and the French colony on the St. Lawrence, the Ottawa controlled the fur trade. They pioneered the routes westward and, according to recognized custom, held possession of such routes. When the Huron, Ottawa, and Algonquian groups from Michigan fled into Wisconsin, the French followed. As mentioned, the primary goal for the French was to control the fur trade and thereby assert a political claim to the upper Mississippi Valley. To accomplish this political-economic goal, the French sent traders, beginning with Nicolas Perrot, to live among the Indians to encourage them to ally themselves and trade exclusively with the French.[91]

An alliance with the French was also on the minds of the Potawatomi, for it meant not only French trade goods but also protection and the status that came with access to French goods. In 1667 the Potawatomi made a visit to Chequamegon and, meeting the French, invited them to visit at Green Bay. The plan was to draw the French into an economic and protective alliance while inducing other groups like the Mascouten, Kickapoo, and Fox in the Green Bay area to channel their beaver pelts through Potawatomi villages. Unknown to the Potawatomi, Perrot also had a plan. As a government agent his instructions were to break up Indian trade monopolies. In the clash of wills that followed Perrot's meeting with the Potawatomi, Perrot prevailed, only because the Potawatomi realized that they needed French assistance.[92]

The Potawatomi were compelled to accept Perrot's terms, but they did so in their own way and without recognizing the parity of the other Green Bay Indian groups. If all the groups were "brothers," the Potawatomi would become the elder brothers. The acceptance of an alliance with the French came after a series of council meetings and an elaborate two-day ritual in which commitments were made to the alliance and prayers offered to the French manito for aid and support.[93]

Potawatomi acceptance of the alliance, however, did not represent subservience to the French. Despite the alliance, the Potawatomi schemed to keep the French out of the trade with the other Algonquian at Green Bay. They also resisted French abuses both in Montreal and from traders living in their villages.[94]

This resistance to French abuse throws light on Potawatomi political structure according to anthropologist James Clifton. He notes that what is conspicuous in all these incidents was the absence of a chief to mediate the disputes. Clifton argues that, at this time, unlike the Miami and perhaps some other Algonquian, the Potawatomi did not have chiefs. The structural units of Potawatomi society were, as noted above, patrilineal clans governed by elders. Internal forces within Potawatomi society often caused clans to splinter or disintegrate, and so it was difficult for elders to impose their will. The fur trade tended to increase this fragility of Potawatomi social structure and gave rise to village "big men," whose power increased while that of the elders declined.[95]

FRENCH MILITARY CAMPAIGN AND THE WISCONSIN INDIANS

The benefit of French trade and protection then had to be balanced against the pressures leading to community disintegration. According to Clifton, status among the Potawatomi could be achieved through gift-giving, but in the intense competition produced by the fur trade, the village big men exhausted not only their own wealth but also often that of their relatives and clan members. This produced sharp discord in the village and led to fragmentation. Although this fission process created multiple villages and extended Potawatomi domain along the Lake Michigan shore from Green Bay to southern Wisconsin, these semiautonomous villages further disrupted Potawatomi unity and weakened political control.[96]

The trade practices of the Potawatomi, however, were not the only cause of disruption to community life. As strong allies of the French, the Potawatomi were affected by French military campaigns against the Iroquois and the British. The French often enlisted Wisconsin Indians, especially the Potawatomi, in these engagements. This further destabilized both social and economic community life. Campaigning in the East, warriors were unable either to hunt or to trap, thus forcing their communities to rely even more on French support.

The Fox-French Conflict

However, not all French wars were in the East or against the British and their Iroquois allies. The French controversy with the Fox Indians simmered all through the late seventeenth century and erupted into war in the eighteenth century. The conflict spread like a virulent disease, infecting other Indian groups and tumbling Wisconsin into war.

73

The first recorded notice of the Fox in Wisconsin was that of Allouez, who met them at Chequamegon between 1665 and 1667.[97] The early years of Fox-French relations were not contentious. The Fox welcomed missionaries and hoped that their presence would protect the Fox from Iroquois attack. Further, they were drawn to the missionaries when they believed that the symbol of the cross protected them in their battles with the Sioux. When this later was found not to be so, the Fox grew, according to the French, "badly disposed towards the new Christianity."[98]

Compared with other Indian groups, the French found the Fox fiercely independent. They were described as "less docile than the Potawatomi" and as a "proud and arrogant people."[99] Friction developed between the Fox and the French perhaps because of this clash of attitudes. When the Fox visited Montreal sometime in the 1660s, they were maltreated by French soldiers, and they suffered insults from French traders in Wisconsin.[100] The Fox also considered the French stingy when they refused to give presents freely. According to Perrot, "Those Savages imagined that whatever their visitors possessed ought to be given them gratis; everything aroused their desires, and yet they had few Beavers to sell."[101] Contrary to the usual Native American practice of giving gifts freely without haggling for goods in return when striking an alliance, Perrot's behavior during his first visit among them probably struck the Fox as less than friendly.

Like the Miami, Mascouten, and Kickapoo, the Fox located their village in 1668 at some distance from Green Bay on the upper Wolf River. To the French, this may have seemed unfriendly.[102] The Fox, after increasing difficulties with French traders, elected to trade for French goods through the Sauk, a people with whom the Fox were often in close alliance.[103]

Differences between the Fox and the French continued to worsen. Warfare between the Fox and the Ojibwa and between the Fox and the Sioux frustrated the French, who found such warfare an interference with the fur trade. French attempts to stop the warfare further alienated the Fox.[104] About 1680, the Fox removed their village from the Wolf River and moved south to the Fox River. There, located astride the main trade route between Green Bay and the Mississippi River, the Fox war with the Sioux intensified. The Fox were now in a good position to curtail French trade with the Sioux. Indeed, this may be why the Fox chose to relocate. Fox harassment of French trade on this waterway—perhaps with the surreptitious help from other Wisconsin Indian groups who were uneasy with the French opening up trade with the Sioux in the early 1700s—further poisoned Fox-French relations. Yet serious Fox-French conflict was avoided. The Fox were now investigating the possibilities of trade with the British.[105]

The smoldering differences between the Fox and the French burst into flame in 1712, when some Fox and Mascouten moved to Detroit to be nearer the source of French goods. A fight erupted between the French with their Indian allies and the Fox-Mascouten village. The Fox and Mascouten were nearly annihilated. The news of this incident traveled quickly to Wisconsin, where the remaining Fox, with their allies among the Winnebago, Mascouten, and Kickapoo, attacked French traders. Eventually the French were able to entice the allies of the Fox back into the French fold, but the Fox continued to fight and disrupt French trade. Fearful of a Fox alliance with the Iroquois and British and angry over the Fox threat to the fur trade, the French began a war of extermination against the Fox. This not only caused uneasiness among the Indian allies of the French but also caused the Sauk to come to the aid of the Fox. Under pressure from the Menominee, Winnebago, and Potawatomi to reach an accord with the Fox, the French finally relented and in 1737 settled into an uneasy peace with the Fox and their allies the Sauk. The Sauk and the Fox, however, by this time had moved to southern Wisconsin, with some taking up residence in Illinois along the Mississippi River.[106]

Yet how did this confrontation between the Fox and the French, which dominated so much of the history of late seventeenth- and early eighteenth-century Wisconsin, reach such an impasse?[107] Aspects of Fox personality may have exacerbated the situation, but the controversy between the Fox and the French has to be understood in the larger context of Fox society. The Fox were basically divided into village bands that acted independently. These village bands were further split into two competing divisions, but since each family, lineage, and clan were equally divided between these two divisions, social cleavage was minimized. This and the loose village band structure tended to reduce the factional divisions that beset Indian groups which had a more structured sociopolitical organization.[108]

Although the loose structure allowed the Fox more flexibility in responding to the environment, it also seemed to weaken the power of the chiefs. The Fox had two principal chiefs, a peace chief and a war chief, drawn from these village bands, yet they probably possessed little power.

According to a nineteenth-century account, Fox chiefs were "made tools of by the warriors and [were] compelled in many instances to act as inferiors and do many mean actions. . . ."[109]

If chiefs possessed little status and power, warriors seemed to possess far more. The social status and respect paid to warriors, "their irreverence for the pretender to authority," combined with a "radically individualistic" personality that rankled under insult, tended to promote Fox warfare.[110]

Thus in Fox society, where village bands were loosely organized, where high status and respect were accorded to "radical individualism," and where the mechanisms for social and political control remained weak, Fox tolerance for meddling and control from outside the community proved low. Two other factors are also significant in explaining the Fox response to the French. The Fox subsistence pattern, based heavily on agriculture rather than on hunting and gathering, made them less dependent than other groups on the fur trade, and thus the Fox risked less in their opposition to the French. The other important factor to consider is the initial threat to Fox security that the French trade with the Sioux represented. These factors, although they do not totally explain the Fox-French conflict, do provide a context for understanding. In the end, however, French military strength and the threat to curtail trade with those groups who allied themselves with the Fox strained Fox society and ended overt Fox resistance.

SUMMARY

Even before the French arrived in Wisconsin, a period of profound change had already set in for Wisconsin Indian communities. The arrival of the French and the fur trade altered the economic pattern of some Indian groups and influenced others, although to a lesser extent. Even though Christianity did not replace traditional beliefs or appear to have much influence, it may have introduced new elements into traditional religion.[111] Both the French and the Wisconsin Indian groups experienced acculturation that began slowly but soon accelerated in pace. Increasing acceptance of the fur trade often led to the restructuring of social and political community organization. Finally, alliances for protection and friendship and the rituals and ceremonies that linked these cross-cultural contacts continued to be important.

Does any pattern emerge that can help explain Wisconsin Indian history during the years of French contact? Certain observations can be made.

When stress and strain are increased, the more complex a society is, the more prone it seems to be to progressive disintegration, first in its economy, then in its social structure, and finally in its value system. If disintegration goes too far, the community can collapse entirely. Before that happens, however, a community generally accepts change and restructures itself.

The Huron and Winnebago, and to a lesser extent the Ottawa and the Menominee, are groups that suffered severe disintegration because of war and disease. To survive they accepted French protection and adjusted their societies to the economics of the fur trade.

The Potawatomi, devastated less by war and disease than the above groups, nevertheless suffered disintegration because of a too rapid conversion to the fur trade. When strain in Potawatomi society increased, their political structure broke down and social disintegration soon followed. Only by altering their political and social structures were they able to survive, but the cost of survival meant community division.

The Sioux, Sauk, Mascouten, Miami, and Kickapoo suffered less from war, disease, and economic disruption during this period. Consequently their societies still functioned in the traditional manner and were less receptive to French religious and cultural influences and to the dislocations of the fur trade.

Two groups, the Ojibwa and the Fox, do not fit the above patterns. Both societies were less structured and not as complex as other Wisconsin groups. Their loose internal structure allowed both to remain more flexible in exploring cultural alternatives. That the Ojibwa and the Fox chose different paths has more to do with their economics and environments than with any positive or negative feeling they had for the French. The Ojibwa who came from a hunting-gathering tradition, were more attracted to French goods, which made their precarious survival easier. The fur trade, however, eventually increased the social complexity of Ojibwa society. The Fox, who maintained an agricultural tradition, needed fewer French goods and so were less attracted to the fur trade, which tended to curtail the practice of agriculture.

Thus responses to French contact by Wisconsin Indian groups were varied. They were a product of the complex interplay of environmental forces, social structures, cultural and economic traditions, political forces, and degrees of disintegration. When the French departed from Wisconsin they left people who were profoundly changed by the French presence, but changed in different ways.

4

The Years of the British

When the news of the French defeat in Montreal in 1760 filtered back to the Wisconsin forests, a certain foreboding and uneasiness gripped the Indian communities. Perhaps only among the Potawatomi did grief over the French military defeat exist. Other groups, amazed and disheartened with French military tactics, demonstrated little commiseration for the French situation. Even before the war, dissatisfaction with French administration of the fur trade led the Menominee and some others into open confrontation with them at Green Bay. The enthusiasm for war at a distance was not high. The arena of conflict was too far east to elicit much response from the Indians in the Green Bay area.[1] Concern among the Wisconsin Indians in 1760–61 proved not to be for the French but for themselves, and it focused on rumors regarding the practices of British fur traders and government agents. French rumors that the British would treat the Indians "meanly" circulated in the Wisconsin forests, and it was with some trepidation that Wisconsin Indians awaited British arrival.

They did not have long to wait. In September 1761, Captain Belfour was ordered to take possession of Fort Michilimackinac and the posts at St. Joseph (Michigan) and Green Bay. At Green Bay, Belfour left Lieutenant James Gorrell to rebuild the old fort, which Gorrell renamed Fort Edward Augusta, and to administer affairs at that post. Gorrell found only one family of Indians, presumably Menominee, in the Green Bay village.[2] Other groups, away on their winter hunt, would not return until early spring. In May, Gorrell began to receive visitors from different Wisconsin Indian communities. They wanted "to know how they would be treated, and were agreeably surprised to find that we were fond of seeing them, and received them civilly, contrary to the account given them

78

by the French."[3] Throughout the spring and summer, official delegations from the Menominee, Winnebago, Sauk, and Fox communities arrived in Green Bay to receive gifts and formalize their relationship with the British representative. The war had produced hardships in their villages, and they were anxious to press requests for trade goods and especially for a gunsmith to fix their guns. The Menominee extended a warm welcome and expressed their hope that British traders would come among them because they had discovered that British goods were less expensive than French goods and often of better quality. This desire was echoed by the Winnebago, Sauk, and Fox delegates.[4]

The Indians also demanded gifts. This posed a dilemma for Gorrell. He not only lacked the requisite supplies to carry out the duties of his office, but also had orders to limit gifts to the Indians, giving only those "necessary to keep them in temper."[5] This last was partly a British move to cut the costs of Indian administration. Gorrell realized that the large number of Indians dependent on his post were accustomed to receiving lavish gifts from the French and would quickly grow dissatisfied with British economic measures that gave French rumors greater weight.

Gorrell remembered that Sir William Johnson, superintendent for Indian Affairs north of the Ohio River, cautioned him that, unless he did his "best to please the Indian," he better not go to Wisconsin. Although he did his best to comply with his orders to limit gifts, the growing necessity to counter French rumors forced a desperate Gorrell to request more presents from his immediate superior in Detroit, Captain Donald Campbell. Campbell refused, reminding Gorrell of his orders to hold back on presents. "These orders made me uneasy, as I was assured I could not keep so large a body of Indians in temper without giving them something, as they had always been used to large presents from the French; and at the same time, if I did not give each nation the same [as] I had given those that had been to see me, all would be lost to me and the service."[6] Gorrell's orders came from Lord Jeffrey Amherst, commander-in-chief of British forces. Amherst had an intense dislike for Indians and believed the French system of gift-giving was ineffective, merely a system of bribes to keep Indians under control. In his enmity for the Indian, Amherst found a sympathetic accomplice in Henry Bouquet, commander at Fort Pitt. Restless tribes, Amherst believed, should be sternly rebuked and punished. "Could it not be contrived to send the Small Pox among those dissatisfied tribes?" he wrote to Bouquet. Bouquet suggested the distribution among the Indians of germ-laden blankets. He also suggested hunting them with English dogs.[7]

Despite limited resources and frequent rumors spread by French Canadians that the British were in danger of Indian attack, Gorrell skillfully maintained good relationships with the various Indian communities. His strongest allies were the Menominee and the Winnebago, but Gorrell also established firm ties with the Sauk, Fox, and Iowa to the south and with the Sioux to the west. Gorrell, however, had some misgivings about the loyalty of the Potawatomi at Milwaukee, misgivings strengthened by warnings from the Sauk and Fox that the Potawatomi were not to be trusted. The Menominee and Winnebago similarly cautioned Gorrell about Ojibwa duplicity, and the Sioux boasted that they would protect the British from any Ojibwa attack.[8]

However, when the attack on the British came it did not come in Wisconsin but at Detroit. British austere economic measures and lack of any consistent Indian policy fanned extensive discontent among the Indians of the Ohio region. The British success in the French and Indian War presented new problems for British colonial administration. Ad hoc policy sometimes created confusion and chaos and proved self-defeating to British attempts to rule the former French territory of the Old Northwest. Officials with little experience had to formulate a plan for governing the interior that would satisfy the vested interests of competing colonies in western lands, fur traders, land speculators, English merchants, and Indians. Indians continued to be a serious problem in the West, and efforts made by Sir William Johnson at Detroit in 1763 to restrict traders to certain posts and set prices for both furs and Indian trade goods were unsuccessful.[9] Traders in alliance with British merchants clamored for greater liberty in setting prices and places for trade while land speculators with support from both colonial governments and London investors schemed to move onto Indian land. Trade practices often degenerated under indecisive and unenforceable policy, and Indians frequently complained of flagrant abuses by traders who plundered and stole. Before a policy juggling the interests of these competing groups could be devised in London, the British found themselves at war with the Indians.[10]

The dissatisfaction brewing for two years spilled over into violence in May of 1763, when Ottawa Indians and their allies under the leadership of Pontiac attacked Detroit.[11] Almost on cue, other British forts and posts were besieged. In June of 1763, Gorrell, at Green Bay, received an urgent message from Captain George Etherington, relating the attack by the Ojibwa on Fort Michilimackinac and its ultimate surrender. Etherington and others were held captive, and Gorrell, along with Menominee, Sauk, Fox, Winnebago, and Sioux allies, went to the rescue. By 1764 only Fort Pitt, Detroit, and Niagara remained in British hands, but by then Indian resolve was ebbing. Running low on supplies, the Indians were forced to negotiate for peace and return to the task of supplying their people with food. Trade nearly ceased during the conflict. The British withstood the sieges but at a heavy cost in life and property.[12]

THE NEED FOR A BRITISH INDIAN POLICY

What came to be known as Pontiac's Conspiracy proved a sobering lesson to the British, dramatically emphasizing the need for a western policy protecting Indian interests. A start had been made before the war when a plan was put in effect to separate colonists from Indians by designating the crest of the Appalachians from Georgia to New England as a dividing line between the two groups. Later known as the Proclamation Line of 1763, it confined colonial settlement to east of the mountains.[13] In 1764, the Lords of Trade in London promulgated the Plan for the Future Management of Indian Affairs. This plan drew upon Johnson's recommendations to limit the northern trade to certain designated posts, which, it was hoped, would eliminate trader abuses. The plan would also allow officials to maintain surveillance over the activities of French traders, set prices for furs and Indian trade goods, and grant licenses to qualified traders who presented bonds for good behavior. Finally the plan prohibited the acquisition of Indian land.[14] Negotiations after the war with Indians in the Ohio Valley and Great Lakes region also promised gifts and a more generous trade policy.[15]

The plan failed. Traders objected to being restricted to posts and prohibited from extending credit to Indians for their winter hunts. The traders pointed out that the plan also created hardships for Indians, who depended heavily on hunting and would be unable to devote either time or resources to travel long distances every year for trade. They argued that furs from the West would not come east but instead find their way into French and Spanish hands beyond the Mississippi. Johnson sought to modify the plan and urged the Lords of Trade to create more posts at places like Sault Ste. Marie, Green Bay, and Prairie du Chien. In London, the Lords of Trade rejected Johnson's suggestions as uneconomical. They decided in 1768 to scrap the plan and return control of the fur trade to the colonies, where it lay before the French and Indian War.[16]

Colonial assemblies, however, showed little inclination to assume this responsibility or the expense for Indian affairs. Furthermore, they refused to accept the home government argument for the need to station

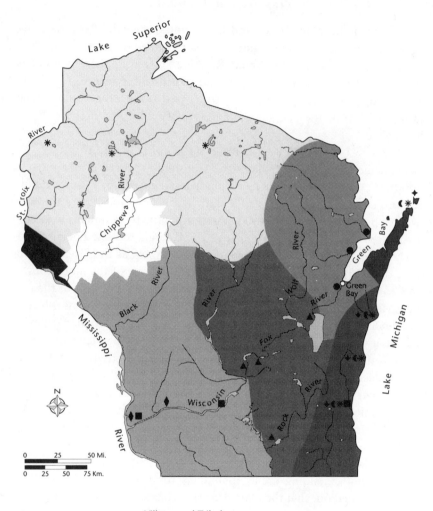

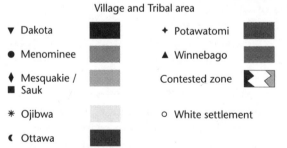

Village and Tribal area

▼ Dakota

● Menominee

♦ Mesquakie /
■ Sauk

✳ Ojibwa

☾ Ottawa

✦ Potawatomi

▲ Winnebago

Contested zone

○ White settlement

Map 4. Indian Villages and Tribal Distributions, c. 1768. Drawn from a portion of map 13 in the *Atlas of Great Lakes Indian History,* edited by Helen Hornbeck Tanner, University of Oklahoma Press, 1987.

troops in the West. The West slid further into chaos while the colonies continued in their indifference and in their disagreement over a fur trade policy. Abuses increased when unscrupulous traders, especially from New York, trading only in rum took advantage of the Indians. Such traders, according to Major Henry Bassett of Detroit, were "the outcasts of all Nations, and the refuse of Mankind" and exacerbated an already worsening situation.[17] Both Sir William Johnson and General Thomas Gage (the latter replaced Amherst in 1763 as commander-in-chief of British forces) were worried about the western situation. Johnson wrote to the governor of New York: " 'Licentiousness' of the frontiersmen in conjunction with the 'artifices' of the French on the Mississippi threatened to bring on an open rupture with the tribes."[18] With the West rapidly slipping out of control, Parliament again groped for a solution to the problem of western security, Indian trade, and colonial discontent. Parliament's answer was the Quebec Act, passed in 1774. Under this act, several of the provisions of the plan of 1764, like confining trade to designated posts, were repeated. But the major provisions placed administration of the West north of the Ohio River and east of the Mississippi River under the governor of Quebec and reinstituted French civil law in the whole area, and the Proclamation Line continued to prohibit colonists from settling in this area.[19]

Although these measures addressed some of the issues that beset British-Indian relations, the Quebec Act was held reprehensible by the original English colonies, and it became another issue leading to their ultimate break with England. In Quebec, however, the act served to allay French prejudice, and in the West, facilitated the fur trade. When the futile attempt to force western Indians to trade at Detroit or Fort Michilimackinac failed, licensed traders were again allowed to trade with Indians in their communities. This not only benefited commerce but also enabled England to enjoy the allegiance of the Sioux, Menominee, Ojibwa, and Winnebago of Wisconsin.

THE EFFECT OF THE AMERICAN REVOLUTION AND
THE WAR OF 1812 ON BRITISH-INDIAN RELATIONS

When the American Revolution erupted, the explosions were primarily felt along the eastern seaboard. There were some skirmishes in the West and indeed a real fear among the colonists over possible British military use of Indian warriors. The military campaigns of both sides in the Old Northwest were indecisive, and although the Americans took some posts in the Ohio and Mississippi valleys, the British retook them, and Wisconsin remained firmly in British hands. Indeed, it was from Wisconsin that the British, under Captain Charles Langlade of Green Bay and Colonel Robert Dickson, launched attacks against American-held positions on the Mississippi. The secret of Britain's success in Wisconsin lay in British control of the fur trade in the region since the French and Indian War. British traders based in Montreal filtered into Wisconsin and maintained a brisk trade, thereby allowing the British not only to control the trade in the western Great Lakes but also, in controlling the trade, to determine the allegiance of the Indian communities. Only the Potawatomi near Milwaukee and the Sauk and Fox communities along with a few Winnebago in Illinois wavered in their support for the British.[20]

The war apparently had little direct effect on the Wisconsin fur trade. Profits for both British traders and merchants were high. The number of pelts and amount of money invested in the trade increased between 1775 and 1779. Thus it was a shock to Dickson, Langlade, and others who had defended Wisconsin to learn that the British at the 1783 Paris conference relinquished the territory to the Americans.[21]

Although through the Treaty of Paris the Americans came into possession of the Old Northwest, the British were slow to depart from the area. From the peace of Paris to the War of 1812, the Wisconsin Territory was American in name but British in fact. British traders continued to navigate the rivers and lakes of Wisconsin and ply their trade throughout the area without interference from American officials.[22]

But this situation would not last, and a profound political, economic, and social revolution would soon engulf the Old Northwest, unleashing forces that would disrupt communities to whom the fur trade seemed a traditional way of life. This change, of course, was felt first in the Ohio River valley, where American settlers moved over the land, cutting down the forest and staking out farms. In the process, they destroyed or drove off the game vital to Indian survival. Traders, watching prime fur areas disappearing under the plow and the survival of the fur trade cast into doubt, surreptitiously urged the Indians to resist in order to protect both their economic interests and their communities. Warfare erupted, and after a series of victories several groups of Indians that had joined together to resist the Americans were defeated at the Battle of Fallen Timbers in 1794. This led to the Treaty of Greenville (1795), which forced the Indians to give up land and brought more social disruption. The traders also, however, must share in the blame for the social disruption in Indian communities. Supplying liquor, traders proved just as damaging to community survival as warfare did. Liquor served to abrogate the influence of chiefs and intensify internal community violence, which further exacerbated community demoralization and disintegration.[23] Even among those chiefs who sought to increase their power through controlling the distribution of liquor, their actions often besmirched their reputations.

Nativistic Revitalization

Under such disturbing conditions, nativistic revitalization movements sprang up. These movements, generally religious in tone, sought cultural renewal at times of social upheaval and community disintegration. The most successful religious revitalization movement was that of Tenskwatawa, or the Shawnee Prophet, who during a trance acquired a prescription for a new Indian society. This prescription, mixed with elements of Christianity, called for a rejection of European goods and a return to traditional ways and nicely complemented the efforts of Tecumseh, the Prophet's half brother, in his attempt to organize an Indian confederacy to prevent American entry into the Old Northwest. Tecumseh and the Prophet spread this religious and political message from the Creek and Choctaw country in the distant South to the Potawatomi and Ojibwa in Canada.[24] Not all Indians accepted the Shawnee formula for survival. Some Indian groups were suspicious of this message, for it called for the rejection of certain traditional religious concepts. Other Indian groups, especially the young warriors, eagerly took up and spread the message and prepared to resist further American advance on their lands.[25]

Because the Wisconsin Indian communities did not suffer the same degree of despair and social disintegration that Indian communities in the Ohio Valley did, they exhibited less enthusiasm for the Shawnee message.[26] Only the Winnebago from southern Wisconsin and northern Illinois, who encountered the effects of an increasing American population, eagerly embraced the Prophet's message.[27]

The remoteness of northern Wisconsin effectively isolated the Menominee, Ojibwa, and some Winnebago and Potawatomi settlements from the dramatic changes taking place to the south. Despite the political fact that Wisconsin was part of the new American nation, the Indians there remained pro-British, some making annual trips to the British at Fort Malden, in Canada opposite Detroit, and trading with traders out of Montreal. They could not hear the chopping of trees in the Ohio Valley or see the fences going up, but in time they would. Deep in the forests of Wisconsin there were undoubtedly rumors of an impending crisis, but life and the fur trade continued unhampered by the events of the population increase to the southeast. The British during the years immediately preceding the War of 1812 anticipated the approaching conflict and pursued a delicate policy of keeping the Indians of the Old Northwest mentally prepared and materially equipped for war, yet, at the same time, counseled restraint.[28]

Given the pressures on Indian communities in the Ohio Valley, an explosion was bound to happen. The flash point was the attack by William Henry Harrison on the Prophet's village. Although this battle, the Battle of Tippecanoe, proved indecisive, Harrison claimed victory and burned the vacated village. But if his goal was to defuse the mounting anger among the Indians of the area and awe them with his might, he failed. Rather than containing the discontent, Harrision's actions merely spread the angry sparks of hate and resistance throughout the Old Northwest. As one American wrote of the Winnebago returning to southern Wisconsin after the Battle of Tippecanoe, they "breathed nothing but war against the United States."[29] The spark kindled by Harrison in the forests of Indiana soon burst into flame when far to the east the new nation, angry over recurring maritime insults from England, declared war.

The British commanders in Canada learned of the declaration of war before their American frontier counterparts did. The British, compelled in 1797 by the Jay Treaty to vacate all their posts in the Old Northwest, now recognized a splendid opportunity for regaining them with the aid of their Indian allies. Seizing the opportunity that foreknowledge of the declaration of war gave them, the British quickly went on the offensive. When war broke out, the upper Northwest fur trade centered at three places: Mackinac Island, Green Bay, and Prairie du Chien, all in British hands although technically American. Because the British dominated the trade and held the allegiance of the French-Canadians who, with their Indian wives, inhabited these posts, it was easy to gain the traders' support. Even before the declaration of war, the British commander at Amherstburg, opposite Detroit, had secretly urged the British trader Robert Dickson to raise an army of Wisconsin Indians and send them against the posts at St. Joseph and Mackinac Island. Dickson's army of Menominee, Winnebago, and Sioux enabled the British in quick succession to surprise the Americans and take Fort Mackinac, St. Joseph, and Detroit. Throughout the Old Northwest, Indians, angry at the encroachment of the Americans on their lands and at Americans' adamant demands for more land, flocked to the British banner. Generous amounts of British supplies were an added inducement.[30]

Although taking these posts was easy, keeping control of them proved a difficult task. While the war dragged on for three years, resupplying food, clothing, and ammunition to the western army and to Indian families severely drained British resources. In 1812 an extremely hard winter followed a summer hit by drought, failed crops, and disappearing game. Dickson, wintering at Lake Winnebago and planning the next year's campaigns, complained, "I am most heartily tired of this distributing of Goods and wish for the Spring. I hear nothing but the cry of hunger from all Quarters."[31] The next two winters were equally severe. Despite hunger, lack of clothes, and bickering among the officers, the British with their French-Canadian and Indian allies maintained control of Prairie du Chien, Green Bay, and other posts in the Old Northwest. Both political and economic ends, in particular the preservation of Wisconsin and the Old Northwest for the fur trade, motivated such supreme sacrifice by the British and their Indian allies. In the end though, the misery, death, and sacrifice came to nothing, for again the peace treaty ending the War of 1812 returned Wisconsin and the Old Northwest to the United States, and British officers retreated to Canada, never to return. The British relinquished the country for both political and economic reasons. The anticipated entry of large numbers of Americans into the area and their effect on the fur trade along with the cost of this competition contributed to the British decision to leave. From the standpoint of Indian communities that had exhausted their resources during the war years, it was time for peace. They may have preferred the old, the British, over the new, the Americans, but they wanted most to return to a period of political and economic stability. The Americans probably seemed to promise this stability.

THE RESPONSE OF WISCONSIN INDIANS
TO BRITISH CONTACT

When the British retreated into Canada, their Indian allies remained behind; so also did the effects of British policy. During the years of British occupation of Wisconsin (1763–1815), despite some movement and founding of new villages, the Indian communities generally remained in the same locations they had occupied at the end of the French regime. In the north along the shore of Lake Superior were the Ojibwa. West and south of Green Bay were the Menominee, and at Lake Winnebago were some Winnebago and Menominee. Mixed villages of primarily Ottawa, but also Ojibwa and Potawatomi occupied the western shore of Lake Michigan. Mixed villages also occurred in the Milwaukee area, where the Potawatomi predominated. Along the lower Wisconsin and Rock rivers in southern Wisconsin were the Sauk and Fox and more Winnebago. The shifting of populations that did occur—the continual drift of Sauk, Fox, and some Winnebago south and west into Illinois and Iowa, the Ojibwa into western Wisconsin and northern Minnesota, and the Potawatomi out of southern Michigan and Indiana—was not in response to British policy but to changing environments, ecological factors, and American pressure.

When the British explorer Jonathan Carver traveled down the Wisconsin River in 1766, he found the Sauk and Fox in four large villages. Of the upper village he wrote, "This is the greatest Indian village I ever saw, containing upwards of three hundred warriors. The town is somthing [*sic*] regularly built containing about 80 large buildings, besides a great number of farm houses in their fields for the conveniance [*sic*] of the squaws while at labour. . . ."[32] Although an epidemic had disrupted one of the Fox communities on the lower Wisconsin, what Carver and later the fur trader Peter Pond noticed were the extensive fields of corn, beans, melons, squash, and tobacco.[33] Pond gives, in his own spelling, the following description of the Sauk and their community:

These People are Cald Saukeas. Thay are of a Good Sise and Well Disposed—Les Inclind to tricks and Bad manners than thare Nighbers. Thay will take of the traders Goods on Credit in the fall for thare youse. In Winter and Except for Axedant thay Pay the Deapt [debt] Verey Well for Indans I mite have sade Inlitened or Sivelised Indans which are in General made worse by the Operation. Thare Villeag is Bilt Cheafely with Plank they Hugh Out of Wood. . . . Sum of thare Huts are Sixtey feet Long and Contanes Several fammalayes. In the fall of ye Year thay Leave thare Huts and Go into the Woods in Quest of Game and Return in the Spring to thare Huts before Planting time. The Women Rase Grate Crops of Corn, Bean, Punkens, Potatoes, Millands [melons] and artikels— the Land is Exaleant—& Clear of Wood Sum Distans from the Villeag. Thare [are] Sum Hundred of Inhabitants.[34]

The river location gave the Sauk and Fox access both to the rich floodplain for agriculture and to traders. Carver and Pond also noticed horses, indicating contact either with Spaniards at St. Louis or Indians farther west. Indeed the Sauk and Fox, although relying primarily on agriculture, now gained much of the meat for their diet hunting large game, like buffalo, from horseback beyond the Mississippi.

In these villages, characterized by a mixed economy, the community prevailed as the economic unit. Although years of fighting and sporadic French contact had taken their toll on Sauk and Fox communities, they continued to function politically and socially. Sometime around 1800, both groups moved to Illinois and the Mississippi Valley. Because agriculture and summer hunts on the plains produced most of what they needed for subsistence, and the lead that they dug from surface mines along the Mississippi could be traded for necessities, the fur trade proved less important and disruptive to them than to their northern neighbors.

Some of the Winnebago also lived along the lower Wisconsin River, along the Rock River to the Mississippi, and near the many small lakes that dotted the prairies in southern Wisconsin. They too were primarily agriculturalists and like the Sauk and Fox began to acquire horses and often hunted buffalo in Iowa. Although the fur trade remained important to these southern Winnebago, their reliance on agriculture buffered them from the economic-social-political shocks that the fur trade imposed on other groups. By the early nineteenth century, however, when American pressure for land arose in southern Wisconsin, the Winnebago there began to suffer the disintegrative pressures of contact. Hence the appeals of the two charismatic Shawnee leaders—Tecumseh's appeal for a confederation to resist American advance and the Shawnee Prophet's spiritual message for a new world—found eager acceptance among disaffected Winnebago and led many to move to the Prophet's village in Indiana.[35]

Farther east and north, the malady of community disintegration infected the Potawatomi, Menominee, and northern Winnebago communities, but for different reasons. The Potawatomi, long the dominant Indian group in the Milwaukee-Chicago area and on the east shore of Lake Michigan up to the St. Joseph River, were, like the Sauk and Fox, both agriculturalists and dependent on the horse for hunting the prairies of Illinois and those west of the Mississippi. They also utilized the canoe for travel and fishing.[36]

In the Treaty of Greenville in 1795, the Potawatomi relinquished some of their lands to the Americans, but the continuing tide of Americans surging westward in the early nineteenth century encroaching on Potawatomi lands thwarted not only Potawatomi expansion but also caused disruption in their communities. Local chiefs, or *okemas,* proliferated rapidly despite American desire to have one chief represent all Potawatomi in official negotiations. If some *okemas* had legitimate claim to the title, most others did not. As Topnebi, a legitimate *okema* of the St. Joseph Potawatomi, who tried without legitimate claim to extend his power over other Potawatomi groups—said, "Too many of our nation aspire to be chiefs—and when they find—they cannot be such in their own Country—they fly to the woods, and impose themselves upon peo-

ple of other tribes, as Chiefs—intrude upon Lands not belonging to
them, and are not only troublesome to us, but to all who meet them."[37]
This flourishing number of *okemas* during the late years of the eighteenth century and into the early years of the nineteenth century added
further discord to Potawatomi communities.

Disruption further increased when aggression once directed outside
the community turned inward. By the beginning of the nineteenth century, however, as anthropologist James Clifton points out, "the frustrations and hostilities of community life [were] curtailed by [Potawatomi]
incorporation into a larger political community; and with ample supplies
of whiskey to act as a solvent for the limited internal controls of men
prone to violence, in-group brawling could become extremely disruptive
to their patterns of community life."[38] Their disintegration derived primarily from direct competition with Americans for land, although the
fur trade and alcohol accelerated Potawatomi demise, as it did that of
other groups. Such were the corrosive effects produced by both American political and economic encroachment and the fur trade that by 1800
the Potawatomi increasingly lost control of their communities and entered a period when the "basic fabric of the Potawatomi tribe would be
dissolved and the tribe would be broken into a number of separate and
sometimes antagonistic parts."[39]

To the north of the Potawatomi, the communities of the Menominee
and the northern Winnebago were beginning to move farther afield from
Green Bay in search of furs and food. Although the Menominee preferred to maintain their villages in the vicinity of Green Bay, their friendship with both the Sioux and the Ojibwa allowed them to hunt in the
game-rich Chippewa River region, the rights to which were bitterly contested by the Sioux and Ojibwa.[40] The choice to maintain residences in
the Green Bay area probably centered on the Menominee's continued dependence on fish and wild rice, especially at times when hunting was
bad. The Winnebago also traveled far to hunt and, like the Menominee,
continued to maintain villages to the south and west of Lake Winnebago,
where they had access to fish, wild rice, and to their corn fields.[41]

North of the Menominee, the Ojibwa on the south shore of Lake Superior continued to expand their villages to the southwest into Sioux territory and also westward into north-central Minnesota. Bloodshed and
war prevailed between the Ojibwa and the Sioux, but the latter by 1810
were also moving westward, where they acquired the horse and turned
more to hunting buffalo on the plains. Some Sioux remained in the Mississippi and Minnesota river valleys and continued to hunt and trap, but

scarcity of game and chronic wars with the Ojibwa taxed community life.[42]

Although British occupancy between 1763 and 1815 led to some relocation of Wisconsin Indian villages, it had a greater effect on village life and organization. The British after Pontiac's uprising attempted to remain at peace with all the Wisconsin Indians. The emphasis on raiding and warfare as the usual path to individual status and recognition among all the Wisconsin nations ran counter to British attempts to maintain peace. The British saw raiding as detrimental to the fur trade and hoped to channel militaristic energies into gathering furs. The result, however, all too often rechanneled aggression into the community—aggression aggravated by the now easy acquisition of alcohol through trade.

Other conflicts affecting Wisconsin Indian communities were the American Revolution and the War of 1812. In both wars, the British employed Wisconsin Indians and linked presents to military activity. This is underscored in a letter of De Peyster, the British commandant at Fort Mackinac: "The Weenippigoes & Menomies . . . know they are not to have goods sent among them unless they strike the enemy. Should they misbehave I hope you will see the necessity of curtailing their presents."[43]

Fighting in the British wars posed critical problems for Wisconsin Indian communities. Men were away for long periods of time, and communities were forced to depend heavily on traders for supplies. Although the wars did not stop the fur trade, they did curtail much of its operation and restricted the flow of trade items now so essential for survival. The War of 1812 proved particularly trying because, as noted above, it coincided with several bad winters and poor harvests and often famine prevailed. Yet the wars did not alter Indian communities as much as the operation of the fur trade.

THE EFFECTS OF THE FUR TRADE

Between 1763 and 1815, all Wisconsin Indian communities (although some more than others) grew increasingly dependent on the fur trade. The fur trade whetted an appetite for European goods; guns, ammunition, traps, cloth, and tools soon became necessities, and the demand for these items multiplied.[44] Yet the fur trade was a more complex operation than the mere exchange of furs for goods. It also involved the exchange of services, supplying traders with food and women, and negotiating alliances and "chief making." As Gorrell's journal makes clear, the services of a gunsmith were also indispensable to the Menominee and the Winnebago. The cheap guns traded to the Indians needed frequent repairs, as did other trade items such as knives and metal cooking utensils.[45] This dependency on foreign metal goods reduced Indian self-sufficiency and forced even greater reliance on the trader and the fur trade. When the British trader Alexander Henry visited the Ojibwa in 1766 at Chequamegon, he found "fifty lodges of Indians there. These people were almost naked, their trade having been interrupted, first by the English invasion of Canada, and next by Pontiac." So deplorable was their situation that in a council with Henry, the "men declared, that unless their demands [goods and credit] were complied with, their wives and children would perish; for there was neither ammunition nor clothing left among them."[46] War and restricted trade produced a deplorable condition at Chequamegon.

Another significant indicator pointing to the effect of the fur trade on Indian communities in Wisconsin was the practice of English traders supplying Indians with goods they once produced for themselves. The Menominee, and undoubtedly other groups as well, now began to acquire birch bark canoes, rolls of birch bark, paddles, nets, and smoked deerskins from British traders. Apparently traders determined that supplying Indians with goods they formerly manufactured would ensure that they would devote more time to hunting.[47]

Wisconsin Indians discovered that traders were eager for commodities other than furs. Among the Sauk, Fox, and Winnebago peoples in southern Wisconsin, trade in agricultural goods, horses, hides, and lead complemented the trade in furs and provided further access to European goods. Northern groups, especially the Winnebago, also traded food to the traders. Carver commented on this when he visited the Winnebago village on Doty Island in Lake Winnebago: "The country here is very pleasant and good land not heavily timbered. They raise plenty of Indian corn, beans, squashes, water melons, Indian tobacco, Indian rice, etc. This town serves as a fine market for traders as they pass this way. They are served in plenty with provisions."[48] The Menominee and Winnebago, along with other Wisconsin Indian communities, traded food and slaves as well as furs for European goods.[49] The trade of greatest importance to the Europeans, however, was in furs.

Besides affecting Indian communities, the fur trade affected the environment. The English explorer David Thompson estimated that in the Lake Superior region it took about 206 square miles to sustain one family.[50] Even then, however, game exhaustion was common. Overkilling of one species affected the ecology of other species. Thompson found that when the deer and beaver populations were exterminated in an area so also were the fox and the wolf because "there is nothing for them to live on."[51]

Although residing in a richer environment than the Ojibwa, the Menominee, Winnebago, and the Wisconsin Potawatomi confronted similar environmental problems. The demand for furs resulted in over-hunting and the depletion of certain furbearing species near village locations. The alternatives were few: hunt different species in the same region, rely on a now-modified traditional economy, and thereby preserve community life; relocate villages or communities near better hunting areas; or travel far afield in search of game. After the 1740s, few groups chose the first. The Ojibwa and Potawatomi elected to relocate their villages, as did some Winnebago. Already seen is Carver's description of the large Winnebago village on Doty Island. By 1810, numerous Winnebago settlements were interspersed among Menominee settlements on either side of Lake Winnebago.[52] After the removal of the Sauk and Fox from the Wisconsin River valley sometime around 1800, many Winnebago, moving closer to their trapping grounds on the Mississippi, settled on the vacated lands.[53] Carver reported in 1766 that the Menominee lived in two large settlements, in their old home on the Menominee River and in their new village on the Fox River near Green Bay, but by 1810 Menominee settlements extended from Green Bay to the Wolf River and to both sides of Lake Winnebago. The American explorer Zebulon Pike also found some Menominee hunting on the Mississippi in 1806.[54]

Either option of moving villages or forcing men to hunt at great distances from the village involved risks for the community. Creating multiple villages could weaken or dissolve the main community. The Ojibwa of Chequamegon are a case in point. To hold onto the territory wrested from the Sioux and to search for new hunting areas, it became necessary for the Ojibwa to expand their settlements beyond Chequamegon. This resulted in the gradual dissolution of Chequamegon as bands broke away and moved into the interior. The Ojibwa family or band with its greater flexibility to meet changing conditions replaced the village as the economic unit. Trapping territories could easily be maintained by a single family or, at most, by a band, and although wild rice and some summer crops helped to sustain the small settlements, the Ojibwa depended heavily on the British trader for supplies.[55]

Hunting far afield presented the danger of enemy attack, especially if a hunter strayed beyond his group's territory. The trader James Goddard found in 1767 that the Ojibwa of Lac Court Oreilles lived in "continual fear being so near the Soux [sic] nation."[56] Most Wisconsin Indians hunted within their nation's boundaries, but when game disappeared in these areas they were forced to accept the risk of hunting in other areas.[57] To minimize the risk of confrontation with other Indian groups in whose territory they hunted, agreements were sought and hunting rights were acquired through formal negotiations and exchanges of gifts and women.[58]

The fur trade also promoted the growth of mixed villages, which were still in evidence in 1810. First encountered during the French period in Wisconsin and especially from the 1660s to the 1680s, when remnants of groups banded together for protection and then later for trade, the trend continued through the British period and into the early nineteenth century. For example, Ojibwa were found not only in Menominee towns but also in the mixed Potawatomi and Ottawa settlements along the west coast of Lake Michigan. There were also a few settlements of Indian renegades or individuals expelled from their communities found in Wisconsin at this time.[59]

As seen in chapter 3, the fragmentation of the old villages and the incorporation of outsiders seriously modified social and political structure. The increasing number of traders—both French and English who resided in Indian villages and took Indian women as wives, concubines, or slaves—contributed to the social and political disintegration of the village. The following description of the "marriage system" in Green Bay in 1816 was probably typical:

> The young people there were generally a cross between the French Canadian and Indian, and marriage between girls of this class and the white men arriving, was of a conventional or business kind, to suit the convenience of the case, the residence of the men not being permanent, or intending to be so. Marriage, therefore, was limited as to time, and was contracted either for life, or for six, or twelve months, as the case might be. . . . In case the lover or husband removed from the place before the expiration of the time agreed on, he had the right—as in the case of the *engager*—to transfer his marital claim . . . to another; so that during the term of the stipulated coverture, the girl might find herself the wife of two or more husbands.[60]

The progeny of these relationships often strained social and ceremonial relations. Discord also erupted over cases of marital infidelity. The transfer of women from man to man may have been acceptable with proper formalities, as was the acceptance of polygamy, but infidelity on the part of the male enraged many Indian women. This seemed to surprise many European males.[61] But perhaps the most insidious influence abetting community decline was the presence of traders as powerful outsiders who sought to influence the weak political infrastructure and encourage entrepreneurial types to ignore traditional customs.

The fur trade generated ethnic pluralism in many communities. It contributed to the decline of leadership patterns through diluting the force of tradition. Leadership in Wisconsin Indian communities was never very assertive except in crisis situations or at times of community hunts or relocation, since it consisted of negotiation and advising and proved most effective when hereditary positions were filled by individuals of character and intelligence. Carver noted this pattern of weak leadership in 1766 and observed, "This nation [Menominee] like almost all other nations of Indians pay but little respect to any authoritative commands and are principally governed by advice when it best suits their inclination."[62]

The absence of strong decisive leadership in Indian communities, however, is not only a cultural manifestation but also has ecological roots. In nonindustrial societies, strong leadership positions are apparently encountered where the environment and technology demand the organization and management of a work force. The Indians of Wisconsin, given their level of technology and environment, practiced hunting, gathering, fishing, and horticulture, tasks easily performed by an individual or family unit. Furthermore the tools and techniques were not specialized, nor did their use require the instruction by an individual with esoteric knowledge. Technical skills necessary for survival in the Wisconsin environment resided in the family, and hence where individuals could perform most tasks of sustenance, leadership remained weak and primarily advisory.[63]

Traders often capitalized on this weak pattern of leadership. Carron, sometimes known as Vieux Carron, a *métis* who came to the Menominee as representative of the Langlades, gained notice through marrying into the community and becoming the speaker for the head chief, a position that brought him to the attention of the Europeans. In time, both he and his sons Tomah and Glode became recognized as chiefs.[64] In 1796, perhaps because his chieftainship was under contention, Tomah requested a medal from the British.[65] Similarly, among the Winnebago, the soldier-trader Sabrevoir de Carrie married Haarpokewinga, or Glory of the Morning. The two sons of this union, Choukeka and Chah-post-kaw-kaw, or Spoon and Buzzard De Corah, became Winnebago chiefs.[66]

Contributing also to the strain on community bonds and the crisis of group identity were: the increased number of adoptions from other groups to replace kinsmen lost in battle; the acquisition of slaves, generally Pawnee from beyond the Mississippi, as a commodity highly valued by both the French and English alike; and the exchange of prospective spouses to consummate defensive and trade alliances. Such alliances often took place at the summer trade fairs at Green Bay and Prairie du Chien. All these forces tended to blur the ethnic identity of Wisconsin Indian communities and resulted in a pan-Indian or pluralistic society.[67]

The naming of chiefs by traders and British officials also diluted the strength of native leadership. Both British officials and traders tried to bring predictability to what they perceived to be the social chaos of Indian life. To accomplish this task, they created chiefs. Official speakers for the chiefs, because they were highly visible in negotiations with Europeans, were often recognized by the latter as chiefs, as in the case of Carron among the Menominee. Furthermore, traders often raised individuals who were popular in the community and good hunters to the rank of chief.[68] Malhiot reveals how this was done with an Ojibwa from Lac de la Triute (Trout Lake) east of Lac du Flambeau, and what was expected: "I gave a coat to 'L'Outarde' and also his flag, and one to 'La Grande Loutre.'" Malhiot then made a speech to L'Outarde:

Kinsman—The coat I have put on thee is sent by the Great Trader; by such coats he distinguishes the most highly considered persons of a tribe. The Flag is a true symbol of a Chief and thou must deem thyself honored by it, because we do not give them to the first comers among the Savages. One must do as thou dost to get one, that is: love the French as thou dost, watch over their preservation and enable them to make up packs of furs. . . . As first chief of the place, thou must make every effort so that all the Savages may come and trade here in the Spring. . . .[69]

Malhiot, however, shortly regretted his choice: "L'Outarde got drunk at Chorette's and did not get sober until today. . . . That man never should have had a coat and still less a flag."[70] Malhiot believed L'Outarde's addiction to liquor to be only part of the problem. According to Malhiot, L'Outarde was a "rogue" with a "black heart" and "very far from perfect." Later, he goes on to say, "I hope, for the public good, both on account of the Savages and of ourselves, and for the benefit of the North West Company, that the flag I gave him will serve as his winding sheet."[71] Of L'Epaule de Canard, Malhiot wrote, he "is the only Savage who deserves a flag. . . . He is a sober, brave Savage, liked by the others, liking the French, capable of sacrificing himself for them; a good man for errands; he does not ask for things, is satisfied with everything that is given him and is a famous hunter."[72] Malhiot's concept of the ideal chief was probably similar to that of other traders.

Competition between traders also produced chiefs, as in a case reported by the fur trader Michel Curot in 1803 in northern Wisconsin. "Pichiquequi when a little Tipsey In the night, told me that Mr. Sayer had given him a chief's capot and a Big Keg [of rum], saying to him to turn away the Savages, and hinder them from paying me their credits, not to furnish me any provisions, that if he succeeded he would give him a chief's coat etc. Next Spring." Pichiquequi's answer to Sayer was that "he was not a chief . . . that he did not command any Savages, that they were also Equal and would go where they liked to trade and that he himself would do the same."[73]

The "made chief" then was to be sober, a pawn of the trader, and one who could control the members of his band and ensure their delivery of furs to the trader. It was a plan for indirect control of the bands or villages through designated individuals. The coats, flags, rum, and preferential treatment of such individuals were more than just bribes; they were meant also to be incentives for other members of the community. The erroneous assumptions—derived from European experience with status individuals and heads of state—that both traders and British officials operated under was that Indian chiefs possessed the power and authority to control the behaviors of their band members. Not even "real," or hereditary chiefs, however, possessed such power. The "making of chiefs" in flagrant violation of native custom led not to stability but to further erosion of social control, jealousy, and sometimes death. Even in small bands, where all the members were related by either blood or marriage, jealousy and violence could erupt when one was accorded preferential treatment and made chief, because, as Curot pointed out in one case, each member of the band believes "himself as Great a Man as an Other."[74]

Although traders attributed problems in the fur trade to alcohol, liquor proved the lubricant of the business. One trader who wintered among the Ojibwa in the Lac du Flambeau country believed rum absolutely necessary to the conduct of the trade.[75] An acute rivalry among traders and their attempts to induce Indians to desert one company for another pushed many traders to provide rum as gifts and have it available as a trade item. In some cases, rum seemed almost the only item of trade.[76] Pike found the Ojibwa in 1805 much "attached to spirituous liquors" and laid the blame for this addition on the traders, "who find it much to their interests to encourage their thirst after an article, which en-

ables them to obtain their peltries at so low a rate, as scarcely to be de-
nominated a consideration, and have reduced the people near the estab-
lishments, to a degree of degradation unparalleled."[77]

The traders who wintered with the Ojibwa and who often became
the focus of small Ojibwa settlements were often forced to move with
them to new locations when the territory became overhunted.[78] This
could be expensive; the expense of relocating combined with the competition from rival companies caused traders to seek to reduce their costs,
often to the detriment of the Indians. Supplying generous amounts of
liquor, often watered down, was one way to economize. Indeed, to get
rum, some Ojibwa played off one trader against another.[79] Although
some traders deplored the use of liquors in the trade and believed it was a
"curse to the Natives," since it destroyed communities, instigated quarrels and revived old ones, and "kept the Indian poor," it was too attractive a trade item to give up.[80]

The dependency on alcohol in many Wisconsin Indian communities—alcohol now made so accessible through trade—not only reflects
the stress and strain in the communities but also contributed much to
their cause. Journals left by fur traders at this time are replete with references to both individual and community quarrels, murders, debauches,
and wife stealing caused by alcohol.[81] These quarrels generated so much
friction that unusual measures were sometimes devised to reduce the
strife. In some communities, it fell to the women to take preventive measures: "The women hid all the Arms, and Knives and left them [men]
nothing but their teeth and fists to fight with."[82] High alcohol consumption, along with the strong value placed on individualism in Ojibwa culture, proved a dangerous combination because, as with other groups,
there were few restraints in Ojibwa society that could compel sobriety
and community harmony. Even murder, often the result of a drunken
spree, was not a matter of community concern but an issue only between
families.[83]

The rampant individualism endemic to Ojibwa culture mixed with alcohol led increasingly to the disintegration of social control. The evolving cultural patterns were no longer determined by ritual sanctions and
culturally approved ecological adjustments but by the priorities of the fur
trade. Band and clan leadership, always weak, could not compete with
the demands, resources, and organization of an external institution like
the fur trade, which could manipulate both warriors and chiefs and, indeed, debase weak leadership institutions by creating new economic and
leadership elites. But the corrosive effect of the fur trade on Ojibwa com-

munities was merely symptomatic of the social disintegration spreading to other Wisconsin groups.

The years from 1760 to 1820 began a period of rapid decline for Wisconsin tribes that would culminate in a crisis situation and the collapse of their mixed economy system in the middle years of the nineteenth century. Except for the Potawatomi and some Winnebago, the American thrust into the Old Northwest in the early years of the century had little or no effect on the Indian communities of Wisconsin until after 1815. The fur trade and new technology were the primary disruptive factors. Communities' economic cycles were disrupted when less energy was expended in harvesting wild rice, fishing, hunting for meat supplies, and gathering, and more time was spent engaged in the hunting and trapping of furs. Over time, this affected the environment and forced communities either to relocate or to watch family groups or individual hunters depart for long periods to hunt in distant places. Following these hunting groups into the interior were fur traders who brought supplies and introduced new technology, thus enabling groups to devote more time to hunting for furs and depleting the local game.

Other factors contributing to disintegration incidental to the fur trade were, as seen, the creation of chiefs and the effects of disease. From the middle of the eighteenth century to the early nineteenth century, as warfare decreased the Wisconsin Indian population increased, but death and disease continued as a source of great anxiety. One of the results of the French and Indian War in Wisconsin was a smallpox epidemic which carried off 300 Menominee and 100 Fox. Because smallpox spread easily, it is likely that other nations also fell victim to the scourge.[84] Deaths now came not only from friction between groups but also from within the community as a result of drunken brawls and disease. Alcohol consumption may also have led to lower resistance to disease, to malnutrition, and to decreased fertility.[85]

Although the nexus between illness and nutrition in Wisconsin Indian communities during the early years of the fur trade has not received much scholarly attention, there may be a connection between the kinds of disease prevalent among Wisconsin Indians and the nutrition levels which corresponded with the new diet that was introduced by the traders and was heavy in sugar, starch, and fat. While nutritional levels may not affect susceptibility to some diseases like smallpox, poor nutrition definitely does increase susceptibility to measles, tuberculosis, diarrhea, and probably influenza.[86]

The more time Wisconsin Indians devoted to the hunt for furs, the

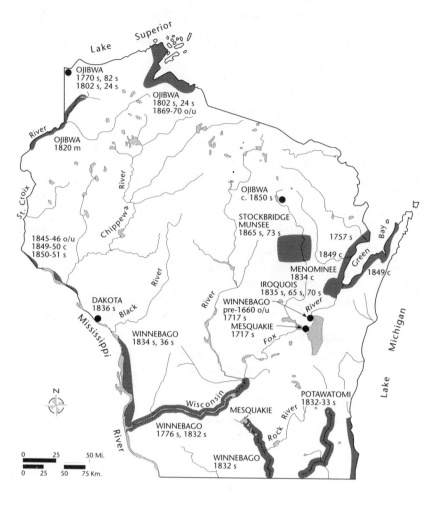

Lake Superior

OJIBWA
1770 s, 82 s
1802 s, 24 s

OJIBWA
1802 s, 24 s
1869-70 o/u

River

OJIBWA
1820 m

St. Croix

Chippewa River

OJIBWA
c. 1850 s

STOCKBRIDGE
MUNSEE
1865 s, 73 s

Green Bay

1757 s

1849 c

1849 c

1845-46 o/u
1849-50 c
1850-51 s

MENOMINEE
1834 c

River

IROQUOIS
1835 s, 65 s, 70 s

River

DAKOTA
1836 s

Black River

WINNEBAGO
pre-1660 o/u
1717 s

MESQUAKIE
1717 s

Fox

Lake Michigan

Mississippi River

WINNEBAGO
1834 s, 36 s

N

POTAWATOMI
1832-33 s

Lake

Wisconsin

MESQUAKIE

Rock River

WINNEBAGO
1776 s, 1832 s

River

WINNEBAGO
1832 s

0   25   50 Mi.

0   25   50   75 Km.

OJIBWA   Indian tribe

●   Indian village

〰️   Generalized region

1757 s   Date of smallpox epidemic

1820 m   Date of measles epidemic

1849 c   Date of cholera epidemic

1660 o/u   Date of epidemic of other or unknown disease

Map 5. Epidemics among Indians, c. 1630–1889. Drawn from a portion of map 32 in the *Atlas of Great Lakes Indian History,* edited by Helen Hornbeck Tanner, University of Oklahoma Press, 1987.

less time they spent exploiting local food sources and the more dependent they became on European foods. The nutritional benefits that wide-range hunting and gathering had provided to the Wisconsin Indian population were lost when a preoccupation with intensive hunting for furs absorbed greater amounts of time and energy. This, combined with a greater reliance on European foods, especially alcohol, undoubtedly resulted in a decline in nutrition and a greater susceptibility to certain diseases.[87]

Change in community composition may also have affected nutritional intake through altered distributional patterns. In traditional hunting and gathering societies, food was shared, and when scarce all suffered equally. The rise of mixed communities containing outsiders, who perhaps did not share in traditional beliefs of food distribution, may have altered the equal allocation of food resources.[88]

THE MIDEWIWIN, OR MEDICINE LODGE

It would, however, be a mistake to see patterns of alcohol abuse, brawling and murder, and community disintegration as the Wisconsin Indians' only responses to their changing world. There was also an integrative spiritual response that pitted "spiritual leaders" against "secular leaders" and against the dissolution of society. The made chiefs held tenuous authority not recognized by the society as a whole. Their power derived from outside the community and depended only on questionable attributes useful to forces external to the community. Their power did not come from sources sanctioned by tradition or custom. Opposed to the made chiefs were spiritual leaders, the leaders of the Midewiwin ceremony. They derived their power and authority in prescriptive ways. They drew upon ancient lore and the power of song and dance, and in so doing reaffirmed the value of tradition and the spiritual dimension. Moreover, the Midewiwin, in using animal skins and shells in its ceremonies, strengthened the community's identity with nature.

The lakes and streams of Wisconsin whose waters carried the fur trade also carried in the eighteenth century the Midewiwin ceremony from the Ojibwa to the Menominee, Winnebago, Sauk, Fox, Potawatomi, and even to the distant Sioux, Miami, and Iowa.[89] Although called different names, such as Medicine Lodge among the Winnebago, Mitawin among the Menominee, and Medicine Dance Society among the Santee Sioux, its mysteries found ready acceptance in communities undergoing profound change and plagued by social and political instability. The ceremony and attendant beliefs seemed to touch a deep responsive chord. This not only gave the Midewiwin wide acceptance within the community but also allowed it to function as both a spiritual and an integrative force.

This acceptance of the Midewiwin among the Algonquian, or the Medicine Lodge as it was called among the non-Algonquian, is important to consider in depth because of what it reveals about Wisconsin Indian communities at this time. There is a debate among anthropologists and historians regarding both the place and date of origin of the Midewiwin. Some consider the Midewiwin to have originated before European contact, perhaps among the Huron.[90] Others have argued—although acknowledging that aspects of the ceremonial complex are probably quite ancient—that the Midewiwin's creation is of a more recent date[91] and that it probably originated among the Ojibwa at Chequamegon.[92] Regardless of whether the Midewiwin is an ancient or postcontact movement, it proved a profound natavistic influence in Wisconsin Indian communities, where beliefs and values were constantly in a state of flux in response to new social circumstances and wrenching social change.[93]

The Midewiwin became a binding force for Indian identity in Wisconsin. As mentioned, it drew upon old values and assumptions of the universe and herbal knowledge. The Midewiwin was a religious society whereby, after payment, nominees were initiated into its mysteries. Over time members graduated through ascending ranks. The leaders or priests possessed a wide range of occult knowledge that included not only healing by herbs but also the ability to "kill," through missiles magically shot into the body, and then bring the dead back to life.[94] The priests or leaders were also the "repositories" of community "traditions, origins, and migrations," which they committed (at least the Ojibwa) to birch bark scrolls with the use of pictographs.[95] These scrolls, constituting the national history, were considered sacred.[96] The performances of the Midewiwin among the Ojibwa, as probably among some other Wisconsin groups, was an occasion of national importance that brought together all the distant communities.[97] Given their esoteric and occult knowledge, the power of the *mide* priests in society was significant, and although they generally remained separate from positions of civil leadership, they probably carried more influence in society than the civil leaders.

The Midewiwin also functioned to strengthen community interests. In his work on the Potawatomi, Clifton claims that the Midewiwin answered the "need for a pan-tribal institution which could aid in the unification of independent clan groups." *Mide* participants also, according to

Clifton, guarded the community from troublemakers and traitors and from situations threatening community security, and in so doing "reinforced traditional norms of conduct" in ways that clan leaders, at least among the Potawatomi, could not.[98]

For any movement like the Midewiwin to survive, it has to fit the economic needs of the community. This the Midewiwin did. By setting up a procedure by which power and medicine could be purchased, it not only redistributed the wealth earned in the fur trade, but it also deemphasized the vision quest, thereby allowing more time to be spent on the traplines. Individuals no longer had to spend days praying and fasting for a vision; now one only had to purchase power and medicine in the Midewiwin.[99]

So given the gradual breakdown of Wisconsin Indian cultures during these years, the growing ineffectiveness of their traditional social, political, and economic institutions, there is little wonder why they turned to religion and in particular to the Midewiwin ceremony. Among the Wisconsin Indians the Midewiwin held open the promise of rebirth or reincarnation after death if one recognized and interpreted the old legends properly and correctly performed the rituals. The Midewiwin redefined their community and their conceptual world. It reinstituted a degree of order and meaning, and at the economic level the Midewiwin redistributed community wealth that the fur trade created.

SUMMARY

The derangement of Wisconsin Indian communities that began even before French contact continued throughout the British occupancy of Wisconsin. During this later period the fur trade became an extremely profitable venture, and it is little wonder that the British sought to keep the Americans out and preserve the region for the harvest of furs rather than develop the land for agriculture and the harvest of crops. Frenchmen, maintaining close kin ties in the Indian villages, remained behind after Britain assumed control and were useful to the British as mediators with the Menominee, Ojibwa, Potawatomi, and Winnebago and with their knowledge of the fur trade.[100] British Indian policy devised just before the Revolution had three priorities: to keep Indian communities satisfied, to prevent intrusion on Indian lands, and to facilitate a just trade policy with the Indians.[101] After the Revolution, British Indian policy and control—through trade and the judicious use of gifts—persisted in Wisconsin.

Both the French and the British sought to rationalize the fur trade.

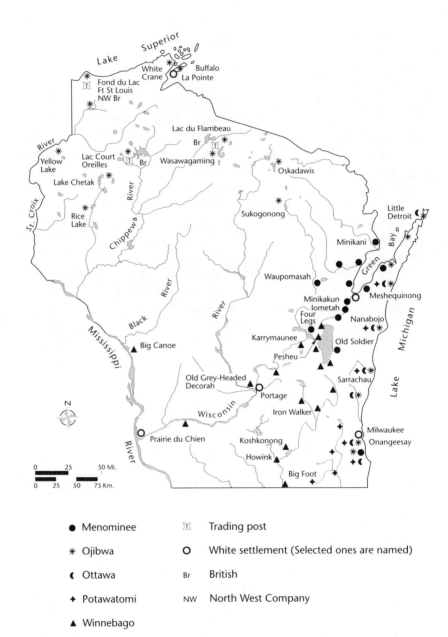

Map 6. Indian Villages, c. 1820. Drawn from a portion of map 20 in the *Atlas of Great Lakes Indian History,* edited by Helen Hornbeck Tanner, University of Oklahoma Press, 1987.

Legend:

- ● Menominee
- ✳ Ojibwa
- ☾ Ottawa
- ✦ Potawatomi
- ▲ Winnebago
- ⊞ Trading post
- ○ White settlement (Selected ones are named)
- Br British
- NW North West Company

They encouraged a managerial elite (made chiefs) who would organize and facilitate the efforts of a work force (community) to maximize profits and thereby realize company goals. Wisconsin Indians, however, frustrated such attempts. Little in their culture led them to capitalize on this plan that clashed with so many of their basic cultural assumptions and the dictates of individualism, equality, and established ecological patterns.

True, after some hesitancy and in differing degrees, Wisconsin Indians accepted the fur trade and the benefits derived from it, benefits that included protection, alliances, goods, and status. But each nation chose to integrate the fur trade complex into its culture in its own way. Although the Indians refused the European model, they did develop their own survival techniques. What Wisconsin Indians did not count on were those deleterious aspects of the trade complex: alcohol, disease, and their effects on the sociopolitical organization.

The most important survival strategy was the Midewiwin. It is possible that the Midewiwin is older than many anthropologists believe, but during the fur trade era its ritual evolved to meet specific community needs, took on new meanings, and performed certain psychological and economic functions. Its strongest appeal seemed to be among those communities that suffered most from the fur trade and contact situation. The Midewiwin probably never realized its full potential as an integrative force. So closely intertwined was the Midewiwin with the fur trade that, when the trade began to decline, so too did the Midewiwin. New problems and social conditions arose, and the Midewiwin—although it continued to operate as a psychological bridge to a traditional past—did not and could not provide solutions.

The fur trade and growing dependency on English goods limited a community's options to deal with its environment. Increases in the number of births in many communities were offset by deaths due to alcohol and disease. Community life suffered when hunters traveled farther afield to seek game and furs. This along with dependence on British goods led to a disinclination among some groups to maintain traditional crafts and a precontact economy. Trade disrupted the political and social order. Elders and headmen continued to lose what small power they had when traders raised up others as chiefs, and real leadership in the community shifted to priests of the Midewiwin ceremony. The new economic order and new environmental pressures dictated new kinds of leadership. In the ceremonies of the Midewiwin, Wisconsin Indians attempted to reform the traditional world and at the same time give some direction to their new social order. But while Wisconsin Indians sought to make sense of their world, the departure of the British between 1815 and 1820 foreshadowed a new world promising even greater disruption and despair.

Potawatomi chief John Young or Nsowakwet. He moved to Wisconsin from Illinois around 1840, and took up residence near Marshfield. According to James Clifton in *Prairie People*, John Young maintained ties with the Prairie Potawatomi of Kansas, fought against the allotment of Potawatomi lands in Kansas, and brought the Dream Dance to the Kansas Potawatomi (393).

Mrs. Katch-ka-mi, daughter of the Potawatomi chief John Young. Except for recent photographs, most of the following pictures present unsmiling subjects. In the late nineteenth century photographers cautioned their subjects not to smile since such facial expressions, they believed, tended to make the individual look foolish and undignified.

Ojibwa woman with baby in front of bark-covered wigwam. There was a sense of urgency in taking such photos. Since photographs portray both people and culture, students of the Indian thought it vital to make a visual record of the culture before it disappeared.

The Menominee family of Kaw-kee-she-uh-quat, with O-Saw-Wiu (Yellow), and Sawano Metámo (South Woman), 1906. They were a Midewiwin Lodge people. Many conservative Menominee live in the traditional community of Zoar on the Menominee Reservation. The Kaw-kee-she-uh-quat family lived in the South Branch area.

A studio photograph of the Potawatomi Simon Kahquados taken about 1919.

A group of Winnebago men playing the moccasin gambling game. According to Paul Radin in *The Winnebago Tribe,* this was a favorite game of the Winnebago and was similar to the well-known shell game where one is made to guess under which shell the pea is placed. In the moccasin game, moccasins serve as the shells, and the person with the stick has to guess in which moccasin the pebble is placed. A singer with a drum sings to try to distract the person in whose moccasin the pebble is placed and to cause him to reveal through gesture or facial expression the moccasin with the pebble (73–75). From a stereograph by H. H. Bennett.

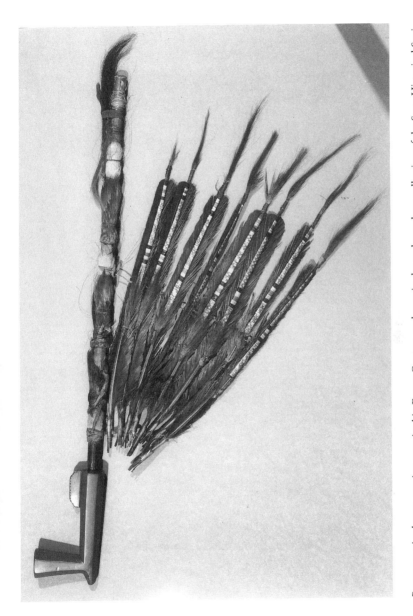

Potawatomi calumet, or pipe, acquired in Forest County, and now in the anthropology collection of the State Historical Society of Wisconsin. It reputedly was made by, or belonged to, Chief Pamobamee of Sheboygan. It has a 5-inch long catlinite bowl, and a 17-inch wooden stem decorated with quillwork, eagle feathers, and horse hair.

113

Menominee medicine dancers. From the dress of the man in the audience on the left, it seems like the photograph was probably taken in the early twentieth century. Until 1900, it was still very difficult, given photographic technology, to take outdoor pictures.

Reed- and-bark-covered Ojibwa Midewiwin lodge. Although information does not specify on which reservation this photograph was taken, it is dated 1948.

Midewiwin lodge on the Lac du Flambeau Reservation near Minocqua. Date unknown but probably early twentieth century.

A Menominee Dream Dance drum, 1945. At that time the drum belonged to John McIntosh. The drum held sacred meaning for groups like the Ojibwa, Potawatomi, and Menominee. As one Menominee, quoted in Thomas Vennum Jr.'s *The Ojibwa Drum*, reported: "Well, we treat [the Drum] as a person. That's the way we [Menominee] was preached [by the Ojibwa] . . . they even make special bed for that Drum. Keep it as a person. We Indians do that just for the sake of God; appreciate, take care of that Drum good, because that's his power. That's why we decorate that Drum, make it look pretty, clean, because it's from God" (61).

Winnebago buffalo clan spring feast lodge. According to Paul Radin's informant in *The Winnebago Tribe*, the buffalo feast could be held in the spring, fall, or midwinter. It always took place in a long lodge and no meat was offered. The feast was held in honor of the Buffalo spirits (195–98, 296–99). Photograph by Charles Van Schaick.

Postcard of Menominee children in front of a reed- and bark-covered wig-wam on the Menominee Reservation in the late 1940s.

Indian school near Hayward, Sawyer County, ca. 1880. Note that most of the children are females, and the few males all have had their hair cut short. Their hair and clothing convey the message that they are just like non-Indians. Often done for health reasons, such haircuts were a physical sign of acculturation. For many male Indians this symbolic rejection of Indian identity brought shame.

120

Ojibwa log house on the Lac Courte Oreilles Reservation belonging to John King, pictured with his wife and Nellie Mustach. Note the old style bark-covered wigwams in the background probably used in summer in preference to the log dwelling, or for storage. Such scenes convey the popular message of the Indians' transition from the old ways, symbolized by the wigwam, to "civilization," represented by the log house.

Stand of timber on the Menominee Reservation near Shawano, in the 1950s. Such timber was important to the Menominee economy and remains today a source of tribal wealth.

Menominee sawmill on the Menominee Reservation at Neopit, as it looked in the 1950s. Built by tribal initiative, the sawmill allowed the Menominee much economic independence, gave employment to tribal members, and provided funds for a tribal hospital.

5

The Arrival of the
Long Knives

The years of increasing American control over the Wisconsin area coincided with a struggle over competing views of the wilderness. The French and the English did not diminish the Indians' landholdings; their interest generally was in furs, not in land. The old interpretation that posited the military, businessmen, government agents, speculators, miners, and lumbermen against fur traders allied with Indians, *métis,* and English and French *engagés* is simplistic. The frontier was a land where people wore many hats. Occupations were not exclusive; one could be fur trader, miner, lumberman, and farmer, all over a period of time or simultaneously. Uncontested, however, was that a restless eastern population was pulsing steadily westward. The third article of the Northwest Ordinance, stipulating "expansion with honor," was intended to set the course of U.S. Indian policy. Expansion, however, all too often took precedence over honor; any instance of the latter was accidental. The preservation of Wisconsin for the Indian and the fur trade had ended.

TAKING THE LAND

Between 1800 and 1850, through subterfuge, retaliation, and sale, Americans in Wisconsin wrested lands from Indians until they occupied with uncertainty lands they once owned. The process of land alienation began as early as 1804, when the American government forced the Sauk and Fox to cede claims to lands in southern Wisconsin, in Missouri, and along the east bank of the Mississippi River.[1] And in the north, some

Menominee capitulated to government pressure and signed away 1,600 square miles of land on the lower Fox River. Other Menominee violently protested this transaction and eventually won its rejection, but the pattern of land cession was clear.[2]

The year 1825 marked the next major step in securing Indian lands. In August of that year, the U.S. government convened a council of Indians from Wisconsin, Michigan, and the Mississippi Valley at Prairie du Chien. With great ceremony and color, decked in their best clothing and in brilliant war paint, dancing to drums, chanting and firing guns, the Indian nations assembled. The council lasted from August 5th to the 15th. United States agents did not seek to acquire lands from the Indians immediately but rather to determine definitive boundaries between Indian nations, which would later facilitate acquisitions.[3]

The Americans at the council emphasized the concept of "tribe." Prior to 1825, this European term denoting a political entity did not adequately describe the fragmenting communities and mixed villages whose national identity was slowly dissolving.[4] The drift toward a pan-Algonquian culture that began with the fur trade and accelerated through intermarriage, the Midewiwin, and a general linguistic similarity (except for the Winnebago and the Sioux), produced a growing behavioral uniformity among Wisconsin Indian groups. This pan-Algonquian trend did not, however, suit the territorial goals of the American government. Since the late 1700s, the government's strategy was to negotiate land cessions with individual tribes rather than with tribal confederations. This, of course, enabled the government to gain concessions by playing off one group of Indians against another rather than having to deal with a unified opposition or confederacy that could strengthen the resolve of weaker groups to resist American offers. Hence, at the Prairie du Chien council, William Clark, territorial governor of Missouri and ex officio superintendent of Indian affairs, determined tribal boundaries and forced a recognition of tribal identity.[5]

The Lead Mining Region

The government soon employed this strategy with the move to acquire the lead mining regions along the Mississippi River south of Prairie du Chien. Lured by visions of wealth, Americans as early as 1821 raced to the lead mines on the Mississippi. Disturbed by this influx of miners, the Indian subagent John Marsh reported, "The mineral riches of the country have caused people to flock into it with a rapidity altogether unparalleled."[6] As previously mentioned, these mines, long worked by the Sauk, Fox, and Winnebago, provided lead that supplemented furs and corn as trade items. The rush of American miners into the area caused anger and consternation among these Indian groups and especially among the Winnebago, because the United States as signatory to the 1825 treaty had acknowledged this as Winnebago land. The dispute in the lead region was only one of many Winnebago grievances in the area, but it was the major one that fueled their discontent and ignited violent passions on both sides.[7] Confrontations erupted involving both sides, and the military tried to maintain a peace.

The Indian agent at Prairie du Chien, Joseph Street, attempted unsuccessfully with the army's aid to eject miners from the region, many of whom had stockaded their camps. To Street's consternation, federal mine agents even issued licenses to the miners. In 1829 a concerned Marsh reported 10,000 illegal miners on Indian lands.[8] The contest over the lead region produced tragic consequences, especially for the Winnebago with the death of Red Bird. His raid in 1827, prompted by rumors of Winnebago deaths at Fort Snelling and attacks on Winnebago women by miners and keelboat men, and his subsequent death in a Prairie du Chien jail caused much bitterness among the Winnebago. A presidential pardon came too late and probably did not mollify many Winnebago, who saw in Red Bird's actions an expression of legitimate revenge rather than a criminal act against Americans.[9]

Unable to remove the miners, the government turned to a familiar solution: force those tribes with claims to the region to cede the area to the United States.[10] The Sauk and Fox, at least from the government's point of view, had already surrendered their claims to the region in the 1804 treaty, and so in July of 1829 the United States government pressed the Ojibwa, Potawatomi, and Ottawa to relinquish their rights to the region. Skirmishes between the Winnebago and miners and the Red Bird incident sealed the fate of Winnebago claims and also forced them to relinquish more land in 1829.[11]

The continual removal of illegal squatters on Indian land posed a serious problem for the military and proved a major weakness in the military's ability to maintain order on the frontier. Removals often resulted in litigation. "Every subaltern in command knows," reported one civilian traveler in the West, "that if he interferes between an Indian and a white man, he will be sued instantly in the courts of the State."[12] The shared land hunger among frontier residents and their intolerance for In-

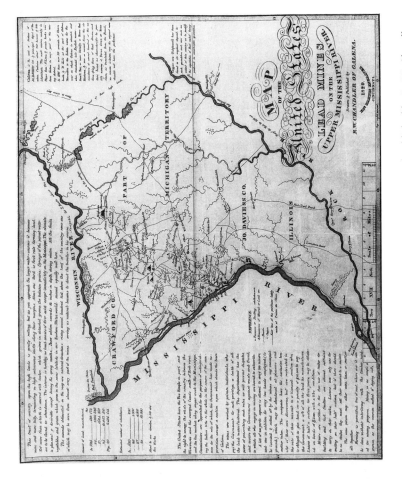

Map 7. Lead Mines on the Upper Mississippi River. Drawn and published by R. W. Chandler of Galena, Illinois, 1829. Courtesy of the Everett D. Graff Collection, The Newberry Library.

127

dian rights prompted some Americans to view the military more as an obstacle to the free pursuit of wealth than as a source of protection.

If frontier settlers were intolerant of Indians, they were also intolerant of each other. The military despaired of the public ever following orders and resented sharing control over the Indians with the Indian agent. Agents, jealous of the military's power, were resentful and often behaved in a petty fashion against both trader and local interests. Indian testimony was often used on both sides. Traders, local merchants, miners, and farmers chafed under any government control and particularly resented Indian agents, who, they thought, stifled opportunity and upset schemes for wealth. Lawsuits were frequent, and frontier lawyers were eager to take both military and Indian agents to court, where local juries repeatedly decided against the government. Faced with this inherent frontier antagonism for government restrictions, government agents often were helpless and ineffective in preserving order.[13]

In this maelstrom of competing interests, Wisconsin tribes petitioned for the redress of their grievances. Unfortunately, their interests proved weaker than those of the frontier community, and when the balance was struck, tribes forfeited their lands. In the clash between two economic systems, the military and the government chose the path of least resistance—the one culturally prescribed by the American public. Pressing tribes to give up their lands proved easier for the military than resisting, if only temporarily, American land hunger.

The Oneida Migration to Wisconsin

Certainly the American appetite for Wisconsin Indian land seemed insatiable. The Menominee received requests from the government in 1821 to provide lands to eastern Indians, primarily some Oneida Iroquois but also Munsee, Stockbridge, and Brothertown, who wished to migrate from New York State and were supported in this by the government as part of its plan to remove eastern Indians to the West.

The Oneida were part of the Iroquois Confederacy, which declined in power after the American Revolution. Before the American Revolution, the Oneida allowed the Stockbridge and Brothertown Indians to settle among them. After the war, American settlers crowded in upon the Oneida and their Indian neighbors and demanded Oneida land. The Oneida were split. Some resisted the pressure and decided to remain in their homeland while others decided to move west. Both the government and the Episcopal Church (the latter maintaining a strong influence among the Oneida) also urged removal. A charismatic part-Mohawk mission-

128

ary, the Reverend Eleazer Williams, had also pushed for Oneida removal in the 1820s. Perhaps with funding from the Ogden Land Company, which sought to purchase all Indian land in New York, Williams led a delegation of the Oneida west to Wisconsin in 1821 to seek a new home in the West.[14]

In 1821, both the Menominee and the Winnebago had agreed to sell land to the Oneida. However, after the first Oneida delegation had come to look over the land, they negotiated for more Wisconsin land in 1822. The Menominee, under pressure from the government, agreed, but the Winnebago, who were against conceding more land, left in disgust and later complained about the concession. Nonetheless, the negotiations enabled Williams to gain for the Oneida a strip of land four miles wide crossing the Fox River. Returning to New York, Williams met with criticism from those Oneida who did not want to move. Under pressure, however, from both the War Department and the Episcopal Church, the Oneida sent another delegation to look over the Wisconsin land later in 1822; this resulted in the first small migration of Oneida to the region in 1823. The small size of the Oneida migration and the realization among the Menominee of the extent of land and resources they had signed away caused them to regret the transaction of 1822, which was reaffirmed in the treaty of 1827.[15] In the treaty of 1827 and the subsequent treaty of 1831, the domain of the Oneida in Wisconsin was whittled down, until in 1838 it amounted to 65,426 acres. Although in 1825 more Oneida followed the first group to Wisconsin, and in 1827 a group of Oneida Methodists known as the Orchard Party arrived there, Iroquois resistance to migration strengthened, and Williams's dreams for a large Iroquois "empire" in the West evaporated. In 1828 a small Stockbridge contingent followed the Oneida and settled near them.[16]

In 1831 the Menominee gave up their claim to more land, that which stretched north from Milwaukee to the Door Peninsula and west to Lake Winnebago. In 1832, the Winnebago were forced to surrender their lands south of the Wisconsin River as a penalty for participating in the Black Hawk War.

The Results of the Black Hawk War
Black Hawk was the leader of a disgruntled band of Sauk who vehemently opposed the treaty of 1804 and the loss of their lands along the Mississippi and Rock rivers in Illinois. Their resistance led to war in 1832 and a tragic retreat northward up the Rock River into Wisconsin. The Sauk in their fight against the Americans received only tepid support

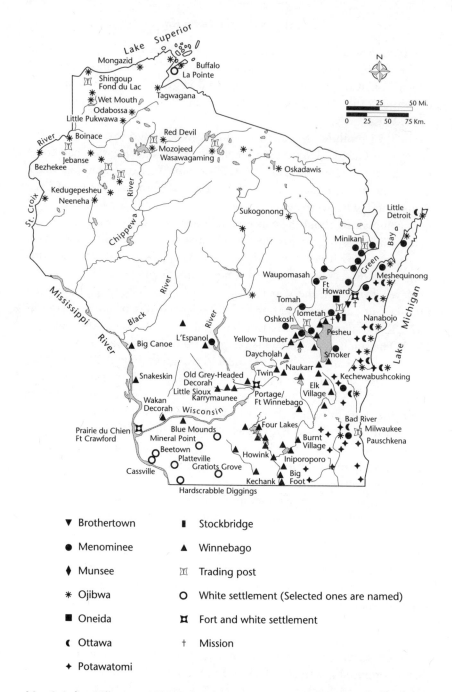

Lake Superior

Mongazid
Buffalo
La Pointe
Shingoup
Fond du Lac
Wet Mouth
Tagwagana
Odabossa
Little Pukwawa
Boinace
Red Devil
Mozojeed
Wasawagaming
Jebanse
Bezhekee
Oskadawis
Kedugepesheu
Neeneha

St. Croix River
Chippewa River
Black River
Wisconsin River

Mississippi River

Sukogonong

Little Detroit
Minikani
Green Bay
Waupomasah
Meshequinong
Ft Howard
Tomah
Lake Michigan
Oshkosh
Iometah
Nanabojo
Yellow Thunder
Pesheu
Daycholah
Smoker
Big Canoe
L'Espanol
Naukarr
Kechewabushcoking
Snakeskin
Old Grey-Headed Decorah
Twin
Elk Village
Little Sioux
Karrymaunee
Portage/
Ft Winnebago
Wakan Decorah
Wisconsin
Bad River
Prairie du Chien
Ft Crawford
Blue Mounds
Four Lakes
Milwaukee
Mineral Point
Burnt Village
Pauschkena
Beetown
Howink
Iniporoporo
Platteville
Gratiots Grove
Cassville
Big Foot
Kechank
Hardscrabble Diggings

▼ Brothertown		▮ Stockbridge	
● Menominee		▲ Winnebago	
♦ Munsee		⌘ Trading post	
✳ Ojibwa		○ White settlement (Selected ones are named)	
▪ Oneida		⌘ Fort and white settlement	
☾ Ottawa		† Mission	
✦ Potawatomi			

Map 8. Indian Villages, c. 1830. Drawn from a portion of map 27 in the *Atlas of Great Lakes Indian History,* edited by Helen Hornbeck Tanner, University of Oklahoma Press, 1987.

from the Winnebago and Potawatomi; their desperate hope for British support never materialized. Rather than joining with Black Hawk, many Winnebago actually remained neutral, undecided, or, as in the case of the mixed-blood interpreter Pierre Paquette, cooperated with American forces in attacking the starving and dispirited Black Hawk band when it made a disordered retreat through southern Wisconsin to the Mississippi.[17]

Despite this northern Winnebago aid to the Americans in effecting the surrender of Black Hawk, it was the earlier support given Black Hawk by some Rock River Winnebago that cost the Winnebago nation its prairie lands south of the Wisconsin River in 1832. Similarly, the Potawatomi, because of the limited support they provided Black Hawk in one of his battles, forfeited all their lands in southeast Wisconsin in 1833. Americans who chased Black Hawk across southern Wisconsin did not hesitate to calculate the prospects offered by the rich prairie lands of that area and quickly grabbed up the lands that the Winnebago and mixed villages of Ojibwa, Ottawa, and Potawatomi relinquished in treaties of 1832 and 1833.[18]

Expansion with Honor?

After the American show of force brought on by the Black Hawk War, tribes offered little further resistance, and the United States government, responding to the demands of anxious settlers, moved rapidly to clear the land of Indian title. Treaty negotiations were often presided over by individuals who later profited from transfer of title. By 1833 nearly all of southern Wisconsin had passed out of tribal control, and Americans soon began eyeing the rich timber and mineral lands of northern Wisconsin. In 1836, approximately 4 million acres of Menominee timber holdings were ceded to the government along with a 48-mile strip of land 3 miles wide on either side of the upper Wisconsin River. In return the Menominee were to receive $20,000 annually for 20 years plus other considerations for a total of $700,000.[19]

The United States concluded the largest real estate transactions in 1837 when it acquired nearly all of western Wisconsin from the Winnebago, Santee Sioux, and Ojibwa. It began for the Winnebago when their delegation, on a visit to the U.S. president to plead for their lands in Wisconsin, signed them all away. Fearful of just this possibility, the Winnebago—who always "observed a certain formalized protocol" in signing treaties, mandating that the signers include a significant representation of leaders of the Bear clan in charge of matters pertaining to land—were careful not to send a delegation that could officially sign a treaty. In Washington, D.C., the delegation was stunned upon receiving immediate pressure to sign a treaty selling all their remaining Wisconsin lands, pressure that they resisted "until it became apparent they would not be allowed to return home unless they signed a treaty." With winter approaching and concerned for the welfare of their families, the delegates signed, protesting that they did so "under duress and that since they had no authority to sell land the government could not expect the tribe to abide by the treaty." Even then the delegation believed that they would be given eight years to move and hoped that within that time a new treaty could be made that would allow them to keep their lands. The treaty, however, actually included a provision that the Winnebago must move out of Wisconsin by the following spring—in eight months, not eight years—to lands provided for them in Iowa and Minnesota.[20] Washington's insistence stemmed in part from Governor Dodge's threat that, if Washington did not remove the Winnebago, he would raise a state militia to remove them forcibly. As the English traveler Captain Marryat pointed out in reference to the Wisconsin scene in 1837, "The Indians . . . are *compelled* to sell—the purchase money being a mere subterfuge, by which it may *appear* as if the lands were not being wrested from them, although, in fact, it is."[21] So much for expansion with honor.

Removing the Winnebago to the West coincided with the growing consensus in the United States since the 1820s that all eastern Indians had little future in the developing nation and should be removed beyond the Mississippi, where, free from the pressures and vices of "civilization," they might yet have another opportunity to adjust to the demands that civilization required of them before it was too late. Understandably, many eastern tribes were reluctant to move to the West and be situated in the midst of warring tribes or former enemies. When spring came many of the Winnebago, who considered the 1837 treaty invalid, chose to remain in Wisconsin, evidently having their own ideas in regard to where they preferred to live and how they wished to adjust to civilization. Two years after the signing of the treaty, General Henry Atkinson was ordered to round up these Winnebago and transport them across the Mississippi, where the Rock River and many of the Portage Winnebago had been relocated on a reservation after 1832. But no sooner had he accomplished the task than many of the Winnebago drifted back to the Wisconsin woods they knew so well.[22]

The lands purchased from the Sioux and the Ojibwa were lands fought over by both groups for years. The Santee Sioux in 1837 relinquished their Wisconsin land, now nearly exhausted of furs and of little use to them for hunting. Most of the Sioux resided west of the Mississippi, and the few who remained on the Wisconsin side moved west apparently without protest. More valuable were the lands the Ojibwa were compelled to give up. Their land was still rich in animals and fish and provided them with an abundance of wild rice. In ceding this land to the United States, however, the Ojibwa retained the right to continue to hunt, fish, and gather rice.[23]

The Lure of Copper and Lumber

Five years later, in 1842, the Ojibwa were prodded to sell still more land. Rumors of large deposits of copper ore along the Lake Superior coast had circulated in the Wisconsin and Michigan regions for years. As early as 1826 at the treaty signed in Fond du Lac (now Duluth), the Ojibwa grudgingly gave permission for the removal of copper from their lands; however, this did not involve any land cession. When this ore proved to be high-grade, pressure mounted to remove the Ojibwa from the copper region. By the treaty of 1842, the Ojibwa were induced to give up lands in Michigan and Wisconsin, thus opening the possibility for commercial mining, lumbering, and fishing to begin. At the discretion of the U.S. president, the Ojibwa could remain on the ceded land until it was needed by settlers.[24]

Lumbering rather than mining prompted the government to return to the Menominee in 1848 and press for their remaining Wisconsin lands. Bowing to commercial pressures, Commissioner of Indian Affairs William Medill vowed no more delay in throwing open all Indian lands for settlement. Resorting to blandishments, flattery, and the threat that if the Menominee refused to sign they could be forcibly removed, Medill gained Menominee assent and the sale of all their Wisconsin lands in partial exchange for 600,000 acres in Minnesota. But the Menominee, unlike the Santee Sioux, did not go quietly into Minnesota. Like the Winnebago, they did not care for their trans-Mississippi lands and were adamantly opposed to removal. Wary of land situated between the warring Sioux and Ojibwa, the Menominee resisted. They pointed out, however, that it was "good country for the white man, for he was more numerous, and could protect himself from those warlike tribes."[25] In 1854, the government rescinded the treaty and provided the Menominee with land for a reservation in Wisconsin on the Wolf River.[26]

Nearly all the treaties during this period were similar in that they provided in exchange for land: an immediate cash payment, goods and cash paid out as annuities over a stipulated number of years, parcels of land given to mixed-bloods, or *métis,* and to Indian wives of whites, payment of individual debts to the traders, and often provisions for farming equipment, blacksmiths, and schools. Treaty commissioners and agents also provided American flags and presented American medals in exchange for British ones.[27]

THE SURGE OF AMERICAN NATIONALISM
AND COMMERCIALISM

The history of expansion in the Old Northwest is a history of more than just the acquisition of land. Nationalism proved very much a vital force. Even after the War of 1812 and into the late 1820s and 1830s, Americans still expressed fear regarding the British presence and their hold over the Indians of the Old Northwest. Besides British traders in American territory, the retention of British medals and flags by the Indians proved especially irksome to American officials because these items represented, or so Americans believed, a lingering allegiance to the British Crown. But if the retention of these symbolic tokens annoyed Americans, Indian travel to the British post at Drummond Island northeast of Mackinac Island was particularly noxious. Upon their departure from Fort Mackinac, the British positioned themselves at Drummond Island, southeast of Sault Ste. Marie, and continued to meet and trade with tribes coming from as far away as the Mississippi Valley and Minnesota.[28]

American officials objected to the British presence on Drummond Island, not only because the British used the site as a "listening post" through which their Indian Department could gain information about American activities from Indians, but also because, through gift giving and trade with the tribes visiting there, the British influenced and meddled with Indians now under American control. An angry Lewis Cass, territorial governor of Michigan, claimed that the influence of these British agents "has been uniformly exerted to hostile and insiduous purposes. . . .They systematically seize every opportunity of poisoning the minds of the Indians." Cass even believed that the British Indian Department had some American chiefs in their employ. To Cass the influences and intrigues emanating from posts like Drummond Island were "revolting to humanity, injurious to us, and incompatible with the amicable relations which have generally subsisted between the United States and Great Britain."[29]

Such statements by Cass and others echoed the wave of anti-British feeling that swept the Old Northwest after 1815 and lingered on well into the 1820s and 1830s. Fears of another British invasion spurred anti-British sentiment and found expression in public animosity against the old traders like John Lawe, Joseph Porlier, and the Grignon brothers at Green Bay. This, combined with racial bias against the large mixed-blood, or *métis*, population, contributed to shrill American demands for Indian removal.

The American fur entrepreneur John Jacob Astor adroitly manipulated this anti-British sentiment. He used it to increase the power of his American Fur Company and drive out of business rival traders in Wisconsin and Michigan who had had links with either of the two British companies, the North West Company or the Hudson's Bay Company. Of course, the American Fur Company had competition from the government trading operation known as the factory system. Government trading posts, or factory stores, were established along the frontier in an attempt to reform Indian trade by providing goods at fair cost and by prohibiting "credits" and the sale of liquor. The fur trade, however, was built around selling liquor and issuing credits to the Indians each fall, so the poorly conceived factory system experiment, while well-intentioned, ultimately failed in 1822.[30]

With the demise of the factory system, the American Fur Company controlled the fur trade in Wisconsin for a while. But the days of large profits in the fur trade were nearly over. By 1825 the beaver was gone in Wisconsin, and large game such as elk and buffalo was gone by the early 1830s.[31] After 1830 muskrats constituted the primarily profits in the fur trade, but the Indians by then were often too weak from lack of food to hunt them. Competition from small independent traders, some who worked out of the many shanties that sprang up around the forts and who traded mostly in liquor and cheap merchandise, cut into the profits of the American Fur Company. Under such conditions, the American Fur Company diversified into commercial fishing and real estate, and then in 1834 collapsed.[32] By then profits were no longer in the fur trade but in selling Indians goods and food on credit and then claiming often inflated or bogus reimbursements from the government at the next treaty cession or annuity payment.[33]

THE DISINTEGRATION OF THE INDIAN COMMUNITIES

When Wisconsin became a state in 1848 the settlements of Green Bay, Prairie du Chien, and Milwaukee were growing rapidly. Plows were breaking the rich prairie lands in southern Wisconsin, and the corn that ripened under the summer sun was no longer Indian corn. The copper once held in reverence by the Ojibwa now attracted Americans who sought to exchange it for gold. Far from the northern soil that had nurtured them, the forests were being converted into homes and barns, and the creak of the mill wheel replaced the sound of the canoe paddle on Wisconsin rivers and streams.

By 1848 the Indians had lost control of their lands and lakes in Wisconsin and were rapidly losing control of their communities, the direction of their lives, and the ability to shape their futures. In confronting these misfortunes, Wisconsin tribes were limited in the actions they could take: they could move to avoid confrontation, or they could either attempt to stem the onrush of settlement through physical force, duplicity, and subterfuge or resist through negotiation and compromise.

The Loss of Collective Memory

In 1854 when the German traveler Johann Georg Kohl visited northern Wisconsin and talked with the Ojibwa people living along the south shore of Lake Superior, he asked one old woman about the old times. She, in turn, complained that she had lost her memory.

The Ojibways have all lost their memory. The Americans have made us weak. Our people do not talk so much about their own affairs now as they used to do. They no longer feel the same pleasure in telling the old stories, and they are forgotten, and the traditions and fables rooted out. You often ask them, but you seldom find any one who can give you the right answer. Our nation is fallen; and this came quite suddenly, since the Long-knives entered our country.

The old times, according to her, were much better. Then the Indians were stronger, they had more faith, they were more pious and possessed a stronger religion. They could fast longer and had better dreams. They lived longer. They had greater control over the animals. Now the Ojibwa's dreams were weak and ineffective.[34]

She told Kohl about the French, English, and Americans who had come among them. The French brought them presents, good solid presents. The Ojibwa loved the French. They came among the Ojibwa and lived with them. The black robes came and were good to the Ojibwa. Frenchmen and Ojibwa hunted together and were happy.[35]

Then the English came. The Ojibwa did not at first like the English but in time accepted them. The English brought more liquor into the country than the French did. When the English fought the Americans, the Ojibwa helped the English and stood up for them. When the war was

136

over the Americans came. They brought even more liquor, which killed more men, and the times became worse. "The presents and the salt pork grew ever worse, and the hunting-grounds have failed: besides more and more land was taken from us." Now it was all over with the Ojibwa. "Their strength is broken, and they have lost their memory. Their tribes have melted away, their chiefs have no voice in the council. Their wise men and priests have no longer good dreams, and the old squaws forget their good stories and families."[36]

Undoubtedly the woman to whom Kohl talked held an idealized image of the past. The collective memory of her people, filtered and burnished through the haze of time, contrasted sharply with current reality. As seen, the Ojibwa experience under the French and the English was not as golden as she claimed. But it is important not to discount her version of history too quickly but rather to remember that the history she presented, distorted as it may have been, had become perhaps the only relevant reality her people possessed, and they acted on it. There was power in the old stories and dreams; they maintained the people's identity, foretold the future, determined the course of future action, and enabled them to rework and supplement their traditions. For many of Wisconsin's Indians, dreams predicted accomplishments in war and in the hunt, and thus the necessity to choose among alternative strategies was removed. Dreams offered assurances for success and protection. Now that the stories were being forgotten and there were no "good dreams" anymore, the future was obscure, the people bewildered, and their strength and very existence became problematic. The old woman's version of history was probably similar to how other tribes viewed their experiences with both Europeans and Americans. Among the Menominee, liquor was seen as a poison destroying the Indian, and although the French and the British sold some liquor to them, the Americans would "sell it to them as long as they [had] any furs."[37] In 1836 an Ojibwa claimed, "Since the Long Knives came among us which is about 20 years everything goes wrong. We are poor. We have few things. We do not know why it is so. It makes us feel very bad."[38] For many Americans, the pioneer experience in Wisconsin proved a positive one. For the native inhabitants of Wisconsin, the conquest meant only a disaster of monumental proportions.

Promises were easily made and just as easily broken. When these promises made by American agents and treaty commissioners were not kept, tribal people questioned the credibility of future promises, and relations became further strained.[39] As an Ojibwa woman told Cass at the Fond du Lac treaty in 1826:

My Father, truly I am poor. At the time when the English People were supporting me, I had plenty to wear, but when you made your appearance, you who are called the Big Knives, you told me that you would support me, that I would be better off than I had been with the English. I am now a good deal poorer than I was then. You have made me a great many promises which you have not fulfilled.[40]

As seen, the depletion of fur-bearing animals near the villages forced migration to areas where such animals were more populous. Given the dependence on the fur trade, it was improbable for communities to abandon the trade and return to a traditional life-style, that is, one centered on fishing, hunting, and gathering, as some of the nativistic movements urged. The price was too high and Indian dependency on trade goods too great. This dependency led to village fragmentation and a scattered population until, finally in the nineteenth century with no refuge left, community life passed into a state of atrophy. Migrations had undercut village social structure and operations, or tested them severely. Cultural norms became grotesquely bent or broken, and authority corrupted by external influences.

The Effects of Alcohol, Unscrupulous Traders, and the Creation of Chiefs

According to Indian agents, alcohol and designing traders were high on the list of corrupting influences.[41] Lewis Cass learned in 1816 that "many of the traders have been extremely active in the Chicago and Green Bay Countries, in souring the minds of the Indians, encouraging the disaffected, exciting their fears and preparing them to oppose the establishment of American posts. . . ."[42] An angry Joseph Street, agent to the Winnebago, castigated traders who held back the Winnebago and encouraged their immorality. According to agent Street, who was no friend of the American Fur Company, "Every attempt to civilize Indians in this section is violently opposed by the agent at this place of the American Fur Company and all their traders. They live on savage ignorance and brutality of the Inds. and lead them into the most debasing immorality, and they strive to keep them ignorant, savage and brutally immoral."[43] A disgusted agent, George Boyd, complained that among the Menominee, their "traders are their chiefs and their headmen nothing. Four or six traders made the treaty of 1836 and I can designate half the number who shall sell the Balance of their land to-morrow."[44] In 1833, agent Street had detected the hands of traders in frustrating government policy to remove the Winnebago from Wisconson.

In consequence, every effort [by traders] has been made since the Treaty to prevent the Indians from going West. And they have now settled down North of the Wiskonsin, in a poor country nearly devoid of game, and are in a fair way to perish or kill themselves with whisky, which last they can get in great abundance from the whites on the South bank of the Wiskonsin.[45]

The reason that traders sought to prevent Indian removal is not hard to see. Although the trade in furs was in decline, keeping Indians supplied was profitable as long as Indian annuity payments continued.

Blame for community disintegration must be placed on both traders and agents who subverted community political institutions through the creation of chiefs.[46] Tribal political leadership extended only so far as the chiefs' reputation. Chiefs led by example. Unfortunately, reputations were easily blemished in the early nineteenth century when chiefs fell victims to bribes and alcohol. As seen, observers as early as 1820 reported that traders often gave chiefs great quantities of alcohol and other bribes to gain trading advantages. Government agents also resorted to bribes and other pressures to gain signatures on treaties, thereby compounding tribal rifts. Such pressure on the Menominee created divisiveness. For instance, after the treaty of 1822, which gave land to the Oneida, "the Menominee separated into two parties, the one adhering to the treaty and the interest of the New York Indians, the other denying them and resisting their rights to any part of the country."[47]

Chiefs who engaged in prolonged bouts of drunkenness and demonstrated evidence of bribes also tended to weaken community reliance on the old leadership. Destroying the reputation of tribal chiefs led inevitably to political control passing from the community to outside forces. As seen above, traders were quick to make a good hunter a chief, and the American Fur Company even handed out their own "chief medals." At treaty negotiations, government commissioners often grew exasperated with the absence of a strong leader and sometimes took steps to correct the situation by creating a chief. Such was the case among the Menominee in 1827. In council before them, Lewis Cass announced:

We have observed for some time the Menomonees to be in a bad situation as to their chiefs. There is no one we can talk to as the head of the nation. If anything should happen, we want some man, who has authority in the nation, that we can look to. You appear like a flock of geese, without a leader, some fly one way and some another. Tomorrow, at the opening of the Council, we shall appoint a principal chief of the Menomonees. We shall make enquiry this afternoon, and try to select the proper man. We shall give him the medal, and expect the Menomonees to respect him.[48]

Indian agents, too, were eager to exert their power and depose a chief and replace him with a puppet they could control or at least with someone more amenable or better able to articulate government policy. Impatient with tribal bickering and stalling tactics and having the perception of chaotic tribal political organization, government agents, often in desperation, created new chiefs for the community. Agent George Boyd's blistering attack on the Menominee chiefs Oshkosh and Amata (A-ya-mah-ta), who prevented the distribution of goods to the Menominee in 1838, is such an example:

I can tell you Sir in a few words, why they refused to extend the *Charity* towards their whole Nation. They are influential Chiefs,—and identified by Blood & marriage with the whole French fraternity of Green Bay,—they can command at all times, all that they can possibly require for the subsistence of their families and Bands, let the times & Scarcity of provisions, be as they may. . . . As for Chief Osh-kosh—I will merely observe, that it has become my duty, to report him, for very exceptionable Conduct . . . and that when their [Menominee] remaining lands within this territory shall be sold to the U. States . . . I would respectfully recommend that He be removed from his situation as first Chief of these people, and that another be appointed in his stead. . . . This man has always *boasted* that He is not the Chief of the U. States Government, *but the Chief of the Traders.* The 2d Chief . . . is I. Amata, and made a chief *at my instigation,* by Governor Porter, in 1832. He is entirely under the direction of the Catholic-Priests—and has done more than any hundred other men of his Nation to defeat the intentions of this Government, in relation to every thing like education, farming etc. for the benefit of their Nation.—He should also be deposed, and another of different materials, placed in his stead.[49]

Under such conditions, it is little wonder that Indian agents frequently complained that chiefs had no power and anarchy seemed to prevail. Some communities had two sets of chiefs: traditional chiefs and "Indian agent" chiefs. This encouraged factionalism and sometimes the breaking away of groups that set up their own communities under band chiefs. A multiplicity of chiefs and communities complicated the communication problem. No longer could communities speak with a single voice or act in unison. Street pointed out, "The fact is the Winnebago government is a wretched one, and the influence of their chiefs small"; this he attributed partly to the wandering nature of the Winnebago and, because of factionalism, their increasing tendency to dissolve into many small communities.[50]

Traditional tribal or band leadership could not be trusted to represent American economic and political interests properly. So puppet leaders were put in place who would articulate these interests to the satisfaction of the dominant society.

Along with meddling traders and the wholesale creation of chiefs, alcohol also continued to be a destructive force to community cohesion and ability to function. Its consumption and concomitant violence eroded further the already debilitated community economy, polity, family organization, and health. At times of annual treaty payments (annuity payments) for land sold to the government, alcohol abuse had its greatest effects. Although selling alcohol to Indians was illegal, it did not stop traders and whiskey sellers from descending like vultures on the "payment grounds" and plying their trade, with only token enforcement of the law by government officials. Dealers in whiskey would encircle the grounds and, upon the completion of the payment, would soon strip the Indians of all their money and anything else they had of value. Agent Street noted, "At every payment of *specie annuity* at Fort Winnebago, the most shameful scenes of drunkenness and murders amongst the Inds. take place. The white people assembling on the ground with large quantity of whiskey, erect booths and regularly dispence intoxicating liquors to the poor Inds. as long as they are able to pay for it."[51]

As one visitor to a Wisconsin Indian payment in 1837 reported, the scene was a virtual orgy, "an entire tribe plunged into drunkenness." He found the scene difficult to describe: the men "with almost no exception, indulging in a profound orgy, staggering, singing, shouting, fighting one another, smoking, or lying in the dust; the women following, or at the most presenting the same spectacle; the maidens, running through the camp and inviting the whites, by gestures and speech, to partake of their favors. You can even then have only a very feeble idea of what passed under my eyes." Several Menominee were accidently killed at this payment, including one baby stifled by its parents.[52]

Personal and public violence proved more than an index of social disarray; it also reflected the high level of rage born out of helplessness and despair. These orgies of violence and disorder had their own wild power and exploded against years of cultural manipulation and the emerging forms of social control. For a people suspended between two markedly different conceptions of culture and society, violence constituted a kind of answer.

DECLINE OF THE FUR TRADE AND A CONTINUED
LOSS OF THE LAND

The continuing decline in fur-bearing animals further strained tribal communities. This decline produced a crisis in the fur trade that soon led to disarray and then to collapse. Just when demand for foreign goods was increasing, the means for paying for these goods declined. Traders, however, were all too willing to sell goods on credit, so debts mounted year by year.[53] Among the Ojibwa, these traders were different from previous traders, who had lived in the communities and who through kinship ties had established sympathy or at least interest in community concerns. The new traders proved "a new class of men, of far different temperaments, whose chief object was to amass fortunes." Such men were considered indifferent and insensitive to the customs and beliefs of a community. Holding themselves aloof, such traders underscored their isolation from the community in which they sought to trade.[54] This shift in behavior emphasized the increasing government control over the Wisconsin Territory and the demise of tribal groups as military forces. These factors reduced the necessity of traders' cultivating political-military alliances; the Indian became merely an economic factor.

When the fur trade died, so did the fur trade culture. Gone were the fur-bearing animals in quantities sufficient to sustain tribal populations.[55] Confronted with growing poverty and increasing debts, tribes were urged to accept the painful alternative of selling off their lands. External pressure from the government and from traders and the need for food, goods, and clothing combined to force tribal land cessions, and in less than 50 years the land was gone. With these cessions came wrenching social dislocation and a gnawing sense of impermanence reflected in Indian reluctance to improve the land and to depend on annuities. As agent Boyd noted for the Menominee in 1840:

These people in general, do not raise enough from the ground to support their families two months in the year. They look to their annuity as their main support and are consequently idle and dispirited. It is my firm belief that they were better fed & clothed before they sold an acre of land to the United States than they are at present—and they will always progress from bad to worse, until they can rid themselves of their half Breed relatives & sell their remaining lands in the territory and remove West of the Mississippi.[56]

The cessions of land that the Ojibwa, Potawatomi, Ottawa, and Winnebago made in 1829, the Menominee made in 1831, and the Winnebago made again in 1832 were small compared with later requests from the U.S. government. In 1836 the Menominee relinquished still more land, this time along the Wolf and Fox rivers and a large section of land west of Green Bay. The Winnebago in 1837 gave up the rest of their lands in Wisconsin, as did also the Sioux. That same year the Ojibwa relinquished their lands across central Wisconsin and then in 1842 ceded the rest of their Wisconsin lands. Finally in 1848, the Menominee were forced to sell their remaining homeland. Even the immigrant Stockbridge were encouraged to sell lands purchased for them from the Menominee and to move across the Mississippi.[57]

The Menominee

The Reverend Jedidiah Morse, a special government commissioner to investigate Indian affairs, explicitly revealed the crisis of land loss and its destructive effects on Menominee society in his 1822 report to the secretary of war. Visiting Green Bay in 1820, Morse "found the Menominee who live on Winnebago Lake, Fox River and near Green Bay, in a state of considerable agitation." Their apprehension grew out of the questionable 1816 treaty, in which some unauthorized tribal members sold some of the most valuable Menominee land. The tribe appeared to Morse to be disoriented and divided, and he noted that "nearly all the *real*, acknowledged chiefs of the nation were strongly opposed to the sale." Their grief and anger over this treaty extended to killing one of the Menominee who had signed it.[58]

This treaty, Morse reported, came at a bad time for the Menominee; one of their old chiefs had just died, and the other was dying. Just when their situation required men of experience and authority to guide them, the Menominee had only three young and inexperienced chiefs to chart the tribe's future. If this situation were not bad enough, there were some among the Menominee who seemed bent on hastening their decline. As the young chiefs complained to Morse, "You see your children here before you, full of grief and sorrow. The moment we turned our backs, this spring, a change took place; and our families and children are all in trouble, in consequence of the conduct of some persons who are not true Menominee."[59] Although the 1816 treaty was never ratified, its presentation and signing caused community fear, dismay, and increased divisiveness.

In negotiations with the Americans, the Menominee were hampered by the French-*métis* population in their midst. They often acted as intermediaries between the tribe and the outside world and wielded political and economic influence. Previous to both American and British rule, the French were an external force on Menominee politics, but under subsequent non-French rule, the vested interests of both French and Menomi-nee grew closer together. As seen already, some French gained positions of political power within the tribe. They also shared with their Menomi-nee relatives the same fears regarding American occupation, but they were also very careful to watch out for what they perceived as their own interests, sometimes to the detriment of Menominee interests. Although it is possible to cite examples of French and *métis* cooperation either with the government or with the American Fur Company, at other times they were guilty of surreptitious attempts to disrupt treaty negotiations.[60] In one case, disturbed over American encroachment, some young Meno-minee, perhaps under French influence, opted to take a direct physical approach. Their fears and distrust spilled over into violence when they attacked and stabbed an American soldier in 1820.[61]

Despite the opposition of some Menominee and the French residents of Green Bay, Menominee leaders recognized the folly of a policy of open confrontation and resistance to American control. It was also obvious that physical force could not alter their situation, and, indeed, they were too weak to resist the more powerful American force. A planned French and Menominee migration to the Red River region in Canada, where Lord Selkirk and the Hudson's Bay Company sought to found a colony, aborted with the death of Selkirk. Whether the Menominee would have left their homeland for Canada is a moot question, for when the colony project collapsed the Menominee were forced into negotiations with the Americans as the only feasible alternative short of going to war.[62]

The Menominee, through astute negotiations, resisted further Ameri-can encroachments for a while. By stalling and by manipulating agents, commissioners, teachers, and missionaries, they were able to set aside the 1816 treaty with the United States government. Such tactics, however, did not always prevail. As seen, in 1821 when the Oneida delegation from New York came to Wisconsin seeking land for settlement, the Me-nominee and Winnebago agreed to grant them a small parcel. When the Oneida pressed for more the following year, the Menominee, on the ad-vice of their French relatives, resisted. In the end though, under heavy pressure and threats from the government, the Menominee finally com-promised and sold.[63]

The Menominee also employed manipulation as a form of resistance and with some success. When their agent refused to relay their com-plaints to Washington, D.C., the Menominee used any visitor that came into their country whom they thought able to relay their message to the Great Father in Washington. Such was the case when the Menominee persuaded two Quakers, Thomas Wistar and Alfred Cope, to carry a message of their grievances to President Zachary Taylor, who was deeply affected by their plight.[64]

The Winnebago

The Winnebago shared with the Menominee some of the same foreboding premonitions regarding their future under American rule. Morse, who gained his information from traders, agents, and personal observation, found them darkly suspicious of Americans and reluctant to have any intercourse with them. They were extremely jealous of their territory and would "suffer no encroachment upon their soil nor any person to pass through it."[65] They attempted to isolate themselves along the upper Fox River, at the Fox-Wisconsin portage, and in mixed Indian villages farther south, and between the Mississippi River and the upper Wisconsin River to the north. Of all the Wisconsin tribes, Morse found them most sympathetic to the British and most inclined to travel to Drummond Island for gifts. When the American government in 1822 pressed the Menominee and Winnebago to sell more land to the Oneida, the Winnebago attended the treaty cession but were adamant in refusing to part with any more land. They claimed they had too little land already.[66]

Like the Menominee, the Winnebago also resorted to negotiation and manipulation to resist the encroachment of settlers and miners on their lands. As noted above, when the government requested more land for the Oneida, the Winnebago refused, claiming they needed all the land that they then possessed. Although government agents scoffed at this reply, the Winnebago, mindful of the disappearance of game and aware of increasing American settlement in southern Wisconsin, were quite right. After the Menominee finally acquiesced to government demands for Oneida land, however, the Winnebago and Menominee, suspicious of Oneida intentions, carefully located the Oneida between them, where they could keep a close watch over Oneida activities.[67] The entry of the Oneida into Wisconsin compounded the uneasiness and confusion that the Winnebago and Menominee were suffering, and they demonstrated their displeasure through harassment of the Oneida and the Americans, killing their pigs, cows, and other livestock became a common occurrence. Winnebago harassment also included firing on Americans traveling on the Fox River.[68]

In the 1820s, however, the Winnebago were more concerned about miners on Winnebago lands along the Mississippi than they were about the Oneida settling near Lake Winnebago. As seen, Americans, in their search for lead, crossed into Winnebago territory and mined Winnebago lead. Confronted with Winnebago complaints of this encroachment, the miners announced, "We have a right to go just where we please."[69] The Winnebago answered with harassment that eventually led to killings. This catapulted the Winnebago into the so-called Winnebago War. As a war it did not amount to very much—a couple Winnebago attacks sparked by whites' molestation of Winnebago women and rumors of two Winnebago deaths at Fort Snelling—but the term does indicate a certain jingoism of the Americans and reflects the intensity of Winnebago concerns.[70]

The Winnebago response was also symptomatic of strains within Winnebago society. These strains surfaced again when the Black Hawk War prompted indecision over what course of action the Winnebago ought to take. As previously discussed, some wanted to fight on the side of Black Hawk, arguing that the Americans were the enemies and that ties of friendship and kinship existed between the Sauk and the Winnebago. Others wanted to fight on the side of the Americans, feeling that doing otherwise would only mean defeat and loss of land and traders. Others did not know what to do and so decided to go hunting, taking themselves out of the path of war. In the end, the Winnebago fought on both sides. With the end of the war, the Winnebago lost more land and were strongly urged to move west of the Mississippi. Instead they chose to remain in the country north of the Wisconsin River. There in a land nearly devoid of game, they faced poverty, lack of food, alcohol abuse, and disease. When their misery increased, the Winnebago fragmented into even smaller wandering groups and began a fugitive existence in their old hunting territory while the government tried to move them west.[71]

The Ojibwa

To the north, the Wisconsin Ojibwa did not feel American pressure or suffer severe community strains until the late 1820s. Small parcels of land in southern Wisconsin were sold by the Ojibwa prior to 1834. In 1837, however, they sold lumbering rights to their pine forests in central Wisconsin but maintained possession of the roots of the trees. Specifically, they were careful not to relinquish the land, that is, the roots of the maples, oaks, or wild rice. These they would hold "in their hand." These they would not sell. At least these are what they thought they were not selling.[72]

From the government point of view, however, the Ojibwa had sold their land in central Wisconsin. In 1842, the Ojibwa sold the rest of their

Wisconsin land that lay along the south shore of Lake Superior. When the Ojibwa thought about resisting this sale, they were admonished by the agent that failure to sell would be met with curtailment of annuities and a prohibition of traders. Thus the agent also possessed economic leverage. He determined who could trade or if anyone could trade with a tribe. Through monetary threats and control of tribal purse strings, the agent could trigger tribal economic collapse and thereby force compliance. Indians may have been ignorant of much of American culture, but they were not stupid. They were fully aware that the agent controlled their economic destiny.[73]

The Ojibwa did resist attempts by their agents and the missionaries to change their culture. Although they sometimes used the missionaries to resist government removal plans, the Ojibwa preferred the Midewiwin and traditional religious practices to Christianity.[74] More difficult for the Ojibwa to combat were the incursions of miners, lumbermen, and farmers into their region.[75] The Ojibwa were in a weak position, decimated by disease, "reduced to abject want," and caught between Americans hungry for Ojibwa lands and resources and their removal to the western plains to live among their enemies; Ojibwa future looked bleak.[76] Making matters even worse, the decline in the fur trade left them with mounting debts. Convinced of their ultimate destruction if they moved west, the Ojibwa decided that if they were to be destroyed they preferred it to be in their old homeland. When orders came for their removal, they refused to move. Pressure by missionaries and other whites on behalf of the Ojibwa forced the government to reconsider and allow the Ojibwa to remain in Wisconsin.[77]

THE COLLAPSE OF THE OLD INFRASTRUCTURE OF WISCONSIN INDIAN COMMUNITIES

All Wisconsin Indian communities suffered structural damage through contact with Americans and vastly altered environments. Besides suffering emotionally from the loss of land, fear of removal, alcohol abuse, and political factionalism, they had to confront starvation and absorb a growing population of *métis,* who were a drain on meager community resources. They endured constant malnutrition and poverty, which taxed community energy and weakened community resolve. Social organizations were redefined and cultural norms grossly twisted when tribes were forced to comply with the often-conflicting demands of agents, military, traders, missionaries, and miners while confronting an army of eastern settlers and epidemic diseases. Tribal communities also endured the infestation of conniving whiskey peddlers and an immoral and lawless frontier element spreading violence, disease, and death.[78] The intermittent fear of periodic food shortages resulting from bad rice harvests or poor hunting and fishing had always been with them. But with the disappearance of large game animals and competition with Americans for the fish and wild rice, Indian survival grew steadily more precarious.[79]

Yet with neither political nor economic control, the tribes, relying on what traditions remained, stubbornly resisted the attempts of agents and missionaries to introduce unwanted changes. Opposition by tribal religious leaders to acculturation ensured the survival of native religion until the tragic epidemics of the 1830s struck. Communities in their weakened condition could not withstand the ravages of measles, or "the great red skin," that racked the Ojibwa in the 1820s or of smallpox and cholera epidemics that swept through the Wisconsin Territory between 1834 and 1837, gutting whole communities. Among the Winnebago, efforts by medicine men to stay the epidemics were futile, and the Winnebago fled their villages, not even taking time to bury their dead.[80] At such a time their religion seemed to fail them. The traditional healers, shamans and herbalists, could do nothing. The songs had lost their power. The spirits seemingly had abandoned them, and no one knew where to go or what to do. The old infrastructure of tradition and economics upon which community once stood, now seriously weakened, began to collapse.

In the old French-British communities of Green Bay, Prairie du Chien, and Milwaukee, American entry brought dramatic changes. Tribal people were no longer welcomed. Neither did the French residents of Green Bay enjoy the influx of Americans, because the latter questioned French property rights and marriage customs. The commercial development of these towns, oriented now to lumber, mining, and agriculture rather than to the fur trade, no longer catered to tribal needs. Indians were welcomed only in the shanties and grog shops along the waterfront, where they, on the credit of their yearly annuities, sporadically boosted the sales of liquor.[81] No longer were Indians feared, by many Americans, or considered a major source of income; now they were considered nuisances who wandered through frontier communities in rags; they were mere obstacles squatting on the land and obstructing development. There was indeed much truth to the Menominee chief's remark at the 1848 treaty cession: "The American never comes unless he wants something! Without a want he never takes us by the hand."[82]

Unfortunately, the dialogue, distorted by cultural expectations on both sides, aggravated the misunderstandings between tribal people and the government. Hearing what was said did not necessarily mean under-standing what was said. When Americans promised a better life to Indi-ans, they meant not what the Indians thought (that is, gifts of clothing, food, tobacco, and a rejuvenated fur trade) but rather a revolutionized style of living. The meaning inherent in the Americans' promise found expression in the Second Annual Message that President James Monroe delivered in 1818:

To civilize them, and even to prevent their extinction, it seems to be indispens-able that their independence as communities should cease, and that control of the United States over them should be complete and undisputed. The hunter state will then be more easily abandoned, and recourse will be had to the acquisition and culture of land and to other pursuits tending to dissolve the ties which con-nect them together as a savage community and to give a new character to every individual.[83]

Thus the promise for a better life meant two different things: one thing to the speaker and another to the listener.

Wisconsin Indian communities experienced chronic disasters similar to those described by the sociologist Kai Erikson. According to Erikson, the psychological crisis produced by chronic disasters like repeated floods, earthquakes, and epidemics "gathers force slowly and insidi-ously, creeping around one's defenses rather than smashing through them."[84] Under conditions of chronic disaster, a person or community cannot effectively mobilize resources to counteract the threat, perhaps because of ignorance or because there is nothing that can be done to avoid the threatening conditions. Studies of communities under chronic stress report the traumatizing effects that people suffer: a numbness of spirit, a susceptibility to anxiety, rage, or depression, a feeling of help-lessness and loss. Both the tendency toward immobilization of resources and these social and psychological symptoms of chronic stress character-ized Wisconsin tribal communities while they coped with perceived threats, attempted to respond to these threats, and, failing that, disinte-grated during the first half of the nineteenth century.[85]

SUMMARY

Despite the efforts of the native peoples of Wisconsin to alter this situa-tion, despite attempts in treaty negotiations to protect their lands and their economies, despite their numerous petitions to agents and other government officials, despite their trips to Washington, D.C., to present their interpretation of treaties and seek redress, their efforts met with meager success. A nation and government intent on economic and geographical expansion could ill afford the luxury of letting abstract and humanitarian ideals determine political realities.

So the native peoples of Wisconsin waited. They waited through numbing poverty. They became separate entities seen flitting among the trees; they wandered on the altered landscape in ragged little bands where the forces pulling them apart were stronger than the forces holding them together. They waited to learn when they would have to move and where and then shape strategies for resistance. They sought leaders who would know what to do and how to respond. They waited in smoky lodges for fevers to break or for death. They waited for the end of emotional terror and physical violence that ripped apart their communities and their lives. They waited, not really knowing for what. They saw their world, their culture, disintegrating; they feared the slide into oblivion.

The role of culture is to edit or translate reality, and when culture fails in this task, when the community fails to offer support and comfort, then people resort to other means to protect themselves and relieve anxiety. As crisis-shocked people, Wisconsin Indians sought ways to shut out or forget both the present and the past. Alcohol helped them to relieve anxiety, to construct a more acceptable reality, or to obliterate reality itself. Alcohol became an addiction stronger than life itself. Killings and physical abuse became part of the pattern of rapid community disintegration. In a world of habitual disasters, where everyone knew death, a loss of both concern and human trust followed the unraveling of community ties.[86]

During the first half of the nineteenth century, many Indians in Wisconsin lived in a state of chronic disaster produced by American government policy and by a physical and social environment that changed more rapidly than tribal adjustment could tolerate or tribal peoples could comprehend. They had lost that solace that community can provide. They lost both the physical and spiritual health that derive from living in a community of kinsmen and friends who care. In the spring of 1848, Wisconsin slipped from a territory to statehood. The snows were gone by May, and the scent of new blossoms filled the air and promised a grand future. The landless native peoples of Wisconsin waited to learn what the summer of statehood would bring.

6

The Shrinking Land

In 1847, the *Missionary Herald* reminded its readers that "the designs of Providence in respect to the Indian tribes generally are dark and mysterious. There are influences at work, of great and increasing power, which threaten their destruction." The editors drew upon a litany of complaints confided to the society by the Reverend Sherman Hall, a missionary among the Ojibwa at La Pointe. Hall was plainly discouraged.

The success of our labors has not been heretofore what we hoped and expected, when we entered the field. . . . They [the Ojibwa] seem to have no idea of any higher good than the gratification of their animal desires; and consequently, when they understand that religion does not supply their temporal wants without their own exertions, but rather requires them to repent of their sins, and abandon their lusts . . . it loses its attraction for them. Most of them who give the best evidence of conversion to God, have never exhibited such pungent conviction of sin, as I have desired to see. . . . It seems to me, therefore, that our prospects for reclaiming them from sin, and of working a revolution in their social and religious condition, are to some extent discouraging.[1]

The bleak situation that Hall described in somewhat simplistic terms was far more complicated in actuality. The Ojibwa at La Pointe and all the Wisconsin tribes were experiencing the convergence of two Indian policies: one, long-standing and embracing all the nation's tribes; the other, targeted at Wisconsin Indians. The former policy was federal and employed the resources of the national government, and the latter was local and motivated by immediate concerns and vested interests. All too often these two policies clashed, aggravating a deplorable situation and making any unified rational response from the tribal peoples of Wisconsin extremely difficult.

Federal Indian policy, as historian Robert F. Berkhofer has shown, grew out of British colonial Indian policy as it had developed among the seaboard colonies.[2] The premise of that policy was rooted in competition over resources, especially land. From the viewpoint of the new American government, the competition had to be eliminated, and in order to do so Indian title to the land must be extinguished and the Indian acculturated, if possible, into American society.

Early Americans considered land important, not only because land-ownership held symbolic and economic significance, but also because it defined identity and bestowed voting rights. Land proved the most accessible form of property in America, and because the foundation of late eighteenth-century government rested on property, one had to be a land-holder to have status and to be able to exercise civil rights. Standing between the American and his social and political rights was the Indian.

To eliminate racial competition over land, the government proposed to extinguish Indian title and promote the Americanization of the Indian. If the Indian would learn to use the land as prescribed by American values, he could keep a portion of it, but to use the land in this way involved acceptance of the values of the dominant society. Once Indians accepted these values, however, they would no longer be Indians, but Americans.

NATIONAL INDIAN POLICY AND FRONTIER PRIORITIES

In 1819, Congress set aside $10,000 as the Civilization Fund and encouraged religious organizations to draw upon it to educate the Indian. The government also sent farmers, blacksmiths, and physicians, who, through example, were to instruct Indians in the proper procedures. Beginning about 1815, America was swept with a reform zeal that continued until the Civil War. "Benevolence," "philanthropy," and "perfectability" were key expressions bantered about by social reformers during this period. Fueled by an optimism that determined all things were possible in a democracy, reformers set out to perfect the world or at least their corner of it. Buttressed by religion, science, a belief in progress and the perfectability of man, reformers argued that the Indian could be altered and led to accept Christianity and civilization if properly encouraged.[3] Caught up with this spirit, the government aided missionary organizations that worked to educate the Indians and spread the gospel among them.[4]

For most Americans, by midcentury, tribalism was the antithesis of the American way with its emphasis on individualism, competition, and private property. Tribalism was static, or so Americans presumed, and represented "communism" and lacked that acquisitive capitalism upon which the marketplace depended. To become an American, the Indian had to be detribalized, had to be torn from the community and made into an individual who could perceive and act upon self-interest. Indians had to be taught the concept of private property and had to learn to comprehend their identity through that concept.

Those who worked with Indians believed this could be accomplished only through the destruction of the reservation. To such workers, the reservation kept Indians enslaved to Indian ways; it allowed them to practice "pagan" rites, to share their hunts, to live on government annuities, to escape the responsibility of educating their children, in short, to do Indian things. In order to educate the Indian to the concept of private property, the reservations had to be divided up and the land turned over in severalty, or small landholdings, to individuals and families. Under such conditions, the Indian would be forced to become a self-supporting farmer, a contributor to society, and a candidate for citizenship. Some treaties since the 1830s contained plans for allotting land to individual Indians, but the General Allotment Act, or Dawes Act, of 1887 was the fullest expression of this idea.[5]

Throughout the late nineteenth and early twentieth centuries, national Indian policy remained the same: force the breakup of tribal entities and move the "newly individualized" Indian toward citizenship. Missionization and education were brought into this effort, as were the breakup of the tribal land base through allotment and the privatization of property. Instituting tribal community police forces and enforcing American law were also involved in this process. Where Indians would not or could not adjust to these conditions, they were moved west into isolated communities in the hopes that with more time they would eventually change or the recalcitrant generation would die off and be replaced with one that was more pliable and receptive to change.[6]

Local interests, however, often obstructed national goals for the Indian. At the local level, the desire for Indian land, timber, and mineral resources won out over any attempts to improve the economic conditions of tribal peoples. All too often government agents were enlisted by local forces to defraud the very people they were assigned to protect.[7]

Local attitudes in Wisconsin reflected the needs of a rapidly growing population. Population increases between 1836—the year Wisconsin became a territory—and 1848 were explosive and in large measure dictated Wisconsin Indian policy. Writing in 1843 in the *Southport American*, a commentator noted that Wisconsin "is teeming with population. . . . Emigration and trade of every kind flood our shores. . . . Our interior is fast filling up with a hardy and industrious . . . and intelligent population. . . . Towns . . . have arisen as if by magic along the shores of our lakes and by the banks of our rivers. These developments illustrate the railway speed at which we advance to empire."[8] Between 1836 and 1850, the U.S. population increased 51 percent; in Wisconsin, during the period, the increase measured 2,514 percent.[9] Change was endemic to the restless Wisconsin population.

In his study of law and economic growth, James Willard Hurst stresses that Americans "used law not so much to hold things steady as to direct change, not to maintain ordered status but to encourage mobility. . . . ."[10] During the first half of the nineteenth century, Americans adroitly applied law to gain possession of the mineral and agricultural lands of southern Wisconsin. The government's halfhearted attempt to retain the mineral region of southwest Wisconsin collapsed under the pressure of settlement. Wisconsin settlers were unsympathetic to the concept of government as landlord and demanded that public land quickly be turned over for sale. They campaigned strenuously for preemption laws that would allow the sale of public lands to squatters.[11]

In a land seemingly blessed with abundant resources, Wisconsin pioneers cheered any government action that would convert these resources to capital and release community energies for development. The public land, however, remained the most obvious resource.[12] Local governments were sympathetic to such demands, for settlement meant wealth and development. Again, according to Hurst, "both political-social and economic objectives highly prized in the first half of the nineteenth century converged to create great pressure to bring the public land to market, fast and in quantity."[13] Along with the ideal of the small independent farmer holding his lands in fee simple went the belief that such farmers released the productive capacity for community development. Land became equated with happiness and with a community's "physical, moral and intellectual" development, or so thought Wisconsin's governor Dewey in 1851.[14]

American pressure for opening public land to private sale combined with a demand for extinguishing Indian titles and moving eastern tribes to the West. In southern Wisconsin, by the 1850s, the tide of native-born Americans and the more recent German, Swedish, and Norwegian immigrants demonstrated little sympathy or patience for Indians occupying good farm land. "To him who should pay for and till the soil, to him it should belong" seemed the ruling national philosophy.[15] Although tribal

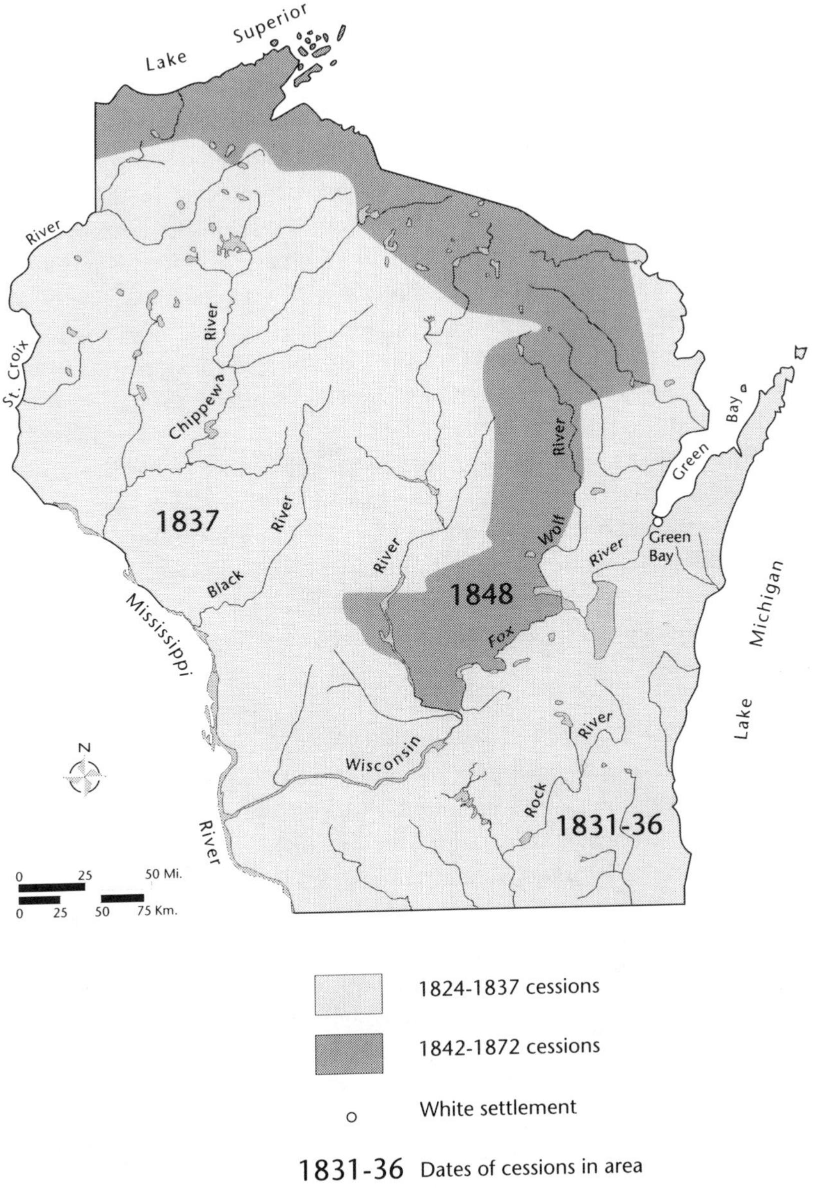
Lake Superior
St. Croix River
Chippewa River
Black River
River
Wisconsin River
Wolf River
Fox River
Green Bay
Green Bay
Lake Michigan
Rock River
Mississippi River
N
1837
1848
1831-36
0 25 50 Mi.
0 25 50 75 Km.
1824-1837 cessions
1842-1872 cessions
White settlement
1831-36 Dates of cessions in area

Map 9. Land Cessions, 1783–1873. Drawn from a portion of map 30 in the *Atlas of Great Lakes Indian History*, edited by Helen Hornbeck Tanner, University of Oklahoma Press, 1987.

people were productive, they were not productive in the same way as American and European immigrants. Tribal peoples devoted their energies to the survival of the local community rather than to stimulating the wealth of the larger community. As seen, these demands affected the Potawatomi and Winnebago tribes in southern Wisconsin.

The explosive energy that Americans displayed in coming to Wisconsin was manifested in other regions of the country when these people tumbled across the Midwest and out onto the plains in their restless search for land and economic opportunity. Here on the treeless plains, lumber was desperately needed, and so even before 1850 the allurement of the pinelands of northern Wisconsin with their potential for wealth began to replace the desire for farmland. The national need for lumber for houses on the plains and for railroads whetted the appetite for these pinelands. Wisconsin businessmen quickly realized that their forests could fulfill this national need.[16]

By the 1860s, a group of lumber companies known collectively as the Pine Ring coveted the timber on the Menominee, Stockbridge, and Ojibwa reservations. Lumbermen, who often poached trees from public land, now poached from reservation lands.[17] When the tribes complained of this practice, lumbermen and land speculators appealed to the government to remove the tribes or force them to relinquish their timber rights, or reserves.

THE INDIAN RESPONSE TO NATIONAL POLICY

Tribal opposition to both national policy and local interests varied and proved uneven in its application and results. Communities weakened by the assault on their land base and by the corrosive influence of alcohol and a declining fur trade were often in straitened conditions and unable to mount serious resistance to commercial interests in their resources.

Within Wisconsin tribes variant versions of community evolved during the late nineteenth century. Groups or factions within tribal communities held different prescriptions of what ought to constitute a community or what life should be like within one; they often emphasized dissimilar aspects of the culture and presented different strategies for adapting to environments and to a constantly changing and enveloping Western culture. If groups varied in response to change, so too did individuals. Some who were culturally marginal were often more receptive to the blandishments offered by a competing culture. Others who were more competitive accepted marginal roles in the dominant culture as a means of strengthening their ability to maneuver in their own. Still others offered resistance when outside forces threatened their position of power, especially if they were in a position of leadership. Although it is important to see how Wisconsin Indians manipulated both the foreign culture and their own to achieve certain ends, it is also important to see what environment and community they sought to preserve.

Unfortunately for the historian, there are few explicit pronouncements made by Indian peoples regarding their choice of alternatives, and, even if these pronouncements were to exist, they still might be suspect. Only the actions of various groups within a tribe can reveal to the historian the differing community aspirations within a specific environment.[18] Among Wisconsin Indian peoples, positions ranged from pro-tradition to pro-acculturation; in this situation, factionalism and environmental conditions both defined the possible and fashioned community life. Turning briefly to the various Wisconsin Indian groups, it is possible to see this process at work.

The Menominee

The Menominee are a good example of how these multiple forces shaped the community. There are several books and articles[19] that offer detailed accounts of Menominee history and their conflicts with the government and with the lobbying efforts of the Pine Ring (again, which represented local lumbering interests), so that history will be treated here only briefly.

The early reservation years for the Menominee continued the disruptive community life that plagued the tribe during the early nineteenth century, but with their settlement in 1854 on a reservation on the upper Wolf River and their fear of removal west of the Mississippi now extinguished, the Menominee began the process of reorganizing their community and adjusting to a different physical and cultural environment. Confined now to a limited land base, they set about trying to survive. Although many Menominee took up farming, the poor sandy soil frustrated their efforts, and two years of starvation followed crop failures. Compelled to return to their old subsistence patterns of hunting, fishing, and gathering to survive, the Menominee quickly discovered that their reservation resources were inadequate, and they were forced to turn to government aid. In further complications to their adjustment to reservation life, they were beset by the state of Wisconsin claiming parts of the reservation and lumbermen and traders finding the Menominee good targets for plundering and the women for seduction.[20]

If the Menominee suffered economically in their move to the reserva-

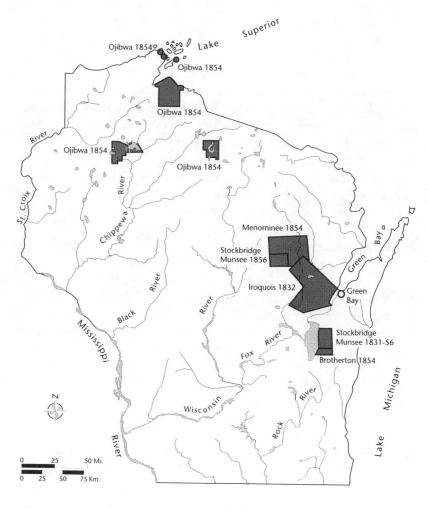

Map 10. Reservations, 1783–1889. Drawn from a portion of map 31 in the *Atlas of Great Lakes Indian History,* edited by Helen Hornbeck Tanner, University of Oklahoma Press, 1987.

158

tion, they also faced a continuing social disintegration. Menominee society broke apart along religious lines when they organized themselves into bands under headmen who chose village sites. One division made up of mixed-bloods and those who favored acculturation constituted the Christian Menominee, who founded settlements on the east side of the Wolf River under such leaders as Aia'miqta, Carron, Lamotte, Akine'bui, Osh'kiqhina'niu, and Wa'ta'sau. Those resisting acculturation and following old Menominee beliefs divided into two groups, generally according to whether they were members of the politically powerful Bear clan or Thunder clan, and located on the west side of the Wolf River. The Bear people settled under Oshkosh, Souligny, Chickeney, and Sha'-wano, and the Thunder people settled farther north under Poegonah, Keso, and Ni'aqtawa'pomi. After 1854, the river band under Keshi'niu and Tshitshikwo'nuwau, the Peshtigo under Asha'wuni'pinas, and the Oconto band under Pikwu'kunao arrived on the reservation and located in other parts of it.[21]

The death of Chief Oshkosh in 1858 brought increased instability. The crisis widened the division between the traditionals and the Christians and sharpened the sphere of discord. The traditional bands wanted A'kwine'mi, Oshkosh's eldest son, appointed chief. The Christians, who were in the majority, wanted Oshkosh's second son, who was a Christian, appointed. Members of the other bands put forth other candidates. The choice finally fell on A'kwine'mi. Adding further political stress, a split developed between the older leaders and the younger men of the tribe when the younger men demanded and received a political role in tribal affairs equal to that of the older leaders.[22]

The mixed-bloods also continued to jockey for influence in tribal decisions and "excited a turbulent and rebellious feeling." Their demands centered primarily on their share of the annuity payments. Charges and countercharges led to an appeal to Washington, D.C., and eventually culminated in 1861 in a decision by the Menominee tribal council to disclaim all "relations with the mixed bloods."[23]

Despite the Christian Menominees' attempts at farming and their attempt to define their community along American lines by employing American agricultural techniques, building frame houses, adopting American-style clothes, and supporting schools and churches, life proved extremely difficult in the 1860s. Supporting the Menominee in this goal were the missionaries and government agents. They, in turn, were aided by Menominee Civil War veterans, who threw their support behind acculturation. Poor harvests in the 1860s brought starvation again to the

Menominee. Commenting on their "almost hopeless poverty," their agent in 1863 pointed to the worthlessness of the land as the primary cause of Menominee misfortune. "It is difficult to conceive of locations more illy adapted to the support and wants of a people but little acquainted with the arts of civilization. . . ."[24]

The traditional Menominee, who continued to practice the Midewiwin, moved to more inaccessible parts of the reservation. They saw themselves as the real Menominee, the upholders of traditional values. Supported by garden plots, fishing, and hunting, they maintained a strict moral code. At their settlements they often entertained conservative members of the Winnebago, Ojibwa, and Potawatomi tribes. Through these intertribal contacts, the Dream Dance was introduced in the 1860s. Performances of the Midewiwin and the Dream Dance embarrassed the Christian Menominee, but some non-Indian local residents found the ceremonies colorful and saw in the traditional Menominee "the real Indian."[25] According to one contemporary local observer:

These Indians are divided into two distinct classes by their religious beliefs, the Christians who have renounced the old customs and modes of worship and the pagans who still hold to the traditions and religious customs of their forefathers. The Christian Indian adopts the civilian dress while the pagan clings to his blanket, breech clout, and leggings. . . . It is a fact worth mentioning and one that should excite grave consideration, that the loathsome diseases [scrofula, consumption] are almost wholly confined to the Christian class. The pagen, firm in his faith with chastity a leading feature in his creed, has escaped largely the curse of these diseases, but he is largely in the minority.[26]

Beginning in the 1870s and continuing into the twentieth century, lumbering became a way of life for many Menominee. Up until the 1870s, they cut lumber only in order to clear lands and build houses. With the end of annuity payments approaching, the Menominee began to look upon their lumber as a valuable resource and in 1863 requested the Bureau of Indian Affairs for permission to cut and sell their pine timber. The bureau refused and instead contracted with the member companies of the Pine Ring to log trees that were dead and down. Unsatisfied with these limits placed on their operations, lumber companies poached standing trees on the reservation, and there were allegations that they deliberately fired the forest to increase the amount of dead timber.[27]

A Menominee committee set up to investigate these charges appealed in 1868 to the Bureau of Indian Affairs to protect their lumber. Lumber companies that had clearcut all the non-Indian lands surrounding the Menominee and Stockbridge reservations now were intent on obtaining

160

the rich reservation pine stands. With the aid of Congressman Philetus Sawyer, the Pine Ring pushed a bill through Congress in 1870 that opened up some of the Menominee timber reserves to sale if the Menominee would agree. This threat posed by the Pine Ring and the government to Menominee lumber and resources brought both the traditionalists and Christians together in defense of Menominee interests. Indeed, attempts by the government to force the Menominee to sell their timber reserves generated mistrust even among the acculturated Christians.[28]

The Menominee were far more receptive to employment as lumbermen than to working as farmers. When they became skilled as lumbermen, they became aware of their own timber wealth and sought to protect it. In lumber camps either on or off the reservation, the experience of being away from home for long periods of time in the fall and winter months, traveling, encountering danger with other men, becoming skilled in certain activities, and being rewarded for one's efforts proved similar to the old Menominee hunting and trapping life.[29]

Protecting their timber resources temporarily brought the Menominee factions together, but their victory in preserving their timber proved a defeat for tribal unity. Victory achieved, the need to work together as a tribe became less critical, and disunity again erupted. Work in the lumber camps brought prosperity and fostered acculturation, and the futility of the old ways became apparent to an increasing number of Menominee. This change in their perception led in the 1880s to what anthropologist Felix Keesing has identified as the "commencement of a modern cultural revolution among the Menominee." Menominee demands for frame houses, education, and health care were part of this "revolution."[30]

The government also recognized the stirrings of this revolution among the Menominee for a new order of things and initiated programs to accelerate the process of acculturation. In 1880, a Menominee police force was set up, and in 1883 a Menominee court system followed. The government instituted an "Indian code" that prohibited "the sun-dance, the scalp-dance, the war-dance—and all other so-called feasts assimilating thereto; plural marriages; the practice of the medicine man; the destruction or theft of property; the payment of or offer to pay . . . the friends or relatives of any Indian girl or women . . . " in exchange for marriage.[31] In 1887 the government also attempted to persuade the Menominee to divide up their land into individual private holdings in accordance with the Dawes Act. This severalty act, passed with the intention of promoting agriculture and inculcating a sense of private property among the tribal peoples of the United States, and also for selling off surplus Indian land to non-Indians after it was divided among tribal people, met with resistance among the Menominee. The traditionalists spear-headed the resistance to allotment, but the acculturated Menominee also recognized the intent of the act and realized the absurdity of dividing up timber land into family holdings, so refused to comply.[32]

Other factors spurring acculturation during these years were the construction of roads and rail lines on or near the Menominee reservation which both employed the Menominee and drew them off the reservation to nearby towns. Off-reservation boarding schools also removed Menominee children from the reservation and introduced them to varied aspects of American life and culture. Education and prosperity made for improved hygienic conditions in the community. A hospital started by the Franciscans in 1886 initiated modern health care among the Menominee and further split the Menominee because there were still many who preferred medicine men.[33]

The life of the acculturated Menominee centered around the tribal lumber mill (started in 1905), the schools, and the Catholic church. Not all Menominee, however, shared the same degree of acculturation or interest in American culture. Traditional Menominee resisted acculturation but split along religious lines in their own community. Despite old-style dress, evasion of schools, performance of traditional ceremonies, and protest over American influence, a division occurred between those who followed the Midewiwin and those who were devotees of the Dream Dance, a ceremony introduced to the Menominee by the Potawatomi and Ojibwa, perhaps as early as 1862.[34] Some Menominee belonged to both the Midewiwin and the Dream Dance religions, but increasingly the Dream Dance advocates saw their ceremonies as a replacement for the corrupted Midewiwin. As the ethnologist Walter J. Hoffman, who attended several Midewiwin ceremonies on the Menominee reservation between 1890 and 1893, noted, "It is asserted by the Menomini that Kisha' Ma'nido became angered at the Indians because the old customs and ceremonials of the Mita'wit became corrupted, and that, desiring to give to the Indians a purer ritual and religious observance, Kisha' Ma'nido gave to them the 'dance.'"[35] By the 1890s, although Hoffman still found Menominee being inducted into the Midewiwin, the number of believers, he claimed, was in decline, suggesting as reasons the many conversions to Christianity, the effects of boarding schools, and the death of old members of the religion.[36] Other reasons may have been the cost to join the Midewiwin as compared with the cost of performing in the Dream Dance and that the Dream Dance "is itself a product of acculturation, and conforms to modern conditions better than the traditional Medicine Dance," or Midewiwin. By the 1920s the Dream Dance would suffer the same fate.[37]

Changes in Menominee society are best recognized through the increasing influence of the federal government on Menominee affairs. Despite the government's attempts to allot the Menominee reservation, tribal voters in 1887 and again in 1919 blocked such moves. The court and police systems, however, were more symbolic of government influence because they were designed to break down traditional Indian political structures. In 1890 several Menominee chiefs—most of them from the traditional faction—were invited to Washington, D.C., and persuaded to relinquish their power and titles of leadership. The implications of this move became apparent after the death of these chiefs, when the government could freely appoint what it considered more acceptable leaders. At the same time the power of the tribal council was circumscribed, and the government began to deal with individual Menominee rather than with the tribe.[38]

One sees this especially in matters of health care and the activities of the government field matron. The field matron's time and efforts were "given principally to improvement of home conditions which must be brought about before there can be material progress toward intelligent citizenship." Home life was the crucible of Indian civilization and as such was a legitimate field for government investigation. "A matron must know personally and intimately every member of the tribe, be able to speak and write their names, be familiar with the location and condition of each home, the number of persons in each family, the health conditions of each, their inclinations and weaknesses, their industry and general habits." As one field matron reported in 1916, most Menominee women were "not willfully neglectful of their child's welfare, but through a mistaken idea of kindness often permit[ted] the child to follow its own inclinations, as to food, habits, etc." This problem could be corrected when the mother was "impressed with the extent of her own responsibility." The field matron urged greater control through laws to check child marriages, to detain wayward girls and boys, to stop "family desertion and other domestic irregularities."[39]

Forcing the Menominee to relinquish their old tribal governing system in favor of direction from Washington, D.C., loosened still further tribal control of the economy and increasingly altered personal relationships. The government Indian agent now became a primary force in Menominee society, and Menominee activities more often fell under government control. A measure of prosperity and economic growth followed these developments. Dependency had its rewards. Neither the dependency nor the rewards, however, benefited all Menominee equally, nor did all Menominee desire these changes that, as will be seen later, contributed to further division in their society.

By 1889, the federal government vigorously urged the lumbering-off of Wisconsin Indian reservations and saw it as a positive measure to bring Indian people into American society. As Secretary of Interior William F. Vilas pointed out in 1889, "The removal of the pine from lands belonging to Indians in severalty is no more to be deplored, if they have enjoyed fair compensation for its value, than the clearing of the forests everywhere before civilized improvement."[40]

The Oneida, Stockbridge, and Brothertown

Similarly to the Menominee, the Oneida, Stockbridge, and Brothertown suffered from American pressure and desire for their lands and timber. For these eastern tribes this was an old scenario and one that had sent them westward to Wisconsin. There, political factionalism, at least among the Oneida and Stockbridge, enabled Americans after the Civil War to gain easy access to their timber and the purchase of their lands. By the early 1860s, Wisconsin settlers and speculators began calling for the opening up of the Oneida reservation and the moving of the Oneida west. Meanwhile, internal strife among the Oneida made it difficult for them to operate under the hereditary tribal council that consisted of one head chief and 12 other "chiefs," who were really headmen of large kin groups or neighborhoods. Besides representing Oneida interests in Washington, D.C., the council controlled access to the land and devised rules for the community. Some Oneida with support from the federal government demanded a change to an elective system, and in 1871 such a system went into operation. Those who did not favor the change to an elected body refused support and "simply ignored its rules concerning land and timber use."[41] Loss of their land and timber resulted in poverty for many Oneida. As one contemporary noted, the Oneida who appeared on the streets of Green Bay and De Pere exhibited an "abject mien" and "shrunken forms"; they were "half-starved, naked [and] destitute. . . ."[42]

The Oneida suffered wrenching change and more community disintegration from the allotment of their reservation, which began in 1874, according to the Oneida John Archiquette, and continued through the 1890s.[43] Because the allotments were not contiguous, economical farming proved to be difficult. After 1900, the allotted land became subject to taxation, and much of it was sold under tax sales and foreclosures and passed into non-Indian hands. By the 1920s little land remained in Oneida hands, and non-Oneida town and county government replaced tribal government.[44] Accelerating the pace of change among the Oneida during this time were the rapid increase in nearby non-Indian settlement and the return of Oneida youth from boarding schools, bringing ideas that "often clashed and bred dissatisfaction with the old ways at Oneida."[45] As with the Menominee, so too with the Oneida: growing dependence on the federal government ushered in changes that had profound ramifications for Oneida society.

Yet despite these changes, the Oneida continued to perform certain traditional Iroquois religious practices, even working some of them into the fabric of Christianity as practiced by Oneida Episcopalians and Methodists. Old beliefs in witches, herbal medicines, and curing ceremonies, as well as funeral practices, served as a link between acculturated Oneida and their Iroquois past.[46]

The Stockbridge-Brothertown fared no better than their Oneida neighbors. Many Brothertown Indians in 1832 elected to divide their lands and accept citizenship, but some of the more conservative opted to join the Stockbridge, who by 1848 were split into two parties over the same issue. By 1846 much of the land the Stockbridge had possessed in the early 1830s had already been lost to non-Indians.[47] Among the Stockbridge, their division into the Citizen Party and the Indian Party was not a split over religion as in some tribes, because members of the two parties often belonged to the same church; rather, they split because of an argument over land and tribal leadership.[48] The Citizen Party wanted to divide the reservation into private family holdings, whereas the Indian Party, more traditionally oriented, sought to maintain the communal reservation and retain the old leadership pattern of chiefs and headmen. They rejected citizenship out of fear that to accept it would "extinguish the Indian State."[49]

The leaders of the Indian Party, men like John W. Quinney and John Metoxen, believed that if the land were divided the Stockbridge would be bought out one at a time until all the land passed out of Indian ownership. Land division also threatened Quinney and Metoxen with loss of power. As headmen they handled annuity money, but with the transition to citizenship all annuities would cease and so would much of their power. Although the allotment of land diminished the leadership roles of Quinney and others, suggesting that their resistance to the allotment may be seen as self-serving, history proved Quinney right.[50]

Selling off their lands, the members of the Stockbridge Indian Party agreed to move west of the Mississippi, but in 1856, after a treaty with the Menominee Indians, they, along with some Brothertown and Munsee Indians, removed to a section of land carved out of the Menominee reservation.[51] Less fortunate than their Menominee neighbors, the Stockbridge were denied access to the timber on their new reservation. The government ruled that the Stockbridge had rights only to occupancy of the soil and that the timber belonged to the government to dispose of as it wished. The government did not hold the timber long. Without notifying the Stockbridge, the Department of Interior sold the timber to a local lumber company with ties to a leading Wisconsin politician.[52]

In 1857, the Stockbridge drafted a new constitution, but it could offer little relief to the sharply divided community, so the Bureau of Indian Affairs assumed control. In 1873 the community remained split while the feud between the Citizen and Indian parties continued because the Indian Party insisted on denying the Citizen Party any of its benefits derived from the treaty of 1871.[53]

The Ojibwa

The Ojibwa situation in northern Wisconsin appeared bleak in 1847, the year before statehood. According to Rev. Hall at La Pointe, "The present is a critical moment with the Ojibwas." Writing to the editors of the *Missionary Herald,* he pointed out: "The tide of immigration as you are well aware, is rapidly rolling in upon them. I fear the fact portends no good to them. . . . The pine lumber on the tributaries of the Mississippi is attracting settlers and lumber men to the ground which they now occupy in that part of the country; and the mines are attracting still more. . . . There is no doubt that the number of adventurers and settlers will every year increase." Unfortunately, Hall reported, these settlers would include a number of "unprincipled men" who would "tend to corrupt and debase" the Ojibwa.[54]

As with the Menominee, much is written about the Ojibwa,[55] so, here too, the focus will be on the Ojibwa attempts to maintain their communities rather than on the details of their history. Between 1848 and 1854, the Ojibwa were nervous about where they would ultimately be forced to move. They treaty they concluded in 1837, in which they agreed to move beyond the Mississippi when required by the president, still clouded their future and filled them with foreboding. Despite the fact that their lands were nearly worthless for farming and the enthusiasm for mining had dissipated somewhat, the Ojibwa were still left in a precarious state of uncertainty regarding their future.[56] The government attempted with little success to induce the Wisconsin Ojibwa to move to Minnesota and in 1850 even required the Ojibwa on the southern shore of Lake Superior to receive their annuities at Sandy Lake in Minnesota. The payment proved a disaster. As related by the missionary at La Pointe:

Autumn came, and notice was sent to the Indians, that their annuity would be ready at Sandy Lake by the 25th of October. The season was so far advanced that many, living at a great distance from the Agency, resolved not to attend the payment. . . . Those who repaired thither, found the goods ready for delivery, but neither money nor agent. He had gone to St. Louis to obtain the necessary funds; but was obliged to return without them, and arrived at Sandy Lake, November 24. The goods were distributed, and the Indians were dismissed December 3. . . . In the meantime, however, there had been much suffering among them. Sickness broke out in their camps early in November, and many deaths occurred. . . . In some instances, eight or nine persons died in twenty-four hours. The fact that the government had not prepared a suitable supply of food of course aggravated the evil.[57]

In 1854, however, the picture brightened for the Ojibwa when the government granted them four reservations. Used to wandering over a wide territory, hunting and gathering or in pursuit of furs, the Ojibwa who took up residence on the Bad River, Red Cliff, Lac du Flambeau, and Lac Court Oreilles reservations did not easily adjust to the confinement that reservation life imposed. Many refused reservation life and continued to range over their former territory hunting, trapping, and fishing, while others competed for jobs with the increasing number of American residents in lumbering, fishing, and farming. Reservation Ojibwa possessed few resources, and without resources they could exercise little power. Federal agents now controlled Ojibwa destiny. Traditionally chiefs held power through generosity and the manipulation of resources, but when these functions disappeared so too did most of the chiefs' power. Rights to the land and land use, once a prerogative of the chiefs, were thrown into question. Agents could countermand chiefs' rulings and further diminish their power. Chiefs now cleared their decisions with the agent or applied to him for permission to make the decision. As one contemporary observed, even in questions where non-Indians or mixed-bloods used Ojibwa land, the chiefs "say they have no authority to stop them."[58]

As seen, the power of the chiefs diminished over the years when fur traders increasingly assumed the function of distributing food and goods. On the reservation, the agent and missionary now assumed these tasks.

The traditional political and economic community was bankrupt, and intratribal discord increased. As with the other Wisconsin tribes, the Ojibwa chiefs no longer exercised a creative role in society. Rather, their role now lay in resisting increasing government control, attempting to guard treaty rights, or officially representing the tribe in signing new treaties.

Even in the last of these official responsibilities, chiefs were threatened by the young men of the tribe who demanded a greater political role.[59] This generational rivalry can be seen in the young Ja-jig-wy-ong's attack on Chief Black Bird's handling of the Ojibwa treaty in 1855. Ja-jig-wy-ong requested to go to Washington, D.C., to handle tribal matters. Black Bird objected, saying, "If I am needed to go to Washington to represent the interests of our people I am ready to go."[60] The shifting nature of Ojibwa politics split communities and increased stress and bad feelings. Strife also characterized the acculturated Christian part of the community. A rift developed between the Catholic and Protestant Ojibwa, which unfortunately was encouraged by the clergy on both sides.[61]

Community disintegration and an acephalous political situation encouraged intrigue and social meddling by government and religious organizations. Those Ojibwa who gave up traditional ways and promoted government influence and programs of acculturation were often rewarded by the government with community positions. Such actions inflamed the suspicions of the extremely individualistic Ojibwa and caused further community discord.

Both missionaries and government agents attempted to induce the Ojibwa to take up farming. Since most reservation lands were unsuitable for farming and the climate unfavorable for agriculture, the Ojibwa looked to the sale of their timber as a more immediate source of economic stability. By the beginning of the 1880s drastic changes were underway. Lumbering began on the Ojibwa reservations. At this time the settlement of Ashland and the economic development of the region brought a flood of non-Indians into the area, resulting in increased drunkenness and crime. The Ojibwa continued to leave their reservations now to work on railroads and ships and in lumber camps, while farming, always a precarious venture, declined.[62]

Although commercial lumbering on the Lac du Flambeau and, to a lesser extent, Lac Court Oreilles reservations provided jobs for the Ojibwa, graft prevented the tribe from receiving its rightful timber profits. The Bureau of Indian Affairs set the price for the timber, and the proceeds from the timber sales were paid to the Ojibwa. Despite this arrangement, poaching by unauthorized lumber companies continued. Nor did this arrangement prevent the predilection for graft and collusion between Indian agents and lumber companies that "defrauded the Indians of much of the return they should have received for their logs."[63]

A sawmill built in 1894 at Lac du Flambeau brought stores and hundreds of non-Indians to work in the lumber camps. Logging also brought Ojibwa employment opportunities. As workers in the mills, as lumbermen, and as "river drivers" the Ojibwa were paid wages and slowly made the transition from a barter economy, which had characterized the fur trade, to a money economy.[64]

Lumbering also offered opportunities for exploitation of the Ojibwa. The Washington-based Indian Rights Association flagged several corrupt practices in a letter to the secretary of the interior in 1902. The letter noted the severe governmental restrictions to which the Ojibwa were held. It strongly suggested that the government agent was in collusion with the J. S. Sterns Lumber Company, which held the monopoly over Ojibwa timber. By virtue of that monopoly, the association charged, the Sterns company held the Ojibwa people powerless. The timber contract bought from the government by J. S. Sterns gave his company "pine forest at much less than the market value." The Sterns company also controlled "the traffic in merchandise on the Indian lands," enabling it to charge "exorbitant prices by reason of these exclusive privileges." According to the charge, "the Indian agent and other employees co-operate to keep out competition." The timber on the Lac Courte Oreilles reservation was sold off in 1872 to lumberman William A. Rust of Eau Claire for what was described as a give-away price. Corruption extended even to the Government Farmer, who exercised tyrannical means and "prostituted his office for mercenary ends."[65]

Logging also brought other changes with the eventual growth of towns around the lumber mills; this meant increased contact with non-Indian Americans and a growing awareness of racial and economic discrimination. "Cultural symbols of inferior status became increasingly clear to the Indians. Inability to speak English, wearing one's hair long, using moccasins and leggings, living in a wigwam, etc., all seemed to carry a stigma."[66] Even in the schools, Ojibwa children were punished for speaking or singing in Ojibwa.[67] Some Ojibwa were able to improve their standard of living, building better homes and buying goods that made their life easier; others, however, were not so fortunate and remained destitute. As one non-Indian resident of Sawyer County wrote:

The Indians are now in destitute circumstances and need some immediate relief. The price paid for the Indians [*sic*] pine is very much less than the value of the timber. In order to induce the Indian to sell his timber he is told by the lumber company that timber adjoining his will be cut and his timber exposed to loss and destruction by fire and the Indian is in that manner and others induced to sell his pine for much less than it is worth. In some instances the Indians' pine is cut without written contract, and when trespass is committed upon the Indians' land he does not receive much of anything for the trespass committed.[68]

There seemed but two alternatives for the Ojibwa: either one attempted to be more like white Americans, or one retreated deeper into the woods and back into one's culture. As with the Menominee, whose traditionalists isolated themselves at places like Zoar, so too with the Ojibwa at Lac du Flambeau, who removed from the town, set up the "Old Village," and minimized their contact with Americans.[69] Here the Ojibwa continued to enact truncated versions of their old rituals and to perform the Midewiwin ceremonies and the Dream Dance. The small size of the community and its distance from the agency symbolized the isolation and shrinking influence of tradition in community life.

The traditionalists, however, were not alone in their agonizing over the world they had lost. Others who rejected many of the traditional ways and struck off to emulate white Americans also experienced loss of influence. Caught in the rivalry between the government and the Catholic schools, suffering indignation from Government Farmers, exploited by both the Indian agent and the J. S. Sterns Lumber Company, discriminated against by local settlers, they lived a controlled existence where, like delinquent children, even their personal life drew sharp scrutiny. Indian agents, not the Ojibwa, called tribal council meetings, and the agendas under consideration were often determined by the agents' priorities. What little power the Ojibwa possessed upon entering reservation life dissipated under increasing government control and a shrinking land and resource base. The Ojibwa community dissolved into a mosaic of competing interests, factions, and personalities, stretched now over four reservations and wandering groups.[70]

The Winnebago

To the south and west of the Ojibwa, the Winnebago lived an even more precarious existence. After 1837 the Winnebago who refused to move west, suffering from poverty and its related ills, felt compelled to live in small settlements to avoid detection and removal. The rapid increase in American settlement in southern Wisconsin and the settlers' misguided fear of Indian attack in western Wisconsin after the 1862 Sioux uprising in Minnesota prompted Wisconsin settlers to call again for Winnebago removal to the West.[71] In the winter of 1871, army troops rounded up about 1,000 Winnebago for removal to Nebraska. About 860 arrived. The Nebraska agent proved less than enthusiastic about his new guests, and by 1875 about 650 had sneaked back to Wisconsin. In 1874 the government again attempted to remove Wisconsin Winnebago to Nebraska but with the same result.[72]

Leading a fugitive existence and living in small encampments, the Winnebago explored ways to remain legally in Wisconsin. One Winnebago named Yellow Thunder took up a homestead. Later others also took up homesteads, making use of an extension of the Homestead Act of 1862 to Indians and following the example of Yellow Thunder, who seemed to have assumed the role of peace chief. In 1881, new legislation enabled even more Winnebago to apply for 80-acre homesteads and provided them with funds to improve the land and purchase equipment. These homesteads were to be tax free for 25 years. Now, as legal residents of Wisconsin, the Winnebago no longer worried about removal, but subsistence and maintenance of a community life still proved difficult. After years of wandering, few had the necessary resources to invest in farming and compete with local white American farmers. Many continued trapping, hunting, and gathering and, with the aid of gardening, annuity payments, and work as farm laborers, eked out a somewhat meagre but relatively independent life. A few even worked in Wild West shows. Some may have sold the timber on their lands, but more often, upon return from hunting and gathering trips, they found it stolen by timber cutters. Unfortunately, much of the land acquired for homesteads proved inferior because most of the good land had long since disappeared from the market. Although homesteads provided security from the threat of removal, Winnebago dispersal over 10 Wisconsin counties sharply restricted close community life.[73]

Most Winnebago in the late nineteenth century continued to live on their land in bark dwellings and, despite attenuated settlements, practiced traditional ways, especially in areas of religious observances, social control, and dress.[74] Besides performing old medicine bundle ceremonies, they regularly held and inducted new members into the Medicine Lodge, but this began to change by the end of the century. Psychologically, the old rituals lent a sense of security to the Winnebago, but in the changing environment in which they now lived the old ceremonies were less effective than previously in helping them deal with problems of economy and health. The old ceremonies, like the Medicine Lodge, important during the fur trade in reminding them of their ties to nature and in distributing excess wealth through initiation fees, lost their attractiveness when nature, as the Winnebago probably conceived it, changed and when poverty continued to plague them. Rituals served to control nature, and in a world where the forces of nature became more predictable and less threatening than the actions of the dominant culture, the old ceremonies gave way to new ones.

Winnebago returning from Nebraska in the late nineteenth century brought back and talked excitedly about a new religion—a religion supported by visions that transported the believers to heaven and allowed them to talk with deceased relatives; a religion that promised a new way of being Indian in an increasingly non-Indian world; a religion that offered a better life if the Winnebago would throw away their old songs and war and medicine bundles, stop smoking and drinking, give up the blessings they received in fasting, and stop Medicine Lodge activities. The spread of this new religion, the Peyote religion, or Native American Church as it was called in Wisconsin, caused fear and some trauma among the traditionally oriented Wisconsin Winnebago, who still depended heavily on medicine bundles and songs for protection.[75] Although some Winnebago eventually joined the new religious movement, others continued to follow the old beliefs, especially the Medicine Lodge ceremony and war bundle ceremonies, resulting in religious factions that would disturb Winnebago society in the future.[76]

In 1906 another blow befell the Winnebago when, previously unknown to them, their homesteads became subject to taxation. Too poor to pay their taxes, many Winnebago lost their lands to a land company before tax-free status was restored. By then much of the remaining land was so divided it proved unproductive for farming.[77]

The Potawatomi

The Winnebago were not the only Wisconsin tribe that wandered without a reservation. The Potawatomi shared this same fugitive status. As seen, in the early 1800s they maintained villages around the lower end of Lake Michigan and northward along the western shore of the lake. In 1833, they gave up their lands in Wisconsin, and in 1837, although fearful of their old enemies the Sioux, many moved west of the Mississippi, where they were joined by other Potawatomi in 1846. Some Potawatomi bands, however, refused to move out onto the dry, treeless plains and fled into Michigan, Indiana, and farther north in Wisconsin, where they joined other Potawatomi. These Wisconsin Potawatomi insisted that they never ceded their lands east of the Milwaukee River, Lake Winnebago, and the Fox River between Lake Winnebago and Green Bay. Although the Menominee claimed some of this land and later ceded it to the United States, the Potawatomi disputed the Menominee claim.[78]

In spite of Potawatomi claims, pressure from encroaching settlers forced the tribe off the rich agricultural lands of southern Wisconsin and into the pineries and cutover lands in the northern part of the state.[79] When other Potawatomi returned from Kansas and settled near Marshfield and Wisconsin Rapids, they too competed with settlers for the rich farm lands and lost. Like their tribesmen farther east near Lake Winnebago, they were driven into the marshes and woods, where they cultivated some crops on small plots of land and lived in obscurity.[80] Numerically superior to the Potawatomi around Marshfield, the Potawatomi around Lake Winnebago, Shawano, and Wittenberg continued to press northward.

Between the years 1850 and 1880, the Potawatomi suffered poverty, starvation, disease, and discrimination. Their economy, based on hunting, gathering, and agriculture, conflicted with logging interests and the new intensive agriculture practiced by Americans. Destruction of the forest through lumbering decreased the animal population and hindered the collecting of medicinal plants. Denied access to the streams and lakes, the Potawatomi were curtailed in their fishing, trapping, and gathering of wild rice.

Relations between Wisconsin Potawatomi and settlers became increasingly strained during the 1860s and 1870s. In the 1860s some Potawatomi, enraged at the tightening restrictions placed on their lifestyle and at their dire poverty, proposed a coalition of western tribes to oppose the U.S. government. This call for a western coalition, coming at the time of the Santee uprising in Minnesota, frightened Indian agents. In 1871 the Potawatomi renewed attempts to organize a western Indian resistance to the United States and sent messages to other tribes calling for a council of the disaffected. Again, this action triggered fear, and settlers began calling for Potawatomi removal. Negotiation began in 1873 for their removal to Kansas.[81] Waves of despair passed through the Potawatomi encampments when news filtered through the forests and across the cutover lands that the government would soon carry out a Potawatomi removal to the West. When the government neglected to act upon its decree, the Potawatomi relaxed slightly, but they still carried the fear of a western diaspora and sought even greater obscurity in the northern forests.[82]

In 1876 Potawatomi resistance to encroaching American pressure took yet another turn. The new religious movement known as the Dream Dance, or Drum Dance, began to sweep through Potawatomi communities and extended, as seen above, to the Ojibwa and Menominee. Many who danced to the beat of the drum believed they were dancing to a new life, dancing to create a better world for the Indian, and that the followers of the new religion would be protected by the power of the drum. Rather than offering physical resistance to invading American communities, the Potawatomi turned to religion to exorcise the social and economic ills that plagued them.[83]

In 1894 the main group of Potawatomi moved from Wittenberg to Forest County, Wisconsin. There they took advantage of the Indian Homestead Act of 1884 and took up homesteads on the cutover lands. Other Potawatomi followed. Unfortunately, poverty also followed them to their new home. Without means to work the land and with few local jobs available, economic depression devastated the two new communities of Wabeno and Stone Lake.[84] In 1901, the Reverend Erik O. Morstad, a Lutheran missionary, took up a mission among the Potawatomi of Forest County. Although Morstad's preaching proved less effective against the Dream Dance and the Midewiwin than he desired, he wrote indignantly of Potawatomi poverty and suffering. Their long fugitive existence made them suspicious of government help. Even in the early twentieth century, they were reluctant to answer census questions.

At some of the camps visited much patience and tact were required to get any information whatever from the Indians. They were sullen and suspicious and still considered themselves refugees and repeatedly said they did not wish to be enrolled. For the most part, they feared that their children would be sent to school or that they would be collected and forcibly removed to Kansas by the government.[85]

Only in 1913, with the lobbying efforts of Morstad and the help of Senator Robert M. La Follette, did Congress appropriate $150,000 for the Potawatomi to buy land and another $100,000 for houses. This provided the Potawatomi a land base, and, although not a reservation, government stipulations prevented its sale to whites.[86] No longer wandering over the land like gypsies "without title to the land," the Potawatomi began to shape a community.[87]

This infusion of aid only partly eased the straitened conditions under which the Potawatomi lived. Arguing before a committee of Congress in 1916 for aid to the Potawatomi, former congressman Thomas F. Konop exclaimed: "They just roamed around over the cut over lands and in the woods that the lumber companies owned. Some worked in the lumber camps, and some did any kind of work they could get. But they just roamed the woods half of them starving. They had no medical attendance. Their condition was deplorable."[88]

Despite government aid, crippling poverty and abject living conditions prevailed. Most of the Potawatomi, like their conservative counterparts among the Ojibwa, Menominee, and Winnebago, shrank from contact with non-Indians and American institutions, preferring to put their faith in the Midewiwin and the Dream, or Drum, Dance. Without education and resources the Potawatomi were unable to compete in the American marketplace, even if they wanted to.

SUMMARY

By the beginning of the twentieth century, significant changes were apparent on Wisconsin Indian reservations and in Indian communities. In both places, polarization increased, pitting traditionalists sharply against the more acculturated members of the community, and the majority, caught in between, were pulled in both directions. Here they shuffled across blurred ideological divisions in their struggle to survive. The majority, absorbed with fitting traditional knowledge to a new environment, concentrated on providing for their families; raising crops; working in lumber camps, saw mills, or as laborers; and hunting game for lumber camps, hotels, or for their own tables. When ill, they used herbs or sought relief from medicine men, conjurers, midwives, and/or white physicians. For most, getting on with life proved a more powerful motivation than adherence to traditional ways or acculturation. When necessary, most shifted easily between utilizing native techniques, hunting and gathering, and working for lumber camps and saw mills. They followed a life-style that intentionally avoided bumping up against a government-imposed system of regulation.

Yet the government proved a dominant presence. The traditionalists, who longed for a return to tribal sovereignty, were in retreat. Likewise was the power of the hereditary chiefs, whose functions were usurped first by traders and missionaries and then by government agents and Indian and civil courts. The old norms, based on traditional values, were now less applicable, their force eroded along with the power of the old tribal council, their power abrogated by progressive government influ-

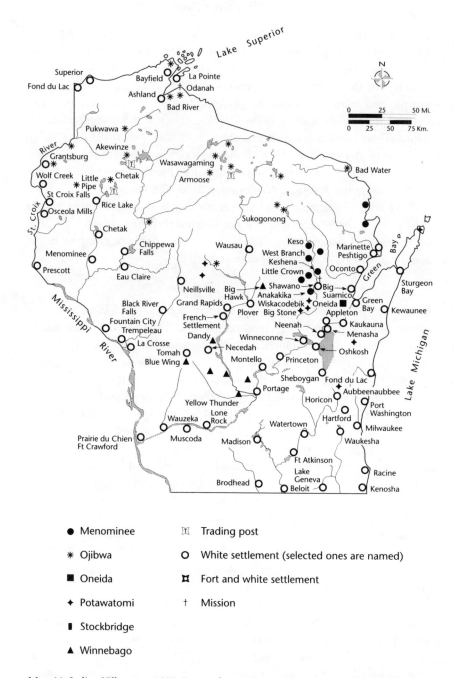

Map 11. Indian Villages, c. 1870. Drawn from a portion of map 33 in the *Atlas of Great Lakes Indian History,* edited by Helen Hornbeck Tanner, University of Oklahoma Press, 1987.

ence, allotment, residence patterns, and education. All these factors affected personal relations and relations with the environment and contributed to a growing dependency on the government. Washington, D.C., now dictated the parameters of both action and opportunity on the reservation.

Given this situation, factionalism increased rather than diminished in Indian communities. During the second half of the nineteenth century much of the factionalism dealt with petty issues and local problems, but it also focused on the direction the community ought to take in regard to the dominant American culture.

While Wisconsin Indians struggled to reconstitute themselves as communities in the second half of the nineteenth century after near collapse during the first half of the century, they lacked the means and the resources to resist local exploitation and the American government's increasing control over their lives and destiny. Their choices were few. They could retreat into the obscurity that a diminishing forest offered, or they could choose to make adjustments to a new environment shaped largely by the dominant American society. Either way, they held second-class status, ricocheting constantly between trying to survive and trying to remain Indian. They lived in a world where ambition and dreams were dulled by government restrictions, discrimination, poverty, alcohol abuse, and disease, where all too often they could not create but waited only to respond.

In a Western civilization that emphasized progress, change, efficiency, and industry, that doubted the ability of nonwhite races to compete and talked openly of bad genes, that promoted full exploitation of both natural and human resources, that pressed for expanded markets and empires—political and economic—in Asia, Africa, and South America, it was difficult for Indian people who spoke for the value of tradition and the dignity of the human spirit to be heard. They were considered, when considered at all, to be anachronistic. Americans saw the verities of the past as useless and quaint and restrictive. Americans believed that tradition held the future hostage and ought to be jettisoned for the sake of progress. In such a "brave new world," the forest and lakes of Wisconsin seemed to many traditional Wisconsin Indians a safer place to reside.

Ojibwa chief's lodge from Lac Courte Oreilles Reservation set up at the 1906 Wisconsin State Fair. Note both reed and bark coverings on the lodge.

Scenes from a Menominee powwow held at Keshena, in 1929. Powwows with dancing and feasting still are an important social event on many reservations often attracting Indians from other reservations, urban centers and even non-Indians.

Van Schaick studio portrait of Iowa Indian, Alex Lonetree and his Winnebago wife Mary Hall Eagle. Alex Lonetree and his wife came to Wisconsin from Nebraska after the last Winnebago removal to the West. Alex was the son of the Iowa chief Old Dave Io Hee. Charles Van Schaick was only one of many photographers who captured Indians on film and most often in studio shots. Besides posing them in Victorian fashion with the man sitting and being the focal point of the picture with the woman standing in the background in less elaborate dress, these photographs also carried messages. Studio shots removed the Indian from the wilds as they were being removed from the land. In the studio, Indian association with the environment was neutralized.

Van Schaick studio portrait of Mary Eagle Wallace of Black River Falls wearing native dress, ca. 1920. Native dress was often important to stress that the subject was Indian. Some photographers actually kept beadwork as props for just this reason, and one can sometimes find the same piece of beadwork on several different Indians posed by the same photographer. This is true of the bandoleer bag, an over- the-shoulder bag, worn by Alex Lonetree.

Postcard of three Winnebago women in tribal dress, with their babies. Photograph taken about 1910 by A.C. Stone.

Ojibwa woman near Odanah, with her son, and samples of baskets and beadwork. This photograph taken about 1913, like many of such photographs, was made into a postcard for tourists. Many Indian families as late as mid-century had stands along the roads of Wisconsin and Michigan where they sold baskets and other Indian-made items to tourists. Wisconsin, along with many other states, encouraged the sale of Indian artifacts to summer visitors and promoted Indian dances and pagents to draw tourists to the state. Such tourist attractions can still can be found at the Wisconsin Dells.

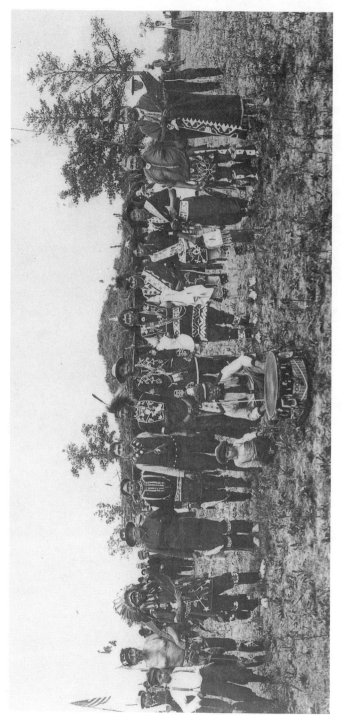

Winnebago dancers photographed near Black River Falls around 1910. In the foreground is what appears to be a Dream Dance drum. How important the Dream Dance was to the Winnebago is difficult to access. Paul Radin does not mention it in his study *The Winnebago Tribe*, and Thomas Vennum, Jr., in his *The Ojibwa Dance Drum* quotes an unnamed source saying, "We gave one Drum to the Winnebago some time ago, but they don't treat them the same as we do. They just use them to have fun with and the drums just go to pieces down there [Black River Falls]" (264).

A posed photograph of Menominee dancers that appeared on a postcard in 1910. Some Indians, like this group, would dance at county fairs.

Three young Potawatomi men. *From left to right*: George Ce-ku-tay, Peter Shomin (Grapes), and Benjamin Wah-mix-i-co. Shomin was a grandson of Chief Shomin of She-boygan County, and Ce-ku-tay was a descendent of Chief Ce-ku-tay. Wah-mix-i-co was a son of Wampun, or Wau-me-gesako, who lived near Manitowoc Rapids.

Five young Ojibwa men in athletic outfits at the Hayward Indian School, Hayward.

Ojibwa Gus Sharlow in World War I army uniform, taken in Hayward. Many Wisconsin Indians along with Indians across the nation volunteered to fight in World War I despite being exempt from the draft since many were not citizens of the United States. Citizenship was extended to all Indians by an act of Congress in 1924.

A studio photograph of two Winnebago World War I soldiers: Hugh Lonetree and Richard Winneshiek, with Lucy Thunder and Nora Olthur. The photograph was taken in the Charles Van Schaick studio in Black River Falls in 1917 or 1918.

A group of Ojibwa with Ojibwa World War I soldiers at a victory celebration on June 19, 1919, at Reserve. In the foreground is Ira O. Isham, Ojibwa interpreter.

This photograph, also from the Van Schaick collection, was taken in the late 1920s, and shows the influence of hair and dress styles of the "roaring twenties." The appearance of the three daughters of Rachel Whitedeer Littlejohn: Florence Littlejohn, Mary Littlejohn, and Ann Littlejohn Lone Tree, with their bobbed hair and fur-trimmed coats, stands in sharp contrast to the dress of their mother.

Winnebago Tom Thunder and his family in the studio of Charles Van Schaick. The pose, so reminiscent of Victorian parlor shots, represents an acculturated Indian family, and may have been the image that the Thunder family wished to record. Some Indians undoubtedly requested photographs of themselves and their families.

A Menominee girl in the 1960s.

An Oneida parent volunteer teacher holding a class in the Milwaukee Indian Community School. Photograph taken in January 1971 by Robert Nandell of the *Milwaukee Journal*.

7

Wandering Like Shadows on a Disappearing Land

According to historian Robert F. Berkhofer, "The 1920s marked a fundamental shift in the scientific and scholarly understanding of the Indian through acceptance of the concept of culture and the ideal of cultural pluralism."[1] Quite true, but this shift in academic viewpoint took a long time to reach and affect the destinies of Wisconsin Indians. World Wars I and II equaled the 1920s' attitudinal shift in importance, not only in altering the public view of the Indian, but also in changing Indian life-style and expectations. The accumulative effect of these events, combined with radical shifts in government policies forged by Commissioner of Indian Affairs John Collier during the depression and war years, eventually resonated through Indian country.

Poverty and disease in the early twentieth century continued to sap the energy and spirit of Wisconsin Indian communities. Despite improved medical delivery systems, tuberculosis proved endemic in the Indian population, largely as a result of living in poorly drained or swampy areas and in overcrowded, unsanitary dwellings. In Odanah on the Bad River reservation, "low places in backyards filled up with stagnant water, rubbish and refuse," and spring thaws caused the Bad River to overflow, spreading raw sewage throughout the town.[2] Smallpox also continued to be a problem, and contact with non-Indians led to the spread of venereal disease, which proved to be one of the leading causes of death among infants.[3] The shabby living conditions where whole families often lived in one room were only partly due to the growing poverty.

195

The Ojibwa, a highly mobile people, were now forced to settle in cramped permanent housing; they were a people with no tradition of carpentry to facilitate building repairs or systems of waste disposal so necessary in a permanent community situation, which led all too often to unsanitary rural slums.

The decline of lumbering in northern Wisconsin (except in places like the Menominee reservation, where replanting produced a sustaining yield forest) left impoverishment in its wake. Among the Ojibwa, interest in agriculture again flickered, but poor soil, the expense of clearing the land, and lack of roads necessary to get produce to market defeated most attempts to eke out a living from the soil.[4]

Of increasing economic significance during this time was the growth of tourism. Guiding hunters and anglers, selling baskets and beadwork, and performing dances, all provided needed employment once the timber was gone. Tourists, however, while contributing cash to the reservation economy, also diminished the land base by purchasing lakefront property on reservations like Lac du Flambeau, leaving the Ojibwa in possession of the unproductive swamp and cutover lands on the reservation.[5]

Reservation communities still remained divided by levels of acculturation and by religion. Some individuals marched confidently into the future, eager to climb the achievement ladder of success, untroubled by the discontinuities between the present and the past. If they doubted this path at all and the implications it held for the reservation community, it was in regard to the old ones and the conservatives, or traditionals, and what their future role would be. In the schoolroom "forcing ground," teachers sifted out bright and talented youth and prodded them toward greater accomplishments. Most of the community, the conservative traditionals and those exhibiting degrees of acculturation, walked hesitantly along the border between the past and the future. This frontier was a dangerous place, intimidating to the unsure, frightening to the unprepared, and incomprehensible to those who saw in its promise merely a mirage devoid of moral substance.

Conservatives among all the tribes marched to different drummers. They still performed ceremonies considered traditional, such as the Dream Dance and the Midewiwin, but each year the steps of the dancers grew slower and memory of the rituals and songs dimmer. The Peyote religion introduced into Wisconsin by the Winnebago penetrated north and east and by 1914 found advocates on the Menominee reservation and even among the Ojibwa.[6] Each year, however, fewer young people attended the traditional ceremonies. Many youth, increasingly unable to speak their native tongue, could not understand the old ceremonies or were not interested in trying to do so. Another factor contributing to the decline of traditional ceremonies was their expense. At a time of extreme poverty, initiation fees and the construction and care of religious paraphernalia, all mitigated against the continuation of these ceremonies. To these factors others may be added: an increasing number of converts to Christianity or to the Native American Church; cheaper secular forms of entertainment; and the death of older believers, who took with them many of the songs, stories, ceremonies, and rituals.[7] The fault lines in the rock of tribal values were widening.

THE EFFECTS OF WORLD WAR I AND ITS AFTERMATH ON THE INDIANS OF WISCONSIN

The advent of World War I shook reservation life; it broke like a storm into the boredom of poverty and the regimented existence imposed by governmental regulations. Although not subject to the draft, Wisconsin Indians, like Indians across the nation, volunteered for service. They joined out of patriotism, boredom, and a yearning for adventure, especially one that fitted so nicely with the old warrior tradition. Others were drawn to cities to work in war-related industries. Desperate economic conditions as well as patriotism contributed to this move.[8]

The darkening skies of World War I masked the growing crisis in Indian communities, but after the war it was apparent to an increasing number of Wisconsin Indians that the old customs had grown even more tattered, and many of the old ways were gone forever. On the reservations and in rural communities, poverty and disease remained. The old ways of "getting by" and "making do" proved more difficult. At the same time, the federal government's awareness of what was wrong did not match its ability to frame solutions.

Up until the 1920s, the operation of the government's unchanging acculturation policy produced mixed results, and it worked very slowly. When the "mighty pulverizing engine" of the General Allotment Act divided up many Indian reservations into private holdings, it also created a large, permanently disadvantaged class of Indians and pockets of rural poverty. Where it was tried among the Ojibwa, allotment brought about the extensive loss of land to Indians. Similar results occurred on other allotted Indian reservations in Wisconsin and across the country.[9]

With the conclusion of the war, many Indians who took part in the war effort returned to Wisconsin and to their reservation. What they found triggered sharp discontent. During the war, both in the military and in urban wartime employment, many Wisconsin Indians gained perceptions of the world beyond reservations; these perceptions harshly illuminated the wretchedness of conditions on the reservation. The return of veterans and others roiled the still waters of apathy. For Indians, as for many Americans, the war shifted their outlook. Even more than the schools they attended, the wartime experience proved a forcing ground for acculturation, self-reliance, and leadership experience. The war experience served as a catalyst, triggering an angry discontent with things as they had been before the war, a discontent that echoed in the press when magazine and newspaper stories juxtaposed reservation poverty with Indian patriotism and valor and exposed troubling problems in Indian education and health. Reflecting the new social science interest in cultural pluralism, critics of government Indian policy began to shift the blame for Indian poverty away from the individual Indian and to fault the Bureau of Indian Affairs (BIA). According to these critics, the government's manipulation and willful misinterpretation of reservation society and economics produced the deplorable state of Indian poverty and lethargy.[10]

Despite the fact that by 1924 over half of the nation's Indians were already citizens, Congress propounded a solution to "the Indian problem" by making all Indians citizens in that year and abandoning them to the melting pot. The successful adaptation that many Indians made to life in the armed forces and to urban environments convinced some politicians that the time was propitious for the government to reduce its commitment to tribal peoples. Indians and others concerned with Indian welfare and fearful of the consequences of such a radical move were less prone to dismiss the government from its responsibility so quickly. Rising anger and discontent on the reservations and among non-Indians sympathetic to the plight of Native Americans forced the government to seek further data on the Indian condition.[11]

In 1928, during the presidency of Herbert Hoover, the Interior Department commissioned the Institute for Government Research (a branch of the consolidation known as the Brookings Institution) to undertake a study of the Indian situation. This followed closely on the critical survey of the Committee of One Hundred, which called for more education and health care for Indians and for better sanitation facilities on Indian reservations.[12] The institute's team of researchers, headed by Dr. Lewis Meriam and including Henry Roe Cloud, a Nebraska Winnebago graduate from Yale, drew upon the latest social science survey techniques in their attempt to assess the Indian condition and the reasons

198

for government failure. Investigators spread across the country, looking at reservation conditions and examining agents' files, and by 1928 compiled an extraordinary 800-page indictment of the government's Indian policy. Commenting on the government's treatment of Indian communities, the report noted: "The Indian Service has not appreciated the fundamental importance of family life and community activities in the social and economic development of a people. The tendency has been rather toward weakening Indian family life and community activities than toward strengthening them." The report went on to fault government efforts to educate Indians as "largely ineffective" and found health care services deplorable when compared with those of the general population.[13] The report, still maintaining the old expectations of eventual assimilation, suggested that before entertaining any idea that Indian reservations could be abolished, Indians would have to be brought up to the same level of health and education as the rest of the American population. Anxiety over worsening economic conditions, however, led America to vote Herbert Hoover out of office before the suggestions of the Meriam Report could be implemented.

RESTRUCTURING THE BUREAU OF INDIAN AFFAIRS AND THE EFFECT ON NATIVE AMERICANS

Swept into the presidency by the worst depression America has ever experienced, Franklin D. Roosevelt appointed people who seized upon the economic situation as an opportunity to inaugurate change. Faced with a national crisis of epic proportions, they labored to control a situation that seemed to worsen daily. Although the tentacles of the depression reached deeply into the middle class, all the poor fell victim to the ruined economy, with blacks and Indians suffering the most. The depression cut through Indian reservations across the country, leaving a path of grinding poverty, disease, starvation, overcrowding, inadequate housing, and death that surpassed what had already existed. Already victimized by discrimination, by political and economic policies that isolated them from mainstream America and participation in national affairs, Indians faced a bleak existence where hope withered and the spirit faltered.[14]

The new administration wasted no time in confronting the abuses set forth in the Meriam Report. Roosevelt appointed John Collier, the tart-tongued critic of the Bureau of Indian Affairs, to take over the bureau and implement a fair Indian policy. With the sureness and zeal of a reformer, Collier moved quickly to foster and preserve Indian community life as he understood it. He sought to reinvigorate a sense of community on Indian reservations across the nation. Collier drew his conception of community from the Pueblo Indians in New Mexico, about which he said, "The discovery which came to me out of this first Pueblo Indian experience deepened and broadened, and changed my sociological perspective once and for all."[15] So even before Collier became commissioner of Indian affairs, he believed Indians had prepared him "for the discovery that deep community yet lived on in the embattled Red Indian."[16] In the ceremonial life of the Pueblo, Collier found institutions, although long under attack, still creative and generating "states of mind, attitudes of mind, earth loyalties and human loyalties."[17]

Collier emerged from these profound emotional experiences and went on to press for the regeneration of other Indian communities and the re-creation of Indian communities that had disappeared. First as a vocal member of the Indian Rights Association and later as commissioner, Collier argued that Indians should be given responsibility, power, and land and be allowed to maintain their culture and practice religious freedom. Collier strove ceaselessly to achieve these goals. With extraordinary virtuosity, he steered through Congress in 1934 the Indian Reorganization (Wheeler-Howard) Act (IRA), which embodied many of the reforms suggested by the Meriam Report. The act recognized and empowered Indian tribal society, promoted an Indian civil service and training program, ended allotments, and made credit available to Indian communities out of a revolving government fund.[18]

The Indian Reorganization Act, however, was not forced upon Indian people; each tribe or reservation elected whether to reject the plan or come under its provisions, which included setting up a tribal government and usually writing a constitution. Although some tribes refused to adopt all or parts of the IRA, many decided that the rewards outweighed the risks. By its structure, the IRA politically favored tribal "progressives" over traditionals. The latter, although they welcomed the new freedom to perform their religious ceremonies and the opportunity to practice old customs and promote tribal arts and crafts, were nevertheless concerned that they would lose power as the progressives gained influence. The development of tribal governments and budgets tended to channel power into the hands of the more Western-educated and hence more often acculturated members of the tribe.[19]

All the Wisconsin tribes except the Winnebago responded quickly to the benefits offered under the IRA and elected to come under its provisions. All but the Menominee and the Lac Court Oreilles drew up constitutions and formed tribal governments which enabled them to acquire critical loans during the bleak depression years. Under the auspices of the IRA, the government transferred land to the Oneida, Potawatomi, and Stockbridge-Munsee and created reservations for the Ojibwa both at Mole Lake and from among the small parcels of land acquired by the Ojibwa in the St. Croix area. Financial aid also came to Wisconsin tribes in the form of desperately needed employment in the Works Progress Administration (WPA; later renamed the Work Projects Administration) and the Civilian Conservation Corps (CCC). Two further benefits under the WPA and the CCC were health and education-training programs. As the depression worsened, Indians who held jobs in the city were let go and, with no other work available, returned to the reservation, taxing meagre resources.[20] By the mid-1930s, a crisis situation existed on Wisconsin Indian reservations. As one observer noted, for the Oneida such aid proved vital for their existence:

In 1935 the W.P.A. came to their aid and played a major part in sustaining the Oneidas. By 1939 some two hundred people were employed in such projects as the building of a dam at Kaukauna, the Writers Project for the purpose of teaching them to read and record their own language, and a house-building project. In 1939 approximately 1,300 of the 1,500 Oneidas were receiving government aid, either surplus commodities, W.P.A., outdoor relief, old-age pensions, dependent-children pensions, or C.C.C. aid.[21]

The Ojibwa

Ojibwa at Lac Courte Oreilles, Red Cliff, Lac du Flambeau, and Bad River voted to accept the IRA, and the last two reservations installed tribal governments. At Lac Courte Oreilles, the motion to write a constitution and form a tribal governing body stirred resistance among the traditionalists, who feared loss of power and influence and wished for a continuation of the old hierarchial chief system. Their resistance proved critical. Traditionalists bristled at the thought of accepting the IRA while outstanding claims against the government stemming from the 1854 La Pointe treaty remained at issue. Mobilizing their forces, the traditionalists mustered enough votes to block acceptance of a constitution and the creation of a tribal government. The BIA superintendent J. C. Cavill, however, interpreted the rejection as merely the work of a disaffected faction of older, uneducated traditionalists who sought to return of what he saw as the corrupt and inefficient system of chiefs and headmen.[22] Government relief measures eventually reached the Lac Courte Oreilles people after being channeled through the Business Committee, which became the de facto tribal government.[23]

Although not as extreme, factionalism also existed at other Ojibwa reservations. Perhaps from fear of their declining status and concern over the increasing role of the federal government in tribal politics, traditionalists attempted to frustrate the plans of tribal councils.[24] These divisions, however, did not appear to some observers to be as important as other Ojibwa problems. The anthropologist A. Irving Hallowell saw Ojibwa resistance to acculturation as a factor of their cultural-psychological makeup. In 1946 at Lac du Flambeau, Hallowell found evidence of traditional ceremonial practices at both Old Village and New Village but remained convinced that the old ways were disappearing rapidly and in the process were affecting Ojibwa personality:

I cannot, of course, go into an extended analysis here of all the various factors that may account for the breakdown of the old personality structure of the Ojibwa under the pressures of acculturation at Flambeau. But I can say that one of the most crucial factors involved seems to be the lack of any positive substitute for that aspect of the aboriginal value system that had its core in religious belief.[25]

Hallowell noted the weakness of their beliefs in emotion-laden queries from traditionalists who asked him whether he thought the Indian religion was "really true."[26] To the Ojibwa's lack of inner resources and their inability to draw upon aboriginal values, Hallowell attributed the high frequency of drunkenness and juvenile delinquency and the ineffectiveness of "externally applied controls."[27] The Lac du Flambeau Ojibwa were "attempting [to achieve] values and goals" that crippled them psychologically and hindered their "positive [cultural] readjustment."[28] At Lac Courte Oreilles, other observers saw similar patterns of cultural decline and noted that "the old social system has largely collapsed" and that "the nearly three centuries of contact with whites has resulted in a steady loss of Indian culture. . . ."[29]

The pattern of rapid cultural change that had characterized late nineteenth- and early twentieth-century Ojibwa communities—when the Ojibwa saw first their forest resources cut down and then much of their allotted lands pass from their control to become recreational areas for non-Ojibwa—continued through the Collier years. During the years previous to the IRA, Ojibwa attempts to resist acculturation and erosion of tradition collided with their extreme need. Their poverty forced many to sell off resources, which in turn exacerbated community instability and factionalism. Fearing that their world would continue to disintegrate and that this would only accelerate with closer ties to the BIA, conservatives rallied to oppose the IRA despite the government's attempts to rectify community disorganization through land purchases and the creation of tribal councils. The psychological trauma inherent in the destruction of the old culture, the loss of dances, songs, religion, and clothing—what James Slotkin termed "cultural decay" in his study *The Menominee Powwow*—observers like Hallowell saw as manifestations of the final stage of Ojibwa community disintegration.[30]

The Menominee

Like the Ojibwa, the Menominee elected to come under the provisions of the IRA, but having set up the Advisory Council and the General Council in 1928 to oversee the tribe's lumber interests, the Menominee decided a new governing body would be unnecessary.[31] The Menominee, who complained for years that government regulations prevented them from assuming control of their own resources, now welcomed the opportunity under the IRA to manage their own affairs. Long impressed with the ineptitude of the government to develop tribal forest resources and operate the tribal sawmill profitably, the Menominee confidently believed they could do better.[32]

Years of negotiation with the government over their timber assets instilled in many of the more acculturated members of the tribe a sense of business acumen and political sophistication that enabled them to assume those economic responsibilities needed to compete successfully with non-Indians. Other factors also contributed to Menominee confidence. Education, employment off the reservation in the nearby urban centers of Green Bay and Milwaukee, dealings with lumbermen and with the increasing number of farmers adjoining the reservation, all equipped many Menominee to protect reservation resources and utilize the opportunities now offered by the IRA. Finally, it should be noted that the Menominee had never agreed to allot their reservation.

As with the Ojibwa, tribal discord prevented a unified response to the problems that plagued the reservation. The Advisory Council acted as the tribal council and conferred with the BIA superintendent on budget and policy. This council, made up of highly acculturated Menominee, often found itself hamstrung by the General Council, which could veto its actions. The General Council, made up of 75 members from the Menominee community at large, was often the scene of raucus political infighting. Factions, suspicions, jockeying among large family groups for power, self-styled tribal leaders, and distrust among the various cultural-economic groups on the reservation contributed to divisiveness in the meetings of the General Council while the groups circled, jousted, and clashed over a myriad of issues. These, however, were not the only problems. The large size of the body, the irregular meetings, the lack of a permanent chairperson, the goal of achieving consensus on each issue, an extraordinary tolerance for unlimited discussion, a proclivity to vote in accordance with tribal leaders rather than on one's own conception of the merits of an issue, and the high degree of absenteeism, all contributed to the General Council's ineffectiveness in working with the Advisory Council.[33]

The schisms in Menominee politics mirrored the divisions in Menominee society. In an elegantly designed psychological study, George Spindler found five social classes in Menominee society.[34] The most distinctive were the "elite acculturated" group at one end of the social continuum and the "native oriented" group at the other end. In between, struggling for acceptance and identity, were the members of the "peyote cult," the "transitional," and the "lower status acculturated." Their struggle, however, often foundered in a mixture of rage, apathy, and despair. New roads and, more significantly, the construction of the sawmill in 1909 increased personal contact, resulting in greater opportunity for friction and discrimination among all the reservation groups.[35] The elite acculturated group was more charitable in their opinion of the native oriented group than in their opinion of the other three classes. As one elite Menominee expressed it, the native oriented "have character. . . . Their moral ethics have not been lost," but the other groups "have lost their moral ethics. . . . They have a loose system of character and spend a lot of time and money drinking and running around."[36]

For Felix Keesing, who lived among the Menominee in the 1930s, it was more than a mere loss of moral ethics; the fault lay, as Hallowell found among the Ojibwa, in the Menominee failure to find replacements for the old lost cultural values:

On the social and political sides the reservation community shows a marked degree of individualism, and not a little anti-social behavior. This may in some measure reflect the ancient personality values. But for the most part it seems a consequence of the passing of customary Indian standards and restraints without adequate substitutions of new controls.[37]

According to Keesing, the federal government must share the blame for the pain and frustration of those Menominee who wandered in the no mans' land between acculturation and the traditional world. The government dissolved traditional Menominee political structure and leadership patterns and instituted in their place a paternal-ward relationship which, as seen earlier, rewarded dependency.[38]

Given the political cross-purposes and infighting, the decades from 1930 to 1950 were not fallow years for the Menominee. Despite charges of indecisiveness and accusations that as a tribe they could not decide how they wanted to shape their world or where they wanted to go,[39] these were years of major accomplishments. They initiated a lawsuit that they eventually won 13 years later. Menominee lumbering and sawmill operations, besides providing jobs on the reservation, generated other kinds of employment and funded education, a hospital, and a health care program. The tribe, however, could not provide jobs for everyone. Some Menominee left to find work in Milwaukee and Chicago, but the tribe was proud of "paying their own way."[40] Economic success did not, however, translate into political success, and tribal bickering among factions and political contentiousness contributed to the continued federal meddling in Menominee politics. Economic success and political disunity also facilitated later government efforts to push for the termination of the Menominee as a federally recognized tribe.

The Winnebago

Unlike the Menominee, whose reservation environment allowed multiple classes and a physical sense of security, the environment of the Wisconsin Winnebago provided little security and proved unconducive to social scaffolding. The Winnebago abstained from voting on the IRA in the 1930s. They did, however, achieve some benefits under the law when they acquired some federally built housing on federal, not tribal, trust lands.[41] With attenuated settlements and no tribal government, the Winnebago lived a rather mobile and independent existence. Since before 1870, when their status of residency in Wisconsin was in question and they moved like shadows across the land, many Winnebago survived by picking other peoples' crops. But something else survived. Possessing no timber or land resources, the Winnebago were not targets for exploitation from lumber companies and realtors and so could work out their own strategy for survival, free from outside pressures and internal economic interests. Whereas among the Menominee and some Ojibwa, reservations increasingly replaced ceremonies as sources of tribal identity, among the Winnebago without reservations, ceremonies were a vital source of community identity; the Winnebago "depended on their ritual cycle and special ceremonies to maintain group cohesiveness."[42] They were also forced to rely on each other economically and psychologically, despite religious factions, and these needs served to bind the desperate settlements together in an extended community.

As among other Wisconsin tribes, so too had formal sanctions or controls for maintaining tribal order long since disappeared among the Winnebago. Major crimes like theft, murder, and rape now fell under the province of state law enforcement agencies. The informal sanctions of gossip, witchcraft, ridicule, and ostracism, however, continued to operate.[43] Even factions, in a negative way, gave definition to Winnebago community.

Some Winnebago owned farms, and many who acquired skills during World War II drifted to urban areas and found employment in factories, but most worked as agricultural laborers. A changed environment altered some prewar activities. Picking and selling wild blueberries, a major economic activity for the Winnebago before the war, declined in the 1940s, when the burned-over areas where the berries had flourished became covered with underbrush. This forced the Winnebago to depend more on harvesting crops like cranberries and cherries for others. Automobiles greatly facilitated this activity, but mechanized pickers in the 1950s began to replace Winnebago labor, causing widespread impoverishment among the unskilled.[44]

After the misery and starkness of the depression, the war years brought increased prosperity to the Winnebago, but in the postwar years, they again lapsed into hard times. Returning veterans offered some community leadership and joined with the Winnebago in Nebraska to press a claim against the government through the United States Indian Claims Commission, set up in 1946, to resolve long-standing Indian grievances. But these positive moves were often offset by the growing intensity of religious factionalism—factionalism probably dating back to the 1880s—among the Winnebago Christian, traditional, and Peyote groups that plunged the tribe into dissension.[45]

A Summary of the Impacts of Collier and the Indian Reorganization Act

Overall, despite its weaknesses, the IRA benefited Wisconsin tribes at a time of deep economic and spiritual depression. The IRA did not, however, reverse the direction of government Indian policy. Despite the IRA's emphasis on the merits of tribal culture and community, it also worked to establish routes for Indian entry into the mainstream of the nation's political and economic life. Thus while the prime objective of government Indian policy—Indian acculturation—remained the same, the means for implementing it differed widely between 1934 and 1961. Encouraged to assume greater responsibility over their own programs and economies, tribes still operated under the administrative guidelines and restrictions of the BIA. This proved a major weakness. The new tribal governing bodies still had to submit their decisions to the Indian agent—now called superintendent—and seek his approval.[46] Collier may have envisioned more of an advisory role for superintendents, but Congress decided they should retain a policy role. Despite these caveats, however, tribes acquired greater control over their destinies than they had before coming under the IRA.[47] Indians could again openly show their cultural pride but, more important, Collier chose to work through communities rather than through individuals. Under Collier, Indians were asked what they wanted rather than summarily told what they would receive or what they could do. Thus Indians now entered the decision-making process and assumed the burden of responsibility for their choices and the task of negotiating with the world beyond the reservation.

Collier left office in 1945,[48] but his legacy, which would continue to influence Indian political action and spur leadership into the 1960s, limped into the 1950s. Realistically, Collier attempted too much. He sought to create communities, to erect social structures, too rapidly and often on crumbling foundations. His plans for a new Indian program that would give tribes greater cultural expression and at the same time an improved standard of living foundered on congressional attacks and budget cuts, on war economics, and to some extent on Indian mistrust. Such factors continually pruned Collier's idealism and effectiveness to bring about change, and Indian communities slipped further into poverty. By the late 1940s many were still destitute.[49]

Collier's record and IRA gains are mixed. When he came into office nearly all the nation's Indians were suffering from a loss of confidence, a loss of self-sufficiency, and a loss of control over their environment. Despite depression economics and congressional attempts in the 1930s to derail Collier's program, he exhibited a managerial deftness in implementing his plans. In Wisconsin, Collier's program of setting up tribal governments, creating reservations for those Ojibwa known sometimes as the Lost Tribes or Bands (the Mole Lake Ojibwa), and acquiring more land for the Forest Potawatomi, Oneida, Stockbridge, and Brothertown did not always have the intended effects. Increased tribal landholdings strengthened identity, but they also subjected tribes to greater government interference and loss of control. This resulted in further erosion of local political organization and increased dependency on the BIA and other government agencies. Indians employed in local BIA offices on training programs received little training and became merely supplementary staff. Only after 1945 were efforts made to provide them with managerial responsibility.[50]

Conservative congressional critics accused Collier of reinstituting tribal communism in advocating tribal rather than individual ownership of land and thereby reversing the gains in Indian acculturation made by previous administrations. Critics pointed to the extensive poverty and desperate conditions on many postwar reservations and blamed Collier's policies rather than war-induced funding cutbacks. While Congress continued to hack away at Collier's reforms, it decided the pace of Indian acculturation was too slow. It began to call for the termination of federal responsibility to select Indian reservations and initiated a program to promote the relocation of Indians from reservations to urban areas. Congress, in its pell-mell rush to reduce the budget through eliminating Indian programs, brushed aside the belief that Indians would cease identifying as Indians and enter American society if their special problems were addressed and now decided that reservations were the problem and that abolishing reservations would dissolve the Indian identity issue. Accordingly, critics in Congress passed house Concurrent Resolution 108, legislating the termination of Indian reservations.[51]

CONGRESS' NEW DIRECTION: THE TERMINATION PROCESS AND THE OPPOSITION TO IT

The termination process involved the withdrawal of special government services, ending government trusteeship over tribal (and individuals') lands and resources, and curtailing any special recognition of Indian status. Along with termination legislation, Congress passed the Relocation–Vocational Training Act, which encouraged the relocation of Indians to urban areas. This last act resulted partly from the failure of an earlier policy to curtail government credit to Indian reservations and to rely on private-sector investment to promote Indian employment. When private funds failed to materialize, Indians were forced to leave reservations in their search for jobs.[52] The Relocation–Vocational Training Act sought to provide job training for reservation Indians and thus to encourage more Indians to seek employment in urban areas.

The relatively sound fiscal position of the Menominee made them a prime target for termination. Much has been written about the termination of the Menominee. Despite their strong attachment to the reservation as a homeland, the need for money proved a greater lure. The court case the Menominee initiated in 1936 against the government for its mismanagement of Menominee forests ended in 1951 with their being awarded $5 million. Requesting that part of the award be paid in per capita payments, the Menominee were shocked to learn in 1953 that such payments would be released only if they "accepted an amendment terminating federal supervision."[53] Holding up the desperately needed funds, the government forced the reluctant Menominee to vote in General Council for the dissolution of their reservation. Fears of termination stalked the Menominee like apparitions. What about the land? What about jobs? What about the old people? These questions festered and could not be suppressed. As one Menominee complained, "We have had over 100 years of leaning on the government's shoulder and suddenly we are asked to change our ways in a few years' time."[54]

The boundaries of the reservation, despite communal divisiveness, and government policy lent an artificial cohesiveness to Menominee society. When those boundaries were removed and government policy changed, the illusion of community strength and integrity collapsed into contentious politics characterized by weak and divided leadership. Lack of information and confusion prevented a united opposition from emerging until the shock of termination was a sobering reality.[55]

The draconian measures to eliminate "the Indian problem" or make it less noticeable by diffusing it in the larger urban or state population struck at the very heart of the reservation community. Termination corroded Indian identity and dissolved attachment to the land while relocation scattered tribal members to cities across the nation. The measures were not well thought out and soon encountered heavy criticism. Perceptively, anthropologist Nancy O. Lurie pointed out, "At the very time that suburbs were burgeoning, commuting was a way of life for much of the nation, and far-sighted people were anticipating greater segmentation of industrial operations and dispersing them to where the people live, Indian policy was based on models of concentrating population in large urban centers."[56] Lurie went on to note that the government's reliance on the myth of the melting pot ignored factors like "the special reliance of Indian people on group identity, group membership and group decisions" and the unlikelihood that unskilled and often uneducated Indians, or anybody else, could flourish in an economy increasingly dependent on skilled labor.[57]

Yet another blow to Wisconsin Indian communities was the passage of Public Law 280 in 1953, which turned over to the states both civil and criminal jurisdiction of Indian reservations. No longer would tribal governments handle such problems in their own communities.[58]

The problem of Indian poverty and isolation that Congress hoped to solve through termination and relocation merely spread to the cities in the 1950s to the 1970s. It ensured the growth of militant pan-Indian urban organizations that fed on the despair and urban discontent pervasive in Indian communities.[59]

If frustrations began to boil in Indian communities in Minneapolis, Milwaukee, Chicago, and St. Paul, they also simmered back on the reservations. It is true that many of the old ways, where they had not disappeared altogether, were in the process of being eclipsed by new activities. The automobile, radio, television, movies, and magazines contributed to the decline, but, as seen above, so too did the loss of the native language among the youth, poverty, education in white-oriented schools, growing acceptance of peyote and Christianity, and urban migration, which depopulated many rural Indian communities.[60] Wisconsin Indians, like all people, were changing, but their adjustments to their new environment evolved out of their collective tribal past; it involved humor combined with attitudes and philosophies that they perceived as distinctly tribal. The ideas and aspirations that were effervescing in Wisconsin Indian communities, both rural and urban, were also fermenting in other Indian communities across the nation. They acquired focus at the American Indian Chicago Conference in 1961.

That conference, organized by anthropologist Sol Tax of the University of Chicago, was a symptom of the unrest, anger, and despair that gripped many Indian communities throughout the nation. The 460 Indian delegates from across America drew up the *Declaration of Indian Purpose*. Drawing upon organizational skills and a new sense of pride, a legacy of the Collier program, the delegates spoke with a single voice.[61] Two other reports on Indian affairs were also issued in 1961, one by an independent study group supported by the Fund for the Republic and another by the government Task Force on Indian Affairs, appointed by President Kennedy. Their messages were similar: end termination and include Indians in the decision-making process. The New Trail, as it was called by the task force, would lead to "equal citizenship, maximum self-sufficiency, and full participation in American life."[62]

The year 1961 was a turning point in Indian affairs. Opposition to termination gave voice to Indians and suddenly they were articulating demands that resonated all the way to Washington, D.C. In Wisconsin the termination of the Menominee seemed to adumbrate the future for other Indian reservations. By the late 1950s the enthusiasm for termination abated in Congress, but in Indian communities its specter would not rest. When the economic destruction that termination brought to the Menominee community became obvious to all, the very threat of termination produced an anxiety, a "spiritual" concern that weighed on all Wisconsin reservation Indians. The reservation was more than land: It was a symbol of identity where communities, although fractured by religious and class differences, could exist; it was a buffer between those who stumbled in the old ways or barely recognized them and the outside impersonal world, which was only dimly understood. With many of the old rituals slipping away, the reservation was all that remained, and its existence was infused with an increasing symbolic meaning for Indian identity.

8

Epilogue: Reading the Past

The closer we exist to a given point in time, the larger its events loom in significance; they tumble forth in a jumble of proceedings, images, and sounds, presenting a kaleidoscopic array of impressions on the mind. Current events are easy to note and describe, but the reasons for them are more difficult to assess compared with events of the past because we have too much data, too little time to reflect upon them, and we are less sure of our own emotional involvement in both cataloging and interpreting the "facts." Although perhaps only an illusion, time seems to allow us greater certainty in constructing readings of the past and drawing out the significance of an event. Do we deceive ourselves that we now see past events as clear and decipherable, after actors contemporary with those events so muddled them? Perhaps. Our confidence in interpretation draws upon an assurance grounded in present ideology. So how do we interpret present events? What guidelines can we use?

Certainly for Wisconsin Indians conceptualizing their tribal pasts and affirming their tribal identities, traditions, and customs are important. For the historian, Native American traditions and customs, or cultural categories, are vital to an understanding of the dynamics of the Indians' past. If the world is recognized through a cultural scheme of classification, as some anthropologists suggest,[1] then it is important to note how cultural categories are maintained, manipulated by outsiders, and changed, and how they engage the world. As noted, for the Ojibwa woman who accused Americans of destroying her people, it was not the loss of land of which she complained, but the thwarting of the Ojibwa expression of cultural categories. She believed that by obstructing the Ojibwa propensity to dream, to tell stories, and to gain power through ceremonies, Americans hindered the functioning of the Ojibwa community. For Indian people, dreams have been a way of foretelling the future. Without dreams and the tales that are often the manifestation of dreams, many Indians stumble in a metaphorical darkness. For many Wisconsin Indians, the old cultural categories are often of little relevance to their new world, and there is doubt and disagreement over what new categories should take the place of the old categories.

Their ability to negotiate their future was severely constricted by the early nineteenth century. It was even more limited by both the British and American practice of utilizing the cultural category of headmen or chiefs to manipulate tribal societies for political and economic ends.

For many, geography is an important component of their cultural scheme. The farther one moves from the land base, the more strongly one may feel emotional stress triggered by his or her estrangement from the security of the tribal community. In his elegant study of the Tewa Indian world view, the Pueblo anthropologist Alfonso Ortiz notes that, for the Tewa Indians, the farther one travels from the pueblo, the more one loses the spiritual power that the pueblo represents.[2] Something like this seems also to work for Wisconsin Indians.[3] Whether one is a traditional or an acculturated Indian, the cultural category of sense of home or belonging triggers a sense of dislocation, loss, and insecurity when the person is confronted with removal to an urban area. The reservation is home, and participation in tribal matters is greater—or at least the influence of the community is felt more deeply—when one lives on the reservation. Both terminating reservations and relocating tribal peoples to urban areas far from their home have diminished the tribal bond.

Urbanization, which often leads to intermarriage with non-Indians or with Indians from other tribes, tends to stretch these ties even further. The trips back home to the reservation become less frequent, and second and third generations grow up learning less about their tribal past than those growing up back on the reservation, unless a concentrated effort is made by parents to prevent this. Even Indian education programs in urban areas often tend to focus more on pan-Indian history and culture than on the history and culture of individual tribes.

There is also a loss of tradition on the reservation when old ways and values are reworked to fit new realities and "new traditions" are devised to replace what is lost. As seen, the Midewiwin declined in the face of poverty and altered environment and gradually gave way among some groups to the newer Dream Dance, or Drum Dance, which in turn lost converts, along with the Midewiwin and Medicine Lodge, to the Native

American Church or to Christianity. Subsequently, the Native American Church became identified with being "traditional Indian." Likewise many of the old dances gave way to the flashier powwow and contest dances from Oklahoma and the Dakotas. New dances brought new songs. New dance outfits replaced the old dance outfits. Just being able to sing and dance lent an aura of being traditional. Does all this change diminish the Indian identity? No. Does it diminish their tribal culture? Probably so, yet it is important to remember that diffusion of art, songs, dances, and cultural elements has been endemic not only to tribal cultures but to non-Indian cultures as well.

All communities, Indian and non-Indian alike, change. Some tourists who visit reservations or powwows expect to see tepees or log cabins. Their image of Indians is derived from movies and television. They want to see Indians in feathered warbonnets and dressed in buckskin. Often their disappointment is edged with sadness, for in their nostalgia for the fixed historical frame, another of their verities has disappeared. They are bothered by houses on the reservations sporting television antennas and satellite dishes in what they think should be islands of history and sense that "the Indian" and a valuable bit of the American past has disappeared. To them, the powwows seem a bit of a sham, and the commercialism of the encircling vendors strikes a jangling incongruous note. But still the beat of the drum and the movement of the dancers rivet their attention.

Just as American communities of the nineteenth century disappeared into history, so too did Native American communities change in response to altered environments and economic realities. This does not mean, however, that they surrendered their sense of being Indian communities. As seen, prior to reservation life, Wisconsin Indian communities realized their identity through traditions, customs, language, kinship, and geography. As anthropologist Marshall Sahlins reminds us, the world is organized according to a scheme of cultural categories which constitute a reference system for a society. When the relationship between cultural categories changes, the cultural structure is transformed. Cultural categories are redefined and acquire new functional values, but these functional reevaluations are also extensions of traditional concepts.[4] Thus Wisconsin Indian communities, forced to abandon or redefine some of the cultural categories that previously distinguished them, nevertheless did not relinquish their identity when they were forced onto reservations. They merely constructed new cultural categories. By the twentieth century, reservation communities recognized their identity in terms of bounded land. The attack on reservations that came through the House Concurrent Resolution 108, designed to terminate them, not only threatened the existence of reservations but also the identity and integrity of the tribal community.

Although this work on Wisconsin Indian communities ends at mid-century, Wisconsin Indians and many non-Indians are now evaluating, interpreting, and reinterpreting the events of the last four centuries in the context of their own experience and their own reading of history. That this history will always be a subject for debate is without doubt, but it is hoped that this history and subsequent ones will generate, not only a better understanding of the cultural-historical roles of both races, but also a better understanding between people.

Notes

Bibliography

Index

Notes

INTRODUCTION: SONGS FROM THE POWWOW

1. The term is Benny Bearskin's. See "Benny Bearskin, 45," in Studs Terkel, *Division Street: America* (New York: Avon Books, 1967), 134.

2. Nicholas C. Peroff, *Menominee Drums: Tribal Termination and Restoration, 1954–1974* (Norman: University of Oklahoma Press, 1982), 121.

3. Peroff, 123.

4. Peroff, 123; Deborah Shames, ed., *Freedom with Reservation: The Menominee Struggle to Save Their Land and People* (Madison: National Committee to Save the Menominee People and Forests, 1972), 18–35. For a shorter discussion of the Menominee and the MEI, see also Nancy Oestreich Lurie, *Wisconsin Indians* (Madison: State Historical Society of Wisconsin, 1980), 51–54.

5. Shames, 69.

6. Lurie, *Wisconsin Indians,* 51–53; Shames, 71–107; Peroff, 197–224.

7. Lurie, *Wisconsin Indians,* 53–54.

8. Lurie, *Wisconsin Indians,* 54.

9. Quoted in Bill Stokes, "Social Call in the Land of the Ojibwas," *Milwaukee Journal,* May 6, 1973, 20.

10. Lurie, *Wisconsin Indians,* 55.

11. Lurie, *Wisconsin Indians,* 56–57.

12. See the articles of Stuart Wilk in the *Milwaukee Sentinel* and Bill Stokes in the *Milwaukee Journal* between 1972 and 1976.

13. Lurie, *Wisconsin Indians,* 57–59.

14. Lurie, *Wisconsin Indians,* 57–63.

15. Nancy Oestreich Lurie, "An American Indian Renascence?" in Stuart Levine and Nancy O. Lurie, eds., *The American Indian Today* (Deland, Fla.: Everett/Edwards, 1965), 187–88. See also Elizabeth Clark Rosenthal, "Culture and the American Indian Community," in Levine and Lurie, 22.

16. George D. Spindler and Louise Spindler, *Dreamers without Power: The Minomini Indians* (New York: Holt, Rinehart and Winston, 1971); Felix M. Keesing, *The Menomini Indians of Wisconsin: A Study of Three Centuries of Cul-*

tural Contact and Change (1939; rpt., Madison: University of Wisconsin Press, 1987); Patricia K. Ourada, *The Menominee Indians: A History* (Norman: University of Oklahoma Press, 1979); Paul Radin, *The Winnebago Tribe* (1923; rpt., Lincoln: University of Nebraska Press, 1970); Nancy Oestreich Lurie, ed., *Mountain Wolf Woman: The Autobiography of a Winnebago Indian* (Ann Arbor: University of Michigan Press, 1961); Harold Hickerson, *The Chippewa and Their Neighbors: A Study in Ethnohistory* (New York: Holt, Rinehart and Winston, 1970); Ronald N. Satz, "Chippewa Treaty Rights: The Reserved Rights of Wisconsin's Chippewa Indians in Historical Perspective," *Transactions of the Wisconsin Academy of Sciences, Arts and Letters* 79, no. 1 (1991); Edmund J. Danziger, *The Chippewa of Lake Superior* (Norman: University of Oklahoma Press, 1979); Thomas J. Vennum, Jr., *Wild Rice and the Ojibway People* (St. Paul: Minnesota Historical Society, 1988); Christopher Vecsey, *Traditional Ojibwa Religion and Its Historical Changes* (Philadelphia: American Philosophical Society, 1983); Gerald Vizenor, *The People Named the Chippewa: Narrative Histories* (Minneapolis: University of Minnesota Press, 1978); Helen Hornbeck Tanner, *The Ojibwa: A Critical Bibliography* (Chicago: The Newberry Library, 1976); Timothy G. Roufs, Comp., *Working Bibliography of Chippewa/Ojibwa/Anishinabe and Related Works* (Duluth: University of Minnesota Lake Superior Basin Studies Center, 1981); James Clifton, *The Prairie People: Continuity and Change in Potawatomi Culture, 1665–1965* (Lawrence: Regents Press of Kansas, 1977); Ruth Landes, *The Mystic Lake Sioux: Sociology of the Mdewakantonwan Santee* (Madison: University of Wisconsin Press, 1968).

17. Lurie, *Wisconsin Indians;* Carol I. Mason, *Introduction to Wisconsin Indians: Prehistory to Statehood* (Salem, Wis.: Sheffield Publishing Co., 1987); John R. Boatman, *My Elders Taught Me: Aspects of Western Great Lakes American Indian Philosophy* (Lanham, Md.: University Press of America, 1982); and John R. Boatman, *Wisconsin American Indian History and Culture: A Survey of Selected Aspects* (Milwaukee: University of Wisconsin–Milwaukee, 1993); and Donald L. Fixico, ed., *An Anthology of Western Great Lakes Indian History* (Milwaukee: American Indian Studies, University of Wisconsin–Milwaukee, 1987).

18. Gerald Vizenor, *Wordarrows: Indians and Whites in the New Fur Trade* (Minneapolis: University of Minnesota Press, 1978), vii.

CHAPTER 1. THE LAND THAT WINTER MADE

1. For a detailed account of Winnebago Trickster figure, see Paul Radin, *The Trickster: A Study in American Indian Mythology* (New York: Schocken Books, 1972). This book was already in press when the author learned that the Winnebago tribe had officially changed its name to Ho-Chunk, the original Siouan name.

2. Louise Phelps Kellogg, ed., *Early Narratives of the Northwest 1634–1699* (New York: Charles Scribner's Sons, 1917), 16.

3. Pierre Esprit Radisson, *The Explorations of Radisson,* ed. Arthur T. Adams (1885; rpt., Minneapolis: Ross and Haines, 1967), 91.

4. Kellogg, *Early Narratives,* 107–18.

5. Radisson, 132.

6. Radisson, 95.

7. Jonathan Carver, *The Journals of Jonathan Carver and Related Documents,* ed. John Parker (St. Paul: Minnesota Historical Society Press, 1976), 127–28.

8. Henry Rowe Schoolcraft, *Schoolcraft's Expedition to Lake Itasca, the Discovery of the Source of the Mississippi,* ed. Philip P. Mason (East Lansing: Michigan State University Press, 1958), 276.

9. Carver, 89, 126–27.

10. Carver, 8.

11. Carver, 84.

12. Henry Rowe Schoolcraft, *Narrative Journal of Travels through the Northwestern Regions of the United States Extending from Detroit through the Great Lakes to the Sources of the Mississippi River in the Year 1820,* ed. Mentor L. Williams (East Lansing: Michigan State University Press, 1953), 238.

13. Leonard Bloomfield, *Menomini Texts,* Publications of the American Ethnological Society, Vol. 12 (New York: G. E. Stechert, 1928), 137–40.

14. Radisson, 90.

15. Radisson, 91.

16. Kellogg, *Early Narratives,* 145–46.

17. Frederick Jackson Turner, *The Character and Influence of the Indian Trade in Wisconsin: A Study of the Trading Post as an Institution* (1891; rpt., Norman: University of Oklahoma Press, 1977), 19–20.

18. Lynne G. Goldstein, *Prehistoric Indians of Wisconsin* (Milwaukee: Milwaukee Public Museum, 1985), 10–11.

19. Nancy Lurie (pers. comm.) questions Winnebagos as rice gathers. However, Thomas Vennum, Jr., cites evidence that the Winnebago did gather wild rice (see his *Wild Rice and the Ojibway People,* 5 and 310 n. 7; see also Radin, *The Winnebago Tribe,* 68; and Helen Hornbeck Tanner et al., eds., *Atlas of Great Lakes Indian History* [Norman: University of Oklahoma Press, 1987], 19).

20. William Cronon, *Changes in the Land: Indians, Colonists, and the Ecology of New England* (New York: Hill and Wang, 1983), 14.

21. Writing about the Indians of New England, Cronon relates how their knowledge of the animal and plant life of the region led to the maximum seasonal utilization of the environment to provide food. Such an awareness of the environment was probably also typical of Wisconsin Indians (see Cronon, chapter 3, especially pp. 37–42).

CHAPTER 2. HOW THEY LIVED IN THE OLD TIME

1. The Menominee were one of many Indian nations or tribes that spoke a language designated as Algonquian. Many of these Algonquian-speaking peoples lived in the Great Lakes area. More detailed information on these Algonquian-speaking peoples can be found in Bruce Trigger, ed., *Handbook of North American Indians,* Vol. 15: *Northeast,* William C. Sturtevant, gen'l. ed. (Washington, D.C.: Smithsonian Institution, 1978). (hereafter cited as *HNAI* 15 *Northeast*).

2. Siouan-speaking peoples generally inhabited the upper Mississippi Valley and spread westward into what is now the Dakotas and later into Montana and adjacent regions of Canada. The major Siouan-speakers today are those groups making up the Sioux nation.

3. Lurie, *Wisconsin Indians,* 11–12; Jack Campisi, "Oneida," in *HNAI* 15 *Northeast,* 481; Laura E. Conkey, Ethel Boissevain, and Ives Goddard, "Indians of Southern New England and Long Island: Late Period," in *HNAI* 15 *Northeast,* 181–82; Ives Goddard, "Delaware," in *HNAI* 15 *Northeast,* 222.

4. Some exceptions to this are Guy E. Gibbon, "Cultural Dynamics and the Development of the Oneota Life Way in Wisconsin," *American Antiquity* 37 (1972): 166–85; Guy E. Gibbon, "A Brief History of Oneota Research in Wisconsin," *Wisconsin Magazine of History* 53 (1970): 278–93; and Janet Doris Spector, "Winnebago Indians, 1634–1829: An Archaeological and Ethnohistorical Investigation" (Ph.D. diss., University of Wisconsin, 1974). See also, James B. Griffin, *Archaeology of Eastern United States* (Chicago: University of Chicago Press, 1952).

5. Bruce G. Trigger, "Cultural Unity and Diversity," in *HNAI* 15 *Northeast,* 798–804.

6. Charles Callender also includes the Menominee—as does Nancy Lurie—and, although Siouan-speakers, the Winnebago in this group (see Charles Callender, "Great Lakes–Riverine Sociopolitical Organization," in *HNAI* 15 *Northeast,* 610–19). Bruce Trigger, however, places the Menominee within the Eastern Collecting Pattern (see Trigger, "Cultural Unity," 798–804). An older classification division separates northern woodland cultures from eastern woodland cultures (see Keesing, 18).

7. Keesing, 613.

8. Trigger, "Cultural Unity," 802.

9. Callender, "Great Lakes–Riverine Sociopolitical Organization," 613–15.

10. I follow Callender here and place the Menominee in the Central Algonquian Pattern. Callender divides his groups by social and political organization, whereas Trigger divides his groups along lines of economics and life style (see Callender, "Great Lakes–Riverine Sociopolitical Organization," 613–15; and Trigger, "Cultural Unity," 802).

11. Callender, "Great Lakes–Riverine Sociopolitical Organization," 615.

12. Bloomfield, *Menomini Texts,* 73.

13. Callender, "Great Lakes–Riverine Sociopolitical Organization," 615.

14. Among the Fox Indians there is a legend relating how, through making a troublesome individual a chief, the people hoped to reform him, since by the very rules of the office he would have to change his ways and live up to the honor of being a chief (see Callender, "Great Lakes–Riverine Sociopolitical Organization," 618; William Jones, "Fox Texts," *Publications of the American Ethnological Society*, Vol. 1 [Leiden, The Netherlands, 1907], 9).

15. Callender, "Great Lakes–Riverine Sociopolitical Organization," 618.

16. Callender, "Great Lakes–Riverine Sociopolitical Organization," 618–19.

17. Vennum, Jr., *Wild Rice and the Ojibway People*, 183–94; Eva Lipps, *Die Reiserate der Ojibwa-Indianer Wirtschaft und Recht eines Erntevolkes* (Berlin: Akademic Verlag, 1956), 224. Keesing designates these regulators as police (p. 40). Note also Francis Densmore, *Chippewa Customs* (1929; rpt., St. Paul: Minnesota Historical Society Press, 1979), 128.

18. In proceeding in this fashion, we must remember that the French often did not fully understand what they were describing. Sometimes different cultural groups were lumped together that should not have been or people from the same cultural group were placed in one large village when actually they represented multiple villages.

19. Jeanne Kay believes that there were multiple Menominee villages during the protohistoric period (see Jeanne Kay, "The Land of La Baye: The Ecological Impact of the Green Bay Fur Trade, 1634–1836" [Ph.D. diss., University of Wisconsin, Madison, 1977], 25).

20. Keesing, 26; Louise Spindler, "Menominee," in *HNAI 15 Northeast*, 709; Alanson Skinner, "A Comparative Sketch of the Menomini," *American Anthropologist*, n.s., 13 (1911): 554 and Alanson Skinner, *Material Culture of the Menomini* (New York: Museum of the American Indian, 1921).

21. Keesing, 34.

22. George Irving Quimby, *Indian Culture and European Trade Goods: The Archaeology of the Historic Period in the Western Great Lakes Region* (Madison: University of Wisconsin Press, 1966), 42.

23. Keesing, 40–41.

24. Keesing, 41.

25. Keesing, 22. For a similar story and legends connected with wild rice, see, Vennum, *Wild Rice and the Ojibway People*, 65; Skinner, "Comparative Sketch," 556–57.

26. Trigger admits that certain features of Ottawa culture, like horticulture, make them a transitional group between the Northern Iroquois Pattern, which emphasizes horticulture, and the Eastern Collecting Pattern, but he nevertheless places them in the latter pattern (Trigger, "Cultural Unity," 803).

27. E. S. Rogers, "Southeastern Ojibwa," in *HNAI 15 Northeast*, 760; Quimby, *Indian Culture*, 122.

28. James G. E. Smith, *Leadership among the Southeastern Ojibwa*, Na-

tional Museum of Canada Publications in Ethnology, No. 7 (Ottawa: National Museums of Canada, 1973), 13.

29. Trigger, "Cultural Unity," 803; George Irving Quimby, *Indian Life in the Upper Great Lakes: 11,000 B.C. to A.D. 1800* (Chicago: University of Chicago Press, 1960), 122. Nancy Lurie (pers. comm.) also points out that Ojibwa did not maintain gardens because they were too far north and the growing season was not long enough.

30. Quimby, *Indian Life,* 122.

31. Quimby, *Indian Life,* 122.

32. Quimby, *Indian Life,* 126; E. S. Rogers, 762–63; Harold Hickerson, *The Southwestern Chippewa: An Ethnohistorical Study,* American Anthropological Association Memoir 92 (Menasha, Wis., 1962), 106; Fred Eggan, *The American Indian* (Chicago: Aldine Publishing Co., 1966), 83–97; Trigger, "Cultural Unity," 798; Ruth Landes, *Ojibwa Sociology.* Columbia University Contribution to Anthropology 29 (New York: Columbia University Press, 1937).

33. Quimby lists the following clans for the Ojibwa: Crane, Loon, Goose, Gull, Catfish, Pike, Sucker, Sturgeon, Whitefish, Merman, Otter, Marten, Moose, Bear, Beaver, Caribou, Wolf, Lynx and Snake (Quimby, *Indian Life,* 126); Ruth Landes, *The Ojibwa Woman.* Columbia University Contribution to Anthropology 31 (New York: Columbia University Press, 1938).

34. James G. E. Smith, 13.

35. Johanna E. Feest and Christian F. Feest, "Ottawa," in *HNAI* 15 *Northeast,* 777; Harold Hickerson, "The Feast of the Dead among the Seventeenth Century Algonkians of the Upper Great Lakes," *American Anthropologist* 62 (1960): 81–107.

36. A. Irving Hallowell, *Culture and Experience,* Philadelphia Anthropological Society, Vol. 4 (Philadelphia: University of Pennsylvania Press, 1955), 103–6 and passim.

37. Vecsey, 160.

38. At least this is the view of Hickerson (see Hickerson, *The Chippewa and Their Neighbors,* 52–54). This is also suggested by Keesing, 48–49, and Vecsey, 174–77. Recent work, however, suggests that the Midewiwin ceremony seemed to exist prior to European contact (see Bruce G. Trigger, *Natives and Newcomers: Canada's "Heroic Age" Reconsidered* [Kingston and Montreal: McGill-Queen's University Press, 1985], 117; and K. E. Kidd, "A Radiocarbon Date on a Midewiwin Scroll from Burntside Lake, Ontario," *Ontario Archaeology* [1981]: 41–43).

39. W. Vernon Kinietz, *The Indians of the Western Great Lakes: 1615–1760* (Ann Arbor: University of Michigan Press, 1965), 321.

40. Trigger, "Cultural Unity," 799.

41. See Spector; Guy E. Gibbon, "The Mississippi Tradition: Oneota Culture," *Wisconsin Archaeologist* 67, nos. 3 and 4 (1986): 314–64. Nancy Lurie (pers. comm.) has expressed doubts about the Oneota-Winnebago tie.

42. Gibbon, "Cultural Dynamics," 182. See also Gibbon, "A Brief History of Oneota Research," 278–93.

43. Lurie, *Wisconsin Indians,* 13.

44. Landes, *The Mystic Lake Sioux,* 29–32.

45. Nancy Oestreich Lurie claims that in the case of the Winnebago, the head chief, or peace chief, was always selected from the Thunder clan although perhaps not always from the same family within that clan (Nancy Oestreich Lurie, "Winnebago," in *HNAI 15 Northeast,* 693).

46. Walter Willard Funmaker, "The Winnebago Black Bear Subclan: A Defended Culture" (Ph.D. diss., University of Minnesota, 1986).

47. Radin, *The Winnebago Tribe,* 152.

48. Ruth Landes, *Ojibwa Religion and the Midewiwin* (Madison: University of Wisconsin Press, 1968), 29.

49. Landes, *Ojibwa Religion,* 29.

50. Landes, *Ojibwa Religion,* 29.

51. Spector, 12–13.

52. Lurie, "Winnebago," 690; Nancy Oestreich Lurie, "Winnebago Protohistory," in Stanley Diamond, ed., *Culture and History: Essays in Honor of Paul Radin* (New York: Columbia University Press, 1960), 790–808.

53. Keesing, 8–9, 49.

54. Radin, *The Winnebago Tribe,* 273–74.

55. Radin, *The Winnebago Tribe,* 64.

56. Keesing, 32.

57. Bloomfield, 71–73.

CHAPTER 3. THE YEARS OF THE FRENCH

1. La Potherie in Emma H. Blair, ed., *The Indian Tribes of the Upper Mississippi Valley and Region of the Great Lakes, as Described by Nicolas Perrot, French Commandant in the Northwest; Bacqueville de la Potherie, French Royal Commissioner to Canada; Morrell Marston, American Army Officer; and Thomas Forsyth, United States Agent at Fort Armstrong,* Vol. 1 (Cleveland: Arthur H. Clark, 1911–12), 293.

2. Bruce C. Trigger, *The Children of Aataentsic: A History of the Huron People to 1600,* Vol. 1 (Montreal: McGill-Queen's University Press, 1976), 354–55; C. W. Butterfield, *History of the Discovery of the Northwest by John Nicolet in 1634 with a Sketch of His Life* (Cincinnati: Robert Clark, 1881), 43.

3. Bruce C. Trigger, *The Huron: Farmers of the North* (New York: Holt, Rinehart and Winston, 1969), 36–40; Trigger, *Natives and Newcomers,* 205–8.

4. Petuns were sometimes called the Tobacco nation or Tionontati in the literature.

5. Trigger, *Natives and Newcomers,* 274–81.

6. Trigger, *Natives and Newcomers,* 285–86.

7. There is some doubt about just when this trip took place, that is, whether

225

it was in 1656 or 1658 (see Arthur T. Adams, ed., *The Explorations of Pierre Esprit Radisson* [Minneapolis: Ross and Haines, 1961], i–xvi).

8. Ray Allen Billington, *Westward Expansion: A History of the American Frontier* (New York: Macmillan, 1960), 103–12.

9. W. J. Eccles, "A Belated View of Harold Adams Innis, *The Fur Trade of Canada,*" *Canadian Historical Review* 60 (1979): 422–23.

10. Charles Callender, "Fox," in *HNAI* 15 *Northeast,* 643.

11. Nancy Oestreich Lurie notes that the Ottawa traded with the Winnebago as early as 1623, and the French had known of this trade (see Lurie's "Winnebago Protohistory," 791).

12. La Potherie in Blair, Vol. 1, 293.

13. La Jeune in Blair, Vol. 2, 486–88. Trigger also suggests that the cause may have originated in the torture of some Winnebago by the Ottawa in 1632 (see Trigger, *The Children of Aataentsic,* 354–56).

14. La Potherie in Blair, Vol. 1, 293; Lurie, "Winnebago Protohistory," 797–98.

15. There seems to be a dispute over whether the Winnebago lived in small villages and then moved to their large village at Red Banks or whether they had always lived in a large village and were in such a village in the mid-1600s. Nancy Lurie claims that they were always in a large village until the fur trade's repeated conflicts and depopulation led them to settle in smaller villages (Lurie, "Winnebago Protohistory," 796). For the first view see Robert L. Hall, *The Archaeology of Carcajou Point, with an Interpretation of the Development of Oneota Culture in Wisconsin,* Vol. 1 (Madison: University of Wisconsin Press, 1962), 156.

16. Lurie, "Winnebago," 691.

17. La Potherie in Blair, Vol. 1, 293–95. After completing this book, Richard White's excellent study was published. See his *The Middle Ground: Indians, Empires, and Republics in the Great Lakes Region, 1650–1815* (New York: Cambridge University Press, 1991), chapter 1, for a supporting discussion of disease and turmoil among both the native Wisconsin Indians and the refugee populations.

18. Lurie, "Winnebago," 691. French documents record epidemics that broke out among the Iroquois and Huron peoples in 1634 and lasted until 1640. It is believed that these epidemics were introduced into the two populations following the arrival of French ships in the St. Lawrence Valley in June of 1634 (Trigger, *Natives and Newcomers,* 239).

19. If the Winnebago did indeed move from smaller villages to one large village, then, as Radin suggests, the consolidation of the population into a large village may have increased the influence of the Bear and Thunder clans, whose power in the smaller villages was most likely diffused. Such shifts in power would have undoubtedly had political ramifications on the other clans (see Paul Radin, "The Influence of the Whites on Winnebago Culture," *Proceedings of the State Historical Society of Wisconsin 1913,* Vol. 61 [Madison, 1914], 142–43).

20. La Potherie in Blair, Vol. 1, 293.

21. Radin, *The Winnebago Tribe*, 58; Lurie, "Winnebago," 692.

22. Studies of other cultures have shown that such conditions, besides inhibiting fertility in women resulting in population decrease, can also retard children's growth and development (D. H. Stott, "Cultural and Natural Checks on Population Growth," in Andrew P. Vayda, ed., *Environment and Cultural Behavior: Ecological Studies in Cultural Anthropology,* published for the American Museum of Natural History [Garden City, N.Y.: Natural History Press, 1969], 102–5).

23. Lurie, "Winnebago Protohistory," 804; La Potherie in Blair, Vol. 1, 293.

24. La Potherie in Blair, Vol. 1, 300.

25. Lurie, "Winnebago Protohistory," 804.

26. La Potherie in Blair, Vol. 1, 301.

27. La Potherie in Blair, Vol. 1, 300–301.

28. James Clifton, "Potawatomi," in *HNAI 15 Northeast,* 731.

29. J. A. Jones, *Winnebago Ethnology: Winnebago Indians* (New York: Garland Publishing Co., 1974), 64.

30. Lurie, "Winnebago," 695.

31. Lurie, "Winnebago," 692.

32. J. Joseph Bauxar, "History of the Illinois Area," in *HNAI 15 Northeast,* 595–97; Ives Goddard, "Mascouten," in *HNAI 15 Northeast,* 668; Charles Callender, "Illinois," in *HNAI 15 Northeast,* 686.

33. Kay, "The Land of La Baye," 398.

34. Louise Phelps Kellogg, "The Fox Indians during the French Regime," *Proceedings of the State Historical Society of Wisconsin for 1907* (Madison, 1908), 172–74; Callender, "Fox," 644; J. A. Jones, 66–67.

35. Quoted in J. A. Jones, 71.

36. See Kay, "The Land of La Baye," 167, for the decline of large game near Green Bay.

37. See Kay, "The Land of La Baye," 167–78, for an excellent discussion on the changing Wisconsin environment during the early eighteenth century.

38. J. A. Jones, 72–73.

39. Lurie, "Winnebago," 692.

40. L. Spindler, 719.

41 La Potherie in Blair, Vol. 1, 303–4.

42. Reuben Gold Thwaites, ed., *The Jesuit Relations and Allied Documents: Travels and Explorations of the Jesuit Missionaries in New France 1610–1791,* Vol. 54 (Cleveland: Burrows Bros., 1899), 235.

43. La Potherie in Blair, Vol. 1, 310–13.

44. La Potherie in Blair, Vol. 1, 313.

45. La Potherie in Blair, Vol. 1, 313.

46. L. Spindler, 719; Keesing, 56–57; Kay, "The Land of La Baye," 90.

47. Thwaites, *Jesuit Relations,* Vol. 54, 197–214.

48. Lyle M. Stone and Donald Chaput, "History of the Upper Great Lakes Area," in *HNAI* 15 *Northeast,* 604; Keesing, 58–62, 79–81.

49. Reuben Gold Thwaites, ed., "The French Regime in Wisconsin, 1634–1727," Part I, in *Wisconsin Historical Collections,* Vol. 16 (Madison: State Historical Society of Wisconsin, 1902), 101 (hereafter cited as *WHC*).

50. The Jesuits were often sought as healers, and in the thinking of most Indians, those who could cure disease could also cause it.

51. Thwaites, "The French Regime," Part 1, 101; Keesing, 81.

52. Keesing, 61.

53. Keesing, 61–62.

54. Keesing, 79.

55. Keesing, 56–57; Kay, "The Land of La Baye," 92, 394.

56. L. Spindler, 719; Quimby, *Indian Life,* 145–46.

57. Keesing, 66.

58. Keesing, 66.

59. Keesing, 66–69.

60. Keesing, 76–77.

61. L. Spindler, 719.

62. Quimby, *Indian Life,* 145–51.

63. Feest and Feest, 792; Elisabeth Tooker, "Wyandot," in *HNAI* 15 *Northeast,* 398–99.

64. Tooker, 399; Stone and Chaput, 602; Feest and Feest, 772–73.

65. Thwaites, *Jesuit Relations,* Vol. 54, 153.

66. Thwaites, *Jesuit Relations,* Vol. 50 (1899), 249–311; Callender, "Illinois," 678; Clifton, "Potawatomi," 226.

67. Louise Phelps Kellogg, *The French Regime in Wisconsin and the Northwest* (Madison: State Historical Society of Wisconsin, 1925), 154. See also Thwaites, "The French Regime," Part 1, 77; and Reuben Gold Thwaites, ed., "The French Regime in Wisconsin, 1728–1743," Part 2 in *WHC,* Vol. 17 (Madison: State Historical Society of Wisconsin, 1906), 1–518.

68. Thwaites, *Jesuit Relations,* Vol. 54, 173, 171.

69. Kellogg, *Early Narratives,* 117.

70. Kellogg, *Early Narratives,* 118.

71. Thwaites, *Jesuit Relations,* Vol. 54, 177.

72. Thwaites, *Jesuit Relations,* Vol. 54, 181.

73. La Potherie in Blair, Vol. 1, 277; Harold Hickerson, *Chippewa Indians,* Vol. 2: *Ethnohistory of Mississippi Bands and Pillager and Winnibigoshish Bands of Chippewa* (New York: Garland Publishing Co., 1974), 45.

74. Hickerson, *The Southwestern Chippewa,* 65–67.

75. Harold Hickerson, *Chippewa Indians,* Vol. 3: *Ethnohistory of Chippewa of Lake Superior* (New York: Garland Publishing Co., 1974), 16–20; Hickerson, *The Southwestern Chippewa,* 67; Blair, Vol. 1, 358–63.

76. Hickerson, *The Southwestern Chippewa,* 69–70.

77. Hickerson, *The Southwestern Chippewa,* 70.

78. Hickerson, *The Chippewa and Their Neighbors,* 66 and passim.

79. Quoted in Ernestine Friedl, "An Attempt at Directed Culture Change; Leadership among the Chippewa, 1640–1948" (Ph.D. diss., Columbia University, New York, 1950), 45.

80. Friedl, "An Attempt at Directed Culture Change," 41–42.

81. Friedl, "An Attempt at Directed Culture Change," 11.

82. Robert E. Ritzenthaler, "Southwestern Chippewa," *HNAI* 15 *Northeast,* 744; Elden Johnson, "The Ojibwa," in Robert F. Spencer, Jesse D. Jennings, et al., eds., *The Native Americans* (New York: Harper and Row, 1965), 398.

83. Ritzenthaler, "Southwestern Chippewa," 744.

84. Hickerson, *The Southwestern Chippewa,* 71–72.

85. Thwaites, *Jesuit Relations,* Vol. 50, 249–311; Clyde H. Wilson, "A New Interpretation of the Wild Rice District of Wisconsin," *American Anthropologist* 58, no. 6 (1956): 1059–64.

86. Charles Callender, "Miami," in *HNAI* 15 *Northeast,* 682, 686; Goddard, 668; Charles Callender et al., "Kickapoo," in *HNAI* 15 *Northeast,* 662; James Silverberg, "The Kickapoo Indians: First One Hundred Years of White Contact," *Wisconsin Archaeologist* 38, no. 3 (1957): 71–85.

87. Wilson, 1059–64.

88. Callender et al., "Kickapoo," 662.

89. Kay, "The Land of La Baye," 102–3, 124–25.

90. Clifton, *The Prairie People,* 39; Clifton, "Potawatomi," 727.

91. Trigger, *Natives and Newcomers,* 194–95; Clifton, *The Prairie People,* 45–55.

92. Clifton, "Potawatomi," 727.

93. Clifton, *The Prairie People,* 50–53.

94. Clifton, *The Prairie People,* 61.

95. Clifton, "Potawatomi," 731.

96. Clifton, "Potawatomi," 731.

97. Thwaites, *Jesuit Relations,* Vol. 50, 288–89; Thwaites, *Jesuit Relations,* Vol. 51, 42–44.

98. Kellogg, "The Fox Indians," 149; Thwaites, *Jesuit Relations,* Vol. 57 (1899), 47.

99. Kellogg, "The Fox Indians," 149.

100. Kellogg, "The Fox Indians," 148.

101. Quoted in Kellogg, "The Fox Indians," 147.

102. Charles Callender, "Sauk," in *HNAI* 15 *Northeast,* 636.

103. Callender, "Sauk," 651.

104. Blair, Vol. 1, 357–62.

105. Kellogg, "The Fox Indians," 154.

106. Callender, "Fox," 644.

107. Some historians note Fox personality, along with their pride and fight-

ing prowess, as the major influence in their conflict with the French (see Kellogg, "The Fox Indians"; Rhoda R. Gilman, "The Fur Trade in the Upper Mississippi Valley, 1630–1850," *Wisconsin Magazine of History* 58 [Autumn 1974–75]: 3–18; J. A. Jones).

108. Callender, "Fox," 640.

109. Thomas Forsyth quoted in Anthony F. C. Wallace, *Prelude to Disaster: The Course of Indian-White Relations Which Led to the Black Hawk War of 1832* (Springfield: Illinois State Historical Library, 1970), 3.

110. Wallace, *Prelude to Disaster*, 3–4; Callender, "Fox," 641.

111. Hickerson, *The Chippewa and Their Neighbors*, 59–63. See also D. Peter MacLeod, "Microbes and Muskets: Smallpox and the Participation of the Amerindian Allies of New France in the Seven Years' War," *Ethnohistory* 39 (Winter 1992): 42–64.

CHAPTER 4. THE YEARS OF THE BRITISH

1. Augustin Grignon, "Seventy-two Years' Recollections of Wisconsin," in *WHC*, Vol. 3 (1857; rpt., Madison: State Historical Society of Wisconsin, 1904), 211; Reuben Gold Thwaites, ed., "The British Regime in Wisconsin": 'Sir William Johnson to colonial secretary, August 6, 1769,' and 'Trader's Report,' in *WHC*, Vol. 18 (Madison: State Historical Society of Wisconsin, 1908), 297–98 and 263–64; William L. Clements, ed., "Rogers's Michillimackinac Journal," in American Antiquarian Society *Proceedings*, n.s. 28, no. 2 (1919): 258–73.

2. James Gorrell, "Lieutenant James Gorrell's Journal of 1762," in *WHC*, Vol. 1 (1855; rpt., Madison: State Historical Society of Wisconsin, 1903), 25–26.

3. Gorrell, 27.

4. Gorrell, 31.

5. Gorrell, 31–32.

6. Gorrell, 32.

7. Quoted in Billington, 138; Robert C. Nesbit, *Wisconsin: A History* (Madison: State Historical Society of Wisconsin, 1973), 39; Alice Smith, *The History of Wisconsin*. Vol. 1: *From Exploration to Statehood* (Madison: Historical Society of Wisconsin, 1973), 57–58.

8. Gorrell, 27, 39–48.

9. Thwaites, "British Regime in Wisconsin": 'Sir Guy Carleton to Lord Shelburne, March 2, 1768, The Western Fur Trade,' 288–92; Reginald Horsman, "British Indian Policy in the Northwest, 1807–1812," *Mississippi Valley Historical Review* 45, no. 1 (June 1958): 51; Robert Allen, "His Majesty's Indian Allies: Native People, the British Crown and the War of 1812," *Michigan Historical Review* 14, no. 2 (Fall 1988): 1–3; W. S. Wallace, "The Beginnings of British Rule in Canada," *Canadian Historical Review* 6 (1925): 209–11; Wayne E. Stevens, *The Northwest Fur Trade, 1703–1800* (Urbana: University of Illinois Press, 1928), 21.

10. Billington, 133–38; Stevens, 21–22.

11. For an account of the widespread disaffection Indians had with British policy at this time, see: David R. Edmunds, *The Potawatomis, Keepers of the Fire* (Norman: University of Oklahoma Press, 1978), 75–80; H. H. Tanner et al., 48; Wilbur R. Jacobs, *Wilderness Politics and Indian Gifts: The Northern Colonial Frontier, 1748–1763* (Lincoln: University of Nebraska Press, 1966), 12; Howard H. Peckham, *Pontiac and the Indian Uprising* (Chicago: University of Chicago Press, 1961).

12. Edmunds, *The Potawatomis*, 87–89; H. H. Tanner et al., 49–50; Billington, 138–39; Stevens, 24. See also Louise P. Kellogg, *The British Regime in Wisconsin* (Madison: State Historical Society of Wisconsin, 1935); and the collection of documents in Thwaites, "The British Regime in Wisconsin," xi–468.

13. Jack M. Sosin, *Whitehall and the Wilderness: The Middle West in British Colonial Policy, 1760–1775* (Lincoln: University of Nebraska Press, 1971), 50–51; Dwight L. Smith, "Mutual Aid and Mutual Distrust: Indian-White Relations in British America, 1701–1763," in Philip Weeks, ed., *The American Indian Experience: A Profile, 1524 to the Present* (Arlington Heights: Forum Press, 1988), 61–62; and Robert F. Berkhofer, Jr., "Barrier to Settlement: British Indian Policy in the Old Northwest, 1783–1794," in David M. Ellis, ed., *The Frontier in American Development: Essays in Honor of Paul Wallace Gates* (Ithaca: Cornell University Press, 1969), 249–76.

14. Kay, "The Land of La Baye," 145; D. L. Smith, 62; Stevens, 23–24.

15. Billington, 139–41.

16. Wilbur R. Jacobs, *Dispossessing the American Indian* (New York: Charles Scribner's Sons, 1972), 75–82; Nesbit, *Wisconsin: A History*, 49–50; Stevens, 30–31.

17. Quoted in Sosin, 218.

18. Sosin, 213; H. H. Tanner et al., 68.

19. Sosin, 211–19; Stevens, 30–40.

20. Clifton, *The Prairie People*, 138–40; Colin G. Calloway, "Suspicion and Self-Interest: The British-Indian Alliance and the Peace of Paris," *The Historian* 48 (1985–86): 55; Nesbit, *Wisconsin: A History*, 49–61; Ernest Alexander Cruikshank, "Robert Dickson, the Indian Trader," in *WHC*, Vol. 12 (Madison: State Historical Society of Wisconsin, 1892): 133–53.

21. Kay, "The Land of La Baye," 145–54; Thwaites, "British Regime in Wisconsin": 'Capt. John Vattas to Gen. Frederick Haldeman, July 1, 1773,' 312–14.

22. Nesbit, *Wisconsin: A History*, 58; Reginald Horsman, "Wisconsin and the War of 1812," *Wisconsin Magazine of History* 46 (Autumn 1962): 3; Calloway, "Suspicion and Self-Interest," 54–55. For an extended treatment of British policy in this period, see Colin G. Calloway, *Crown and Calumet: British-Indian Relations, 1783–1815* (Norman: University of Oklahoma Press, 1987).

23. Reginald Horsman, *Expansion and American Indian Policy, 1783–1812* (East Lansing: Michigan State University Press, 1967), 84–103.

24. R. David Edmunds, *The Shawnee Prophet* (Lincoln: University of Nebraska Press, 1983), 118; Clifton, *The Prairie People*, 193–94; John Tanner, *A Narrative of the Captivity and Adventures of John Tanner*, ed. Edwin James (Minneapolis: Ross and Haines, 1956), 144–47; William Whipple Warren, *History of the Ojibways, Based upon Tradition and Oral Statements* (St. Paul: Minnesota Historical Society Press, 1984), 322–25.

25. Edmunds, *The Shawnee Prophet*, chapters 4–5; Clifton, *The Prairie People*, 193–94.

26. John Tanner, 102–3.

27. Edmunds, *The Shawnee Prophet*, 72, 97; Horsman, "Wisconsin and the War of 1812," 4.

28. Horsman, "British Indian Policy," 60–62; R. Allen, 6; see also George Chalou, "The Red Pawns Go to War: British-American Indian Relations, 1810–1815" (Ph.D. diss., Indiana University, 1971).

29. Quoted in Edmunds, *The Shawnee Prophet*, 97.

30. Horsman, "British Indian Policy," 63–66; Horsman, "Wisconsin and the War of 1812," 3; R. Allen, 9–11; Cruikshank, 133–53; see also "Dickson and Grignon Papers—1812–1815," in *WHC*, Vol. 11 (Madison: State Historical Society of Wisconsin, 1888), 271–315.

31. "Dickson and Grignon Papers," 282. See also "Prairie du Chien Documents, 1814–15": 'Capt. Thomas Anderson to Lieut. Col. R. McDouall, 18 October 1814,' in *WHC*, Vol. 9 (Madison: State Historical Society of Wisconsin, 1882), 269–72; R. Allen, 18; Horsman, "British Indian Policy," 62–63; Kerry A. Trask, "Settlement in a Half-Savage Land: Life and Loss in the Metis Community of La Baye," *Michigan Historical Review* 15 (Spring 1989): 19.

32. Carver, 83.

33. Carver, 84.

34. Peter Pond, "The Narrative of Peter Pond," in Charles M. Gates, ed., *Five Fur Traders of the Northwest* (St. Paul: Minnesota Historical Society Press, 1965), 40.

35. Quoted in Edmunds, *The Shawnee Prophet*, 97.

36. Clifton, *The Prairie People*, 160–61.

37. Clifton, *The Prairie People*, 171.

38. Clifton, *The Prairie People*, 159.

39. Clifton, *The Prairie People*, 173.

40. Keesing, 84–92; Hickerson, *The Chippewa and Their Neighbors*, 84–88; Kay, "The Land of La Baye," 167–73; Jeanne Kay, "Wisconsin Indian Hunting Patterns, 1634–1836," *Annals of the Association of American Geographers* 69, no. 3 (September 1979), 412.

41. Kay, "The Land of La Baye," 170–71.

42. Hickerson, *The Chippewa and Their Neighbors*, 80–88; H. H. Tanner et

al., 97–98; see also Gary C. Anderson, *Kinsmen of Another Kind: Dakota-White Relations in the Upper Mississippi Valley, 1650–1862* (Lincoln: University of Nebraska Press, 1984).

43. Keesing, 89.

44. Kay, "The Land of La Baye," 403, 413.

45. Gorrell, 30.

46. Alexander Henry, *Travels and Adventures in Canada and the Indian Territories between the Years 1760 and 1776* (1921; rpt., Ann Arbor: University Microfilms, Inc., 1966), 195–96.

47. Keesing, 88–89.

48. Carver, 79; Pond, 33–35.

49. Grignon, 256–58; Russell M. Magnaghi, "Red Slavery in the Great Lakes Country during the French and British Regimes," *Old Northwest* 12, no. 2 (Summer 1986): 201–17. Trask points out these slaves, generally termed Panis (probably Pawnee taken in war during western buffalo hunts), were owned primarily by the elite trader families. Although slavery was not extensive, it was "nevertheless . . . a social fact of life in fur trade era La Baye" (p. 11).

50. David Thompson, *David Thompson's Narrative 1784–1812*, ed. R. Glover (Toronto: The Champlain Society, 1962), 219.

51. Thompson, 208–9.

52. Some Winnebago settlements stretched down the Rock River into Illinois, along the Wisconsin River to Prairie du Chien, and on the Mississippi River, but these probably reflect the movement of the southern Winnebago. On Winnebago settlement around Lake Winnebago, see H. H. Tanner et al., 144.

53. Note H. H. Tanner et al., 88–89; Kay, "The Land of La Baye," 170, 178; Kay, "Wisconsin Indian Hunting Patterns," 412–13. See also J. A. Jones.

54. Carver, 74; Keesing, 90–91; Hickerson, *The Chippewa and Their Neighbors*, 86–88.

55. Consequently, Ojibwa bands frequently shifted their wintering grounds, thus permitting animal populations, if given enough time, to return to former levels. Unfortunately, too often environmental changes, animal diseases, and demand for furs did not allow such time.

56. James Stanley Goddard, "Journal of a Voyage, 1766–67," ed. Carolyn Gilman in Carver, 189.

57. Kay, "Wisconsin Indian Hunting Patterns," 412; Tanner, 64. See also Patricia Albers and Jeanne Kay, "Sharing the Land: A Study in American Indian Territoriality," in Thomas E. Ross and Tyrel G. Moore, eds., *A Cultural Geography of North American Indians* (Boulder: Westview Press, 1987); Jeanne Kay, "Native Americans in the Fur Trade and Wildlife Depletion," Environmental Review 9 (Summer 1985): 18–30.

58. Kay, "Wisconsin Indian Hunting Patterns," 412; Warren, 268–69.

59. Grignon, 264; Carver, 200; Kay, "The Land of La Baye," 169.

60. James W. Biddle, "Recollections of Green Bay in 1816–17," in *WHC*,

Vol. 1 (1855; rpt., Madison: State Historical Society of Wisconsin, 1903), 58–59; "Lawe and Grignon Papers, 1794–1821," in *WHC,* Vol. 10 (Madison: State Historical Society of Wisconsin, 1883–85), 139–40; Trask, 1–27; Donald Jackson, ed., *The Journals of Zebulon Montgomery Pike: With Letters and Related Documents,* Vol. 1 (Norman: University of Oklahoma Press, 1966), 198–99.

    61. Biddle, 59.

    62. Carver, 76.

    63. Anthony Leeds, "Ecological Determinants of Chieftainship among the Yaruro Indians of Venezuela," in Andrew P. Vayda, ed., *Environment and Cultural Behavior: Ecological Studies in Cultural Anthropology,* published for the American Musem of Natural History (Garden City, N.Y.: Natural History Press, 1969), 377–94.

    64. Keesing, 88; Walter J. Hoffman, "The Midēwiwin of 'Grand Medicine Society' of the Ojibwa," in *7th Annual Report of the Bureau of American Ethnology for the Years 1885–1886* (Washington, D.C.: Bureau of American Ethnology, 1891), 50–51.

    65. Thwaites, "British Regime in Wisconsin," 446–47.

    66. Carver, 79 fn. 49; Nancy Oestreich [Lurie], "Trends of Change in Patterns of Child Care and Training among the Wisconsin Winnebago," *Wisconsin Archaeologist* 29, n.s. (September–December 1948): 50.

    67. Stone and Chaput, 605–6; Magnaghi, 201–17.

    68. Friedl, "An Attempt at Directed Culture Change," 63–66.

    69. François Victor Malhiot, "A Wisconsin Fur-Trader's Journal, 1804–05," in *WHC,* Vol. 19 (Madison: State Historical Society of Wisconsin, 1910), 195–96.

    70. Malhiot, 202.

    71. Malhiot, 203.

    72. Malhiot, 203–4.

    73. Michel Curot, "A Wisconsin Fur-Trader's Journal, 1803–04," in *WHC,* Vol. 20 (Madison: State Historical Society of Wisconsin, 1911), 423.

    74. Curot, 464.

    75. Malhiot, 188–89.

    76. Kay, "The Land of La Baye," 162; Malhiot, 163–233.

    77. Jackson, *The Journals of Zebulon Montgomery Pike,* 217.

    78. Friedl, "An Attempt at Directed Culture Change," 94.

    79. Curot, 419–20.

    80. Thompson, 209.

    81. Malhiot, 188–89, fn. 66, and passim; Curot, 418–24, 433–44, and passim; see also Thomas Connor, "The Diary of Thomas Connor," in Charles M. Gates, ed., *Five Fur Traders in the Northwest* (St. Paul: Minnesota Historical Society, 1965), 257–58 and passim.

    82. Thompson, 209; Warren, 301.

83. Friedl, "An Attempt at Directed Culture Change," 84. Friedl also points out that no Ojibwa "had authority to intervene in order to prevent physical violence" (p. 84).

84. Calloway, "Suspicion and Self-Interest," 56; Thompson, 234–38; Gorrell, 30. Kay does not believe that epidemics were a major factor in the disintegration of Indian communities after 1750 ("The Land of La Baye," 164). Gorrell, however, presents evidence to the contrary, as does Moses Paquette in Reuben Gold Thwaites, ed., "The Wisconsin Winnebagoes: An Interview with Moses Paquette," in *WHC*, Vol. 12 (Madison: State Historical Society of Wisconsin, 1892), 401–2. See also Henry F. Dobyns, *Their Number Become Thinned: Native American Population Dynamics in Eastern North America* (Knoxville: University of Tennessee Press, 1983): 8–32.

85. David H. Van Thiel, Judith Gavaler, and Roger Lester, "Ethanol Inhibition of Vitamin A Metabolism in the Testes: Possible Mechanism for Sterility in Alcoholics," *Science* 186 (December 6, 1974), 941–42.

86. "The Relationship of Nutrition, Disease, and Social Conditions: A Graphical Presentation," *Journal of Interdisciplinary History* 14, no. 2 (Autumn 1983): 503–6. Note also S. Boyd Eaton and Melvin Konner, who point out that in hunting societies "protein contributed twice to nearly five times the proportion of total calories that it does for [contemporary] Americans . . . [however, hunting societies] ate much less fat than we do, and the fat they ate was substantially different from ours" ("Paleolithic Nutrition: Consideration of Its Natural and Current Implications," *New England Journal of Medicine* 312, no. 5 [January 31, 1985], 288); and Alfred W. Crosby, who notes a possible correlation between diet and disease among the Maori of New Zealand after contact with Europeans (Alfred W. Crosby, *Ecological Imperialism. The Biological Expansion of Europe, 900–1900* [Cambridge: Cambridge University Press, 1986], 242). Ann G. Carmichael, "Infection, Hidden Hunger, and History," *Journal of Interdisciplinary History* 14, no. 2 (Autumn 1983).

87. See Gretel H. Pelto and Pertti J. Pelto, "Diet and Delocalization: Dietary Changes since 1750," *Journal of Interdisciplinary History* 14, no. 2 (Autumn 1983): 507–8, for a discussion of diet and delocalization.

88. Carmichael, 260. Such a high carbohydrate diet would have negatively affected lactating females (Ann G. Carmichael, pers. comm.).

89. Landes, *Ojibwa Religion*, 177–78; Landes, *The Mystic Lake Sioux*, 57–60; Carver, 108–10. Among the Winnebago, the Midewiwin was known as the Medicine Lodge.

90. Kidd, 41–43; Trigger, *Natives and Newcomers*, 117; but see also Ritzenthaler, "Southwestern Chippewa," 755; Keesing, 48.

91. Hickerson, "The Chippewa and Their Neighbors," 52–63; Stone and Chaput, 605–6; Clifton, *The Prairie People*, 125.

92. Hickerson, "The Chippewa and Their Neighbors," 57; Warren, 65–67, 77–81; Vecsey, 174–79.

93. At such times, nativistic movements arise, enabling communities to adapt traditional social values to meet the demands of the new social reality. A good example of such movements is the Handsome Lake religion among the Iroquois or the Ghost Dance religion among the Plains Indians (see Anthony F. C. Wallace, *The Death and Rebirth of the Seneca* [New York: Alfred A. Knopf, 1969]; James Mooney, "The Ghost Dance Religion and the Sioux Outbreak of 1890," in *14th Annual Report of the Bureau of American Ethnology for the Years 1892–1893,* Part 1 [Washington, D.C.: Bureau of American Ethnology, 1896], 653–1136; Robert F. Berkhofer, Jr., "Faith and Factionalism among the Senecas: Theory and Ethnohistory," *Ethnohistory* 12, no. 2 [1965]: 99–112).

94. Vecsey, 179; Radin, *The Winnebago Tribe,* 311–30.

95. Hickerson, "The Chippewa and Their Neighbors," 52. See also Hoffman, "The Midēwiwin," 67.

96. See Selwyn Dewdney, *The Sacred Scrolls of the Southern Ojibway* (Toronto: University of Toronto Press, 1975) and Albert Reagan, "Picture Writing of the Chippewa Indians," *Wisconsin Archeologist* 6 (1927): 80–83.

97. Hickerson, "The Chippewa and Their Neighbors," 52; Ritzenthaler, "Southwestern Chippewa," 754–55; Keesing, 48–49; and Warren.

98. Clifton, *The Prairie People,* 125. See also Keesing, 49; and Hoffman, "The Midēwiwin," 68–137, for the Midewiwin integrative force among the Menominee.

99. Vecsey, 183. In regard to deemphasis of the vision quest, Nancy Lurie (pers. comm.) says that this did not occur among the Winnebago.

100. Keesing, 84.

101. Sosin, 250.

CHAPTER 5: THE ARRIVAL OF THE LONG KNIVES

1. For works that examine this 1804 treaty with the Sauk and Fox, see: Wiliam T. Hagen, *The Sac and Fox Indians* (Norman: University of Oklahoma Press, 1958); Donald Jackson, ed., *Black Hawk, an Autobiography* (Urbana: University of Illinois Press, 1964); Ellen M. Whitney, ed., *The Black Hawk War, 1831–1832,* 3 vols., Collections of the Illinois State Historical Library, Vols. 35–37 (Springfield: Illinois State Historical Library, 1970–75); and Wallace, *Prelude to Disaster.*

2. Stephen J. Herzberg, "The Menominee Indians: From Treaty to Termination," *Wisconsin Magazine of History* 60 (Summer 1977): 271. Herzberg points out that Lewis Cass, territorial governor of Michigan, opposed the treaty, but on "practical rather than humanitarian" grounds. See also Francis Paul Prucha and Donald F. Carmony, eds., "A Memorandum of Lewis Cass Concerning a System for the Regulation of Indian Affairs," *Wisconsin Magazine of History* 52 (Autumn 1968): 35–50.

3. Danziger, 75.

4. Stone and Chaput, 605.

5. Government rationale in making treaties with Indian tribes is explored in: Wallace, *Prelude to Disaster*; Horsman, *Expansion and American Indian Policy*; Francis Paul Prucha, *American Indian Policy in the Formative Years: The Indian Trade and Intercourse Acts, 1790–1834* (Cambridge, Mass.: Harvard University Press, 1962); Robert F. Berkhofer, Jr., *The White Man's Indian: Images of the American Indian from Columbus to the Present* (New York: Alfred A. Knopf, 1978), part 4.

6. Quoted in Prucha, *American Indian Policy*, 180.

7. Martin Zanger, "Red Bird," in R. David Edmunds, ed., *American Indian Leaders: Studies in Diversity* (Lincoln: University of Nebraska Press, 1980), 64–87; Martin Zanger, "Conflicting Concepts of Justice: A Winnebago Murder Trial on the Illinois Frontier," *Journal of the Illinois State Historical Society* 73 (1980): 263–76.

8. Prucha, *American Indian Policy*, 180; Zanger, "Conflicting Concepts of Justice."

9. Joseph Street to secretary of war (copy), November 15, 1827, Joseph M. Street Papers, SHSW; Zanger, "Red Bird," 64–87. For accounts of attempts to orchestrate Winnebago removal, see: Joseph Street to Elias K. Kane, February 26, 1830, Elias Kent Kane Papers, 1830, CHS; Joseph Street to Elbert Herring (copy), June 4, 1834, Joseph M. Street Papers, SHSW; Elbert Herring to William Clark, April 2, 1833, Joseph M. Street Papers, SHSW; Joseph Street to secretary of war (copy), May 20, 1831, Joseph M. Street Papers, SHSW.

10. Lurie, "Winnebago," 697–98; Prucha, *American Indian Policy*, 178–81; A. Smith, 129–30.

11. Prucha, *American Indian Policy*, 178–81; Lurie, "Winnebago," 697–98; Lurie, *Wisconsin Indians*, 19; Zanger, "Red Bird"; [William J. Snelling], "Early Days at Prairie du Chien and Winnebago Outbreak of 1827," in *WHC*, Vol. 5 (Madison: State Historical Society of Wisconsin, 1907), 123–53.

12. Quoted in Prucha, *American Indian Policy*, 182.

13. Prucha, *American Indian Policy*, 183.

14. Albert G. Ellis, "Some Accounts of the Advent of the New York Indians into Wisconsin," in *WHC*, Vol. 2 (Madison: State Historical Society of Wisconsin, 1856), 415–49; Albert G. Ellis, "Recollections of Rev. Eleazer Williams," in *WHC*, Vol. 8 (1879; rpt., Madison: State Historical Society of Wisconsin, 1908), 322–52; Lyman C. Draper, "Additional Notes on Eleazer Williams," in *WHC*, Vol. 8 (1879; rpt., Madison: State Historical Society of Wisconsin, 1908), 353–69; Robert E. Ritzenthaler, "The Oneida Indians of Wisconsin," *Bulletin of the Public Museum of the City of Milwaukee* 19, no. 1 (November 1950): 9–14; Campisi, "Oneida," 485–86; Jack Campisi, "The Oneida Treaty Period, 1783–1838," in Jack Campisi and Laurence M. Hauptman, eds., *The Oneida Indian Experience: Two Perspectives* (Syracuse: Syracuse University Press, 1988), 48–64; Reginald Horsman, "The Wisconsin Oneidas in the Preallotment Years," in Campisi and Hauptman, 66.

15. Ritzenthaler, "The Oneida Indians of Wisconsin," 12.

16. Rizenthaler, "The Oneida Indians of Wisconsin," 9–14; Horsman, "The Wisconsin Oneidas," 65–88.

17. John T. de La Ronde, "Personal Narrative," in *WHC*, Vol. 7 (1876; rpt., Madison: State Historical Society of Wisconsin, 1908): 350; Nancy Oestreich Lurie, "In Search of Chaetar: New Findings on Black Hawk's Surrender," *Wisconsin Magazine of History* 71, no. 3 (Spring 1988): 161–83; Jackson, *Black Hawk, An Autobiography*; Whitney; Wallace, *Prelude to Disaster*.

18. Lurie, *Wisconsin Indians*, 18–19; Lurie, "In Search of Chaetar," 161–83; Whitney; Wallace, *Prelude to Disaster*. See also a new study by Roger L. Nichols, *Black Hawk and the Warrior's Path* (Arlington Heights, Ill.: Harlan Davidson, 1992).

19. A. Smith, 145; Robert H. Keller, "An Economic History of Indian Treaties in the Great Lakes Region," *American Indian Journal* 4 (February 1978): 2–20.

20. Lurie, "Winnebago," 699.

21. Frederick Marryat, "An English Officer's Description of Wisconsin in 1837," in *WHC*, Vol. 14 (Madison: State Historical Society of Wisconsin, 1898): 139 (his emphasis).

22. A. Smith, 146; Lurie, "Winnebago," 699–700. See Ronald Satz, *American Indian Policy in the Jacksonian Era* (Lincoln: University of Nebraska Press, 1975) on the removal of the southern tribes.

23. A. Smith, 146–48; Thomas L. McKenney, *Sketches of a Tour to the Lakes* (1827; rpt., Minneapolis: Ross and Haines, 1959), 457–68.

24. A. Smith, 148–49; Gurdon Saltonstall Hubbard, *The Autobiography of Gurdon Saltonstall Hubbard* (Chicago: R. R. Donnelly and Sons, 1911), 47–70. An extensive discussion of the making of this treaty and the Ojibwa understanding of what was involved is found in Satz, "Chippewa Treaty Rights," 33–49.

25. Keesing, 141.

26. Keesing, 142–43.

27. Keesing, 141; Lurie, "Winnebago," 698.

28. Attempts to counter British influence and Indian trips to British posts were made as early as 1809 (see N. Boilvin to James Madison, July 28, 1809, Boilvin file 1809, Boilvin Papers, SHSW. See also William H. Keating, *Narrative of an Expedition to the Source of St. Peter's River, Lake Winnepeek, Lake of the Woods, etc. etc., Performed in the Year of 1823, by Order of the Hon. J. C. Calhoun, Secretary of War, under the Command of Stephen H. Long, Major U.S.T.E.*, 2 vols. (Philadelphia: H. C. Carey and I. Lea, 1824), 339; and John S. Galbraith, "British-American Competition in the Border Fur Trade of the 1820s," *Minnesota History* 36 (September 1959): 247. Felix Keesing cites William Powell, official interpreter to the Menominee, who claimed that the Menominee were still making trips to Drummond Island for gifts as late as 1830 (Keesing, 129).

29. Prucha and Carmony, 41–44; H. R. Schoolcraft to L. Cass, July 18, 1822, Records of the Michigan Superintendency of Indian Affairs, 1814–51, Roll 65, Letters Sent, National Archives. See also Jedediah Morse, *A Report to the Secretary of War of the United States on Indian Affairs* (New Haven: Converse, 1822), 45; and John D. Haeger, "A Time of Change: Green Bay, 1815–1834," *Wisconsin Magazine of History* 54 (1970–71): 285–98.

30. Failure of the factory system must also be attributed to the facts that liquor could not be kept out of the woods, factories were located often far from Indian settlements, factory goods purchased for the trade were often of poor quality and not appropriate for the trade, and to the American Fur Company's lobbying efforts against the factory system in Washington (see Morse; and Herman Viola, *Thomas L. McKenney: Architect of America's Early Indian Policy, 1816–1830* (Chicago: Swallow Press, 1974).

31. Jeanne Kay, "John Lawe: Green Bay Trader," *Wisconsin Magazine of History* 64 (Autumn 1980): 8; Schoolcraft, *Narrative Journal of Travels,* 238.

32. Stanislauss [Chappue?] to John Lawe, June 17, 1837, Grignon, Lawe, Porlier Papers, SHSW; Samuel Abbott to John Lawe, August 18, 1842, Grignon, Lawe, Porlier Papers, SHSW; A. Smith, 121.

33. A. Smith, 114.

34. Johann Georg Kohl, *Kitchi-Gami: Life among the Lake Superior Ojibway* (St. Paul: Minnesota Historical Society Press, 1985), 367–72.

35. Kohl, 367–72.

36. Kohl, 367–72.

37. Jackson Kemper, "Journal of an Episcopalian Missionary's Tour to Green Bay, 1834," in *WHC,* Vol. 14 (Madison: State Historical Society of Wisconsin, 1898), 424. For the importance of dreams among the Indians in Wisconsin, see Vecsey; Victor Barnouw, *Wisconsin Chippewa Myths and Tales* (Madison: University of Wisconsin Press, 1977); Paul Radin, *The Autobiography of a Winnebago Indian* (1920; rpt., New York: Dover, 1963). For Algonquians in particular, see John Heckewelder, *History, Manners, and Customs of the Indian Nations Who Once Inhabited Pennsylvania and the Neighboring States* (1876; rpt., New York: Arno Press, 1971); A. Irving Hallowell, *The Role of Conjuring in Saulteaux Society* (New York: Octagon Books, 1971); and White.

38. Edmund F. Ely, Diaries, October 25, 1836, Vols. 9–20, Edmund Ely Papers, SHSW.

39. Simon Senderl, "Berichte der Leopoldine Stiftung," Vol. 7, 1834, typescript, p. 3, Simon Senderl Papers, SHSW. A more detailed account of government manipulation and misinterpretation in the treaty process is in Satz, "Chippewa Treaty Rights," 13–49.

40. "Chippewa Indian Statement of the Treaties between the Chippewa and the United States from 1825 to 1864 from the Chippewa Standpoint," SC-O/40, 2, SHSW.

41. Joseph M. Street to Montfort Stokes, August 26, 1833, Joseph M. Street Papers, SHSW.

42. Reuben Gold Thwaites, "The Fur Trade in Wisconsin, 1815–1817," in *WHC*, Vol. 19 (Madison: State Historical Society of Wisconsin, 1910), 421–24.

43. Joseph M. Street to Montfort Stokes, August 26, 1833, Joseph M. Street Papers, SHSW.

44. [George Boyd], "Menominee," n.d., Vol. 7, 80, George Boyd Papers, SHSW.

45. Joseph M. Street to Montfort Stokes, August 26, 1833, Joseph M. Street Papers, SHSW. For other accounts of the negative influence of traders on Wisconsin Indians, see Alfred Cope, "Mission to the Menominee: A Quaker's Green Bay Diary," *Wisconsin Magazine of History* 49, no. 4 (Summer 1966): 312, 323; and 50, no. 1 (Autumn 1966): 25; Warren, 393–94; Ellis, "Advent of the New York Indians into Wisconsin," 423–29; Kemper, 424, 439, 443; H. H. Tanner, 423–46.

46. See, for example, John Haney to ———, n.d., John Haney Papers, SHSW.

47. Ellis, "Advent of the New York Indians into Wisconsin," 429.

48. Quoted in Ellis, "Advent of the New York Indians into Wisconsin," 430 fn.

49. George Boyd quoted in John Porter Bloom, ed., *The Territorial Papers of the United States,* Vol. 27: *The Territory of Wisconsin* (Washington, D.C.: National Archives, 1969), 940 (his emphasis).

50. Joseph M. Street to secretary of war, November 15, 1827, Joseph M. Street Papers, SHSW. See also Thomas Forsyth on the weakness of Sauk, Fox, Winnebago, Ojibwa and Potawatomi chiefs (Forsyth to Lewis Cass, July 20, 1823, Forsyth Letterbook, Vol. 4, 172–75, Thomas Forsyth Papers, SHSW). For this phenomenon among the Oneida and other Iroquois, see Ellis, "Advent of the New York Indians into Wisconsin," 426.

51. Joseph M. Street to Gov. Dodge, January 11, 1837, Joseph M. Street Papers, SHSW; see also Joseph M. Street to secretary of war, May 20, 1831, Joseph M. Street Papers, SHSW.

52. Gustave de Neveu, "A Menominee Indian Payment in 1838," *Wisconsin Historical Society Proceedings, 1910,* Vol. 58 (Madison, 1911), 161–62; James Madison Boyd, "Menominee Indian Payment in 1837," folder 7, in H. B. Tanner Papers, SHSW; see Simon Senderl, "Berichte der Leopoldine Stiftung," Vol. 7, 1834, typescript, p. 3, Simon Senderl Papers, SHSW, for a similar scene at the Menominee payment in 1833. These bouts of excessive behavior may have operated as a positive biological adaptation to long periods of stress. See Robert M. Sapolsky, *Why Zebras Don't Get Ulcers* (New York: W.H. Freeman, 1994.)

53. [Boyd], "Menominee," n.d., Vol. 7, 80, George Boyd Papers, SHSW.

54. Warren, 385.

55. For the exhaustion of game in the area, see James Allen, "Journal and Let-

ters of Lieutenant James Allen," in Schoolcraft, *Schoolcraft's Expedition to Lake Itasca,* 186; Schoolcraft, *Narrative Journal of Travels,* 90–91; Danziger, 71.

56. George Boyd, "Statement of the Number of Each Tribe . . . ," September 30, 1840, Vol. 8, George Boyd Papers, SHSW.

57. A. Smith, 143–50; Ritzenthaler, "Southwestern Chippewa," 745; Clifton, "Potawatomi," 737; Keesing, 127–47; Haeger, 285–98.

58. Morse, 15, 52–54.

59. Morse, 52–54; Keesing, 96–98.

60. R. Lawrence to Col. M. Neil, March 16, 1825, Vol. 2, George Boyd Papers, SHSW; Ellis, "Advent of the New York Indians into Wisconsin," 425–27. French attempts to disrupt negotiations could be seen as late as 1848 (see Cope, 50, no. 1: 19).

61. Morse, 15; Ellis, "Advent of the New York Indians into Wisconsin," 424–25, on the French.

62. Keesing, 95.

63. Keesing, 98–99; Ellis, "Advent of the New York Indians into Wisconsin," 428–33; Ritzenthaler, "The Oneida Indians of Wisconsin," 11–12.

64. Cope, 50, no. 1: 38–40, and 50, no. 3: 234.

65. Morse, 48; Marryat, 152; Samuel Stambaugh, "Report on the Quality and Condition of Wisconsin Territory, 1831," in *WHC,* Vol. 15 (Madison: State Historical Society of Wisconsin, 1900), 429–35; George Boyd to G. B. Porter, March 31, 1833, Vol. 8, George Boyd Papers, SHSW; "Winnebago Hostilities," in *WHC,* Vol. 20 (Madison: State Historical Society of Wisconsin, 1911), 139–44.

66. Morse, 48–49; Ellis, "Advent of the New York Indians into Wisconsin," 425; Lurie, "Winnebago," 697.

67. Ellis, "Advent of the New York Indians into Wisconsin," 425–26.

68. Keesing, 96.

69. Andrew Jackson Turner, "The History of Fort Winnebago," in *WHC,* Vol. 14 (Madison: State Historical Society of Wisconsin, 1898), 66–67.

70. Joseph M. Street, Correspondence no. 7, December 11, 1827, Joseph M. Street Papers, SHSW; Zanger, "Red Bird," 64–87; Zanger, "Conflicting Concepts of Justice," 263–76 and [William J. Snelling] "Early Days at Prairie du Chien and Winnebago Outbreak of 1827," in *WHC,* Vol. 5 (1868; rpt., Madison: State Historical Society of Wisconsin, 1907), 123–53.

71. Lurie, "In Search of Chaetar," 163–83; Whitney.

72. "Chippewa Indian Statement of the Treaties . . . ," 2a–3, SHSW. See also Satz, "Chippewa Treaty Rights."

73. Robert Stuart to Alfred Brunson, March 10, 1843, Alfred Brunson, "Letterbook, 1835–43, 135–40, Brunson Papers, SHSW. The threat to deprive Indians of traders unless they complied with government requests can also be seen in comments by the Sioux (see Joseph M. Street, "Treaty Session of 1836," Vol. 73, Green Bay–Prairie du Chien Papers, SHSW).

74. J. Allen, 185–86; Danziger, 85–86; John Nelson Davidson, "Mission on Chequamegon Bay," in *WHC*, Vol. 12 (Madison: State Historical Society of Wisconsin, 1892): 448; Edmund F. Ely, Diaries, Vol. 1, p. 22, Edmund Ely Papers, SHSW.

75. Danziger, 68, 77.

76. Alfred Brunson to Robert Stuart, January 5, 1843, Alfred Brunson Letterbook, September 24, 1842—February 27, 1844, 14–15, Brunson Papers, SHSW.

77. Danziger, 87–89; James Clifton, "Wisconsin Death March: Explaining the Extremes in the Old Northwest Indian Removal," *Transactions of the Wisconsin Academy of Sciences, Arts and Letters* 75 (1987): 1–39.

78. See George Boyd to Henry Dodge, September 17, 1839, Vol. 8, George Boyd Papers, SHSW; Alfred Brunson to J. D. Doty, January 6, 1843, Alfred Brunson Letterbook, September 24, 1842—February 27, 1844, 37–70, Brunson Papers, SHSW; [Snelling], 124.

79. See George Boyd to Elbert Herring, November 18, 1834, and George Boyd to G. B. Porter, January 31, 1833, George Boyd Papers, SHSW; John Haney Journal, December 31, 1842, John Haney Papers, 1835–46, SHSW.

80. Warren, 335; Thwaites, "The Wisconsin Winnebagoes," 401–2; George Boyd to John Mason, April 15–30, 1834, George Boyd to C. A. Harris, February 5, 1838, and George Boyd to C. A. Harris, March 15, 1838, Vol. 8, George Boyd Papers, SHSW.

81. Cope, 49, no. 4: 310. See also Jacqueline L. Peterson, "The People In Between: Indian-White Marriage and the Genesis of a Métis Society in the Great Lakes Regions, 1680–1830" (Ph.D. diss., University of Illinois at Chicago, 1981).

82. Louis B. Porlier, "Narrative by Louis B. Porlier," in *WHC*, Vol. 15 (Madison: State Historical Society of Wisconsin, 1900), 446–47; Keesing, 140.

83. Quoted in Schoolcraft, *Narrative Journal of Travels*, 283.

84. Kai T. Erikson, *Everything in Its Path: Destruction of Community in the Buffalo Creek Flood* (New York: Simon and Schuster, 1972), 255.

85. In his book on American Indian policy, historian Ronald N. Satz uses the sociological term "social anomie" to describe the mental condition that Erikson describes as the result of "chronic disasters." According to Satz, the American government's efforts at forced acculturation of Indian peoples led to social anomie, or "a situation induced by a tremendous conflict of norms which manifests itself in confusion, disorientation, disorganization, and antisocial behavior" (Satz, *American Indian Policy*, 275).

86. See de Neveu, 161–62; James Madison Boyd, "Menominee Indian Payment in 1837," folder 7, in H. B. Tanner Papers, SHSW.

CHAPTER 6. THE SHRINKING LAND

1. Sherman Hall, "Prospects of the Ojibwa Mission," *Missionary Herald* 43 (1847): 161–62.

2. Berkhofer, *The White Man's Indian*, 134–35.

3. Francis Paul Prucha, *The Great Father: The United States Government and the American Indian,* Vol. 1 (Lincoln: University of Nebraska Press, 1984), 283–84. For studies on social reform during this period see, Ronald Walters, *American Reformers, 1815–1860* (New York: Hill and Wang, 1978); David Brion Davis, *Antebellum American Culture: An Interpretive Anthology* (Lexington, Mass.: D.C. Heath, 1979).

4. Berkhofer, *The White Man's Indian;* Michael C. Coleman, "Not Race, but Grace: Presbyterian Missionaries and the American Indian, 1837–1893," *Journal of American History* 67 (June 1975): 41–60; R. Pierce Beaver, "American Missionary Efforts to Influence Government Indian Policy," *Journal of Church and State* 5 (May 1963): 77–94; R. Pierce Beaver, "Church, State, and the Nation," *Journal of Church and State* 4 (May 1962): 11–30; R. Pierce Beaver, *Church, State and the American Indians: Two and a Half Centuries of Partnership in Missions between Protestant Churches and Government* (St. Louis: Concordia Publishing House, 1966).

5. See, for instance, William T. Hagen, "Justifying Dispossession of the Indians: The Land Utilization Argument," in Christopher Vecsey and Robert W. Venables, eds., *American Indian Environments: Ecological Issues in Native American History* (Syracuse: Syracuse University Press, 1980), 65–80; and Wilcomb E. Washburn, *The Assault on Indian Tribalism: The General Allotment Law (Dawes Act) of 1887* (Philadelphia: J. P. Lippencott, 1975).

6. Robert C. Nesbit, *The History of Wisconsin,* Vol. 3: *Urbanization and Industrialization, 1873–1893* (Madison: State Historical Society of Wisconsin, 1985), 420; Danziger, 91–109; Berkhofer, *The White Man's Indian,* 166–75; William T. Hagen, *Indian Police and Judges: Experiments in Acculturation and Control* (New Haven: Yale University Press, 1966).

7. Nesbit, *History of Wisconsin,* 420–22.

8. A. Smith, 464–65.

9. Quoted in A. Smith, 465.

10. James Willard Hurst, *Law and Economic Growth* (Madison: University of Wisconsin Press, 1984), 20.

11. A. Smith, 237–38; Hurst, 15; Nesbit, *History of Wisconsin,* 136–37; Richard Current, *Wisconsin: A Bicentennial History* (New York: W. W. Norton, 1977), 110.

12. Nesbit, *History of Wisconsin,* 180.

13. Hurst, 24.

14. Quoted in Hurst, 25–26.

15. Quoted in Willard H. Titus, "Observations on the Menominee Indians," *Wisconsin Magazine of History* 14 (September–June 1930–31), 93.

16. La Ronde, 358; Hurst, 118–19; Nesbit, *History of Wisconsin,* 297–98; Danziger, 100.

17. Keesing, 153; Campisi, "Oneida," 487; Titus, "Observations on the Menominee Indians," 93.

18. For a discussion of problems historians encounter in dealing with this aspect of Indian history, see Robert F. Berkhofer, Jr., "The Political Context of a New Indian History," *Pacific Historical Review* 40, no. 3 (August 1971): 357–82.

19. Keesing, chapters 6 and 7; S. J. Herzberg, 277–95; Spindler and Spindler; L. Spindler, 708–24; Walter J. Hoffman, "The Menomini Indians," in *14th Annual Report of the Bureau of American Ethnology for the Years 1892–1893*, Part 1 (Washington, D.C.: GPO, 1896); Ourada.

20. Keesing, 148–53.

21. Keesing, 151–52.

22. Keesing, 152–58; Ourada, 134–36.

23. Quoted in Keesing, 158.

24. Quoted in Keesing, 158–59. See also Herzberg, 275–76; Ourada, 141–42.

25. Titus, "Observations on the Menominee Indians," 98–105; Thomas J. Vennum, *The Ojibwa Dance Drum: Its History and Construction*, Smithsonian Folklife Studies, No. 2 (Washington, D.C.: Smithsonian Institution, 1982), 45–49.

26. Titus, "Observations on the Menominee Indians," 96.

27. Herzberg, 277.

28. Nesbit, *History of Wisconsin*, 424; Current, 557; Herzberg, 277; Ourada, 142–45.

29. Ourada, 147; Herzberg, 277. For a similar case of cultural fit and occupation, see Morris Freilich, "Cultural Persistence among the Modern Iroquois," *Anthropos* 53, nos. 3–4 (1958): 473–83.

30. Keesing, 176; Ourada, 151.

31. Quoted in Keesing, 191.

32. Herzberg, 282–83.

33. Keesing, 190–191.

34. Hoffman, "The Menomini Indians," 137; Keesing, 181, 213–14.

35. Hoffman, "The Menomini Indians," 157–58.

36. Hoffman, "The Menomini Indians," 137–38.

37. James S. Slotkin, *The Menomini Powwow: A Study in Cultural Decay*, Milwaukee Public Museum Publication in Anthropology (Milwaukee: Milwaukee Public Museum, 1957), 131; Samuel A. Barrett, "The Dream Dance of the Chippewa and Menominee Indians of Northern Wisconsin," *Bulletin of the Public Museum of the City of Milwaukee* 1 (1911): 251–406; Vennum, *The Ojibwa Dance Drum*, 46–49.

38. Herzberg, 282–83; Gary Orfield, "The War on Menominee Poverty," *Wisconsin Indian Research Journal* 1 (October 1965): 54, 57; Keesing, 176–93; Ourada, 179–80.

39. H. P. Marble, "The Field Matron in Indian Work," in *Report of the Thirty-Fourth Annual Lake Mohonk Conference on the Indian and Other Dependent Peoples* (n.p., 1916), 106–7.

40. Quoted in Danziger, 102.

41. Campisi, "Oneida," 486–87. For an Oneida view of this time, see the Diary of John Archiquette, 1868–74, especially the entry for January 9, 1871, Green Bay Papers, SHSW.

42. Albert G. Ellis, "Fifty-four Years' Recollections of Men and Events in Wisconsin," in *WHC*, Vol. 7 (1876; rpt., Madison: State Historical Society of Wisconsin, 1908), 225.

43. Diary of John Archiquette, entry for April 22, 1874, Green Bay Papers, SHSW. Campisi puts the date for allotting Oneida land as 1892 (see Campisi, "Oneida," 487).

44. Ritzenthaler, "The Oneida Indians of Wisconsin," 13–14; Campisi, "Oneida," 487.

45. Ritzenthaler, "The Oneida Indians of Wisconsin," 13–14.

46. Campisi, "Oneida," 486.

47. Cutting Marsh to John Tawse, letter draft, 1848, Cutting Marsh Papers, SHSW; T. J. Brasser, "Mahican," in *HNAI 15 Northeast*, 209–10.

48. Cutting Marsh to John Tawse, letter draft, June 11, 1847, Cutting Marsh Papers, SHSW.

49. Cutting Marsh to John Tawse, letter draft, June 11, 1847, and Marsh to Tawse, letter draft, n.d., Cutting Marsh Papers, SHSW.

50. Cope, 49, no. 4: 316; Cutting Marsh to John Tawse, letter draft, 1848, Cutting Marsh Papers, SHSW; W. A. Titus, "A Brief Account of the Stockbridge," *Wisconsin Magazine of History* 30 (1946–47): 423–32; W. A. Titus, "Historical Spots in Wisconsin. Brothertown: A Wisconsin Story with a New England Background," *Wisconsin Magazine of History* 21 (September–June 1937–38): 293–300; Sherman Hall, "Ojibwas," *Missionary Herald* 45 (1849): 15; John Chapin, "Sketch of Cutting Marsh," in *WHC*, Vol. 15 (Madison: State Historical Society of Wisconsin, 1900), 25–38; Brasser, 210.

51. Joseph Schafer, *The Winnebago–Horicon Basin: A Type Study in Western History* (Madison: State Historical Society of Wisconsin, 1937), 58–65; Brasser, 210; Titus, "A Brief Account of the Stockbridge," 429; George E. Fay, comp., *Treaties between the Menominee Indians and the United States of America, 1817–1859*, Miscellaneous Series, No. 3 University of Wisconsin–Oshkosh, Museum of Anthropology, 1965.

52. Schafer, 74; Current, 557.

53. J. Adams Papers, September 11, 1873, SHSW.

54. Hall, "Prospects of the Ojibwa Mission," 161.

55. See, for example: Ritzenthaler, "Southwestern Chippewa," 743–59; Hickerson, *The Chippewa and Their Neighbors*; Hickerson, *The Southwestern Chippewa*; Densmore; Satz, "Chippewa Treaty Rights"; Danziger; and Vennum, *Wild Rice and the Ojibway People*.

56. Hall, "Ojibwas," 15; Danziger, 87–88.

57. "Ojibwas," *Missionary Herald* 47 (1851): 100–101. See also Clifton, "Wisconsin Death March," 1–39; Satz, "Chippewa Treaty Rights," 51–59.

58. Leonard Wheeler to C. K. Drew, letter draft, March 1, 1860, Leonard Wheeler Papers, SHSW.

59. Harold Hickerson, "The Chippewa of the Upper Great Lakes: A Study in Sociopolitical Change," in Eleanor B. Leacock and Nancy Oestreich Lurie, eds., *North American Indians in Historical Perspective* (New York: Random House, 1971), 183–89. As an example of this last remaining function for chiefs, see comments of Ojibwa Chief Ngonab in "Diary of Lake Superior Trip," 1873, William F. Vilas Papers, SHSW.

60. Black Bird to G. Manypenny, October 1855, Leonard Wheeler Papers, SHSW. See also "Council of Indians—Odanah, July 6, 1856," Leonard Wheeler Papers, SHSW.

61. Black Bird to G. Manypenny, October 1855, Leonard Wheeler Papers, SHSW.

62. Danziger, 93–97.

63. Robert F. Fries, *Empire in Pine: The Study of Lumbering in Wisconsin, 1830–1900* (Madison: State Historical Society of Wisconsin, 1951), 202; Nesbit, *The History of Wisconsin,* 431. Similar unscrupulous acts also prevailed on the other reservations in Wisconsin.

64. Danziger, 104; John Gillin, "Acquired Drives in Culture Contact," *American Anthropologist* 44 (October–December 1942): 545–54.

65. S. M. Brosius to the secretary of the interior, November 15, 1902, S. W. Campbell Papers, SHSW; Matthew K. Sniffen, "The Need of Protecting the Indians' Interests," *Report of the Twenty-eighth Annual Meeting of the Lake Mohonk Conference* (n.p.: Lake Mohonk Conference, 1910), 17.

66. Gillin, 551. Gillin interviewed "eleven men who passed through these changes" (p. 550).

67. Gillin, 552.

68. Ira O. Isham to John J. Jenkins, May 14, 1906, S. W. Campbell Papers, SHSW. See also other letters in the Campbell Papers about the destitute condition of the Ojibwa Indians at this time.

69. Gillin, 551.

70. See Melissa Meyer, "Tradition and the Market: The Social Relations of the White Earth Anishinaabeg, 1889–1920" (Ph.D. diss., University of Minnesota, 1985), for similiar results at the Ojibwa White Earth reservation in Minnesota.

71. Nesbit, *History of Wisconsin,* 259.

72. Thwaites, "The Wisconsin Winnebagoes," 401–16; Louise Phelps Kellogg, "The Removal of the Winnebago," *Transactions of the Wisconsin Academy of Sciences, Arts and Letters* 21 (1924): 25–29; Nesbit, *The History of Wisconsin,* 358–59; Lurie, "Winnebago," 699; Current, 421–24, 557–58.

73. See, for example, Radin, *The Autobiography of a Winnebago Indian;* and Helen Miner Miller, Nadine Day Sieber, and Nancy Oestreich Lurie, *The Wisconsin Winnebago People: Historical Background of the Wisconsin Winnebago*

Indian People, rev. ed. (n.p.: Wisconsin Winnebago Business Committee, 1967), 2; Lurie, *Mountain Wolf Woman;* Lurie, "Winnebago," 702–4.

74. Lurie, "Winnebago," 702–3; Thwaites, "The Wisconsin Winnebagoes," 419.

75. Radin, *The Autobiography of a Winnebago Indian,* 48–67; Lurie, *Mountain Wolf Woman,* 39–51.

76. Nancy Oestreich Lurie, "Two Dollars," in Solon T. Kimball and James B. Watson, eds., *Crossing Cultural Boundaries: The Anthropological Experience* (San Francisco: Chandler Publishing Co., 1972), 158–61.

77. Lurie, "Winnebago," 704.

78. Publius V. Lawson, "The Potawatomi," *Wisconsin Archaeologist* 19 (April 1920): 98.

79. Robert E. Ritzenthaler, "The Potawatomi Indians of Wisconsin," *Bulletin of the Public Museum of the City of Milwaukee* 19, no. 3 (1953): 106–7.

80. Lawson, 107–9; William H. Hodge, "The Indians of Wisconsin," *State of Wisconsin 1975 Blue Book* (Madison: Department of Administration, 1975): 145–48.

81. Clifton, *The Prairie People,* 382–83.

82. Lawson, 99–105; Clifton, *The Prairie People,* 382–83.

83. Vennum, *The Ojibwa Dance Drum,* 76–155; Clifton, *The Prairie People,* 383.

84. Lawson, 105; Clifton, "Potawatomi," 738. A small group of Potawatomi who returned from Kansas and were known as the Skunk Hill band chose to remain in central Wisconsin near Wisconsin Rapids (see Clifton, *The Prairie People,* 311).

85. Quoted in Alexander E. Morstad, *The Reverend Erik Olsen Morstad: His Missionary Work among the Wisconsin Pottawatomie Indians* (Clearwater, Fla.: Eldnar Press, 1971), 40–41.

86. Morstad, 18; Huron H. Smith, "Ethnobotany of the Forest Potawatomi Indians," *Bulletin of the Public Museum of the City of Milwaukee* 7, no. 1 (May 9, 1933), 13; Ritzenthaler, "Potawatomi Indians of Wisconsin," 108, 111.

87. Morstad quoted in Lawson, 103.

88. Quoted in Lawson, 104.

CHAPTER 7. WANDERING LIKE SHADOWS ON A DISAPPEARING LAND

1. Berkhofer, *The White Man's Indian,* 176.

2. Danziger, 120.

3. Danziger, 119–22.

4. Danziger, 114–19.

5. Danziger, 118; Hallowell, *Culture and Experience,* 339–40.

6. Vecsey, 196; Robert E. Ritzenthaler, "Chippewa Preoccupation with Health; Changes in a Traditional Attitude Resulting from Modern Health Prob-

lems," *Bulletin of the Public Museum of the City of Milwaukee* 19, no. 4 (December 1953): 189; Fred K. Blessing, "Discovery of a Chippewa Peyote Cult in Minnesota," *Minnesota Archaeologist* 23 (June 1961): 1–8.

7. Vecsey, 188–90; Slotkin, 9–16; Vennum, *The Ojibwa Dance Drum,* 132–47. Nancy Lurie (pers. comm.) points out that conversion to Christianity among the Winnebago was not extensive. She also notes that World War I served to revitalize some of the old ceremonies among the Winnebago.

8. Lurie, *Wisconsin Indians,* 25; Robert E. Ritzenthaler and Mary Sellers, "Indians in an Urban Situation: A Preliminary Report," typescript in Oneida Indian Folder 1956–3/1960, p. 3, Illinois-Wisconsin Friends Committee for American Indians Papers, SHSW.

9. Quote of Theodore Roosevelt in Theodore H. Haas, "The Legal Aspects of Indian Affairs from 1887 to 1957," *Annals of the American Academy of Political and Social Science* 311 (May 1957): 16.

10. Berkhofer, *The White Man's Indian,* 179–80; Vine Deloria and Clifford M. Lytle, *American Indians, American Justice* (Austin: University of Texas Press, 1983), 42.

11. Berkhofer, *The White Man's Indian,* 179–82; Deloria and Lytle, 42–44.

12. Deloria and Lytle, 41–42.

13. Lewis Meriam et al., *The Problem of Indian Administration,* Institute for Government Research, Studies in Administration (Baltimore: Johns Hopkins University Press, 1928), 15, 12, 3; quoted in Felix S. Cohen, *Handbook of Federal Indian Law, with Reference Tables and Index* (1942; rpt., Albuquerque: University of New Mexico Press, 1972), 27.

14. John Collier, *From Every Zenith* (Denver: Sage Books, 1963), 126.

15. Collier, *From Every Zenith,* 123.

16. Collier, *From Every Zenith,* 126. For a fuller assessment of Collier's career see: Kenneth R. Philp, *John Collier's Crusade for Indian Reform, 1920–1954* (Tucson: University of Arizona Press, 1977); Kenneth R. Philp, "John Collier and the Indians of the Americas: The Dream and the Reality," *Prologue* 11 (Spring 1979): 5–21; Graham D. Taylor, "Anthropologists, Reformers, and the Indian New Deal," *Prologue* 7 (Fall 1975): 151–62; Graham D. Taylor, *The New Deal and American Indian Tribalism: The Administration of the Indian Reorganization Act, 1934–45* (Lincoln: University of Nebraska Press, 1980); Kenneth R. Philp, "John Collier, 1933–45," in Robert M. Kvasnicka and Herman J. Viola, eds., *The Commissioners of Indian Affairs, 1824–1977* (Lincoln: University of Nebraska Press, 1979), 273–82; and Lawrence C. Kelley, "John Collier and the Indian New Deal: An Assessment," in Jane F. Smith and Robert M. Kvasnicka, eds., *Indian-White Relations: A Persistent Paradox* (Washington, D.C.: Howard University Press, 1976), 227–41.

17. John Collier, *The Indians of the Americas* (New York: W. W. Norton, 1947), 154–57. See also Taylor, *The New Deal and American Indian Tribalism.*

18. Collier, *The Indians of the Americas,* 154–57. As an example of the de-

pressed state of Indian affairs, see the case of Oklahoma Indians as presented by B. T. Quinten in "Oklahoma Tribes, the Great Depression, and the Indian Bureau," in Bernard Sternsher, ed., *Hitting Home: The Great Depression in Town and Country* (Chicago: Quadrangle Books, 1970): 200–216.

19. For an extended discussion of this, see D'Arcy McNickle, *Native American Tribalism: Indian Survivals and Renewals* (New York: Oxford University Press, 1973); and Hazel W. Hertzberg, *The Search for an American Indian Identity: Modern Pan-Indian Movement* (Syracuse: Syracuse University Press, 1971).

20. Ritzenthaler and Sellers, "Indians in an Urban Situation," typescript in Oneida Indian Folder 1956–3/1960, p. 31, Illinois-Wisconsin Friends Committee for American Indians Papers, SHSW.

21. Ritzenthaler, "The Oneida Indians of Wisconsin," 15.

22. Danziger, 136–37.

23. Danziger, 137; Friedl, "An Attempt at Directed Culture Change," 288–92; and Ernestine Friedl, "Persistence in Chippewa Culture and Personality," *American Anthropologist* 58 (October 1956): 814–25.

24. Danziger, 137.

25. Hallowell, *Culture and Experience,* 357.

26. Hallowell, *Culture and Experience,* 365.

27. Hallowell, *Culture and Experience,* 357.

28. Hallowell, *Culture and Experience,* 357; William Caudill, "Psychological Characteristics of Acculturated Wisconsin Ojibwa Children," *American Anthropologist* 51 (July–September 1949): 409–27; Gillin, 545–54.

29. Ritzenthaler, "Chippewa Preoccupation with Health," 177.

30. Slotkin, 9; Hallowell, *Culture and Experience,* 342–44.

31. Lurie, *Wisconsin Indians,* 41.

32. See Herzberg, 267–329, for an excellent discussion of Menominee lumbering and Robert E. Ritzenthaler, "The Menominee Indian Sawmill: A Successful Community Project," *Wisconsin Archeologist* 32 (1951): 69–74.

33. George D. Spindler, *Sociocultural and Psychological Processes in Menomini Acculturation* (Berkeley: University of California Press, 1955), 54–56: Peroff, 41–42.

34. G. D. Spindler, 107–19.

35. For a map showing this residential pattern, see Keesing, 223.

36. Quoted in Spindler and Spindler, 180.

37. Keesing, 246.

38. Keesing, 246.

39. This view is expressed by Peroff in *Menominee Drums* and by David W. Ames and Burton R. Fisher in "The Menominee Termination Crisis: Barriers in the Way of a Rapid Cultural Transition," *Human Organization* 18 (Fall 1959): 101–11.

40. Ames and Fisher, 102.

41. Lurie, *Wisconsin Indians,* 41.

42. Lurie, "Two Dollars," 159. See also Oestreich [Lurie], "Trends of Change," 40–140; and Nancy Oestreich [Lurie], "Cultural Change among the Wisconsin Winnebago," *Wisconsin Archaeologist* 25, no. 4 (1944): 124–25; Hallowell, *Culture and Experience;* and Slotkin.

43. Oestreich [Lurie], "Trends of Change," 61–62.

44. Lurie, "Winnebago," 704–5.

45. Lurie, "Winnebago," 704–5. Not all factionalism arose internally. In the 1950s, some Winnebago obtained employment dancing for tourists at the Wisconsin Dells. Here they were severely exploited. Whether the "dancing" involved a case of involuntary servitude was open to question, but a representative from the Wisconsin State Department of Public Welfare was "sufficiently impressed" that there had been at "the Dells a tragic history of exploitation [and] abuse" (Walter Taylor to Paxton Hart, March 25, 1960, Illinois-Wisconsin Friends Committee for American Indians Papers, SHSW). An American Legion Post that ran the show apparently sowed "dissension among the performers." Another observer noted, "I was left with the impression that the Indians are being exploited by a group who are apparently just staying within the bounds of legality. Apparently, . . . they are able to keep the tribe divided, and in fear of their jobs so that they will not testify against the Legion group" (Larry Wasson to Paxton Hart, April 25, 1960; see also Taylor to Hart, March 25, 1960, both in Illinois-Wisconsin Friends Committee for American Indians Papers, SHSW.

46. Lurie, *Wisconsin Indians,* 26.

47. Lurie, *Wisconsin Indians,* 26; Danziger, 134–70; Berkhofer, *The White Man's Indian,* 186.

48. Collier, *From Every Zenith,* 303–5.

49. Note Graham D. Taylor, "The Tribal Alternative to Bureaucracy: The Indian's New Deal, 1933–1945," *Journal of the West* 13 (January 1974): 128–42.

50. Philp, *John Collier's Crusade,* 243.

51. Nancy Oestreich Lurie, "The Voice of the American Indian: Report on the American Indian Chicago Conference," *Current Anthropology* 2 (1961): 480; Deloria and Lytle, 15–21.

52. Kenneth R. Philp, *Indian Self-Rule: First-hand Accounts of Indian-White Relations from Roosevelt to Reagan* (Salt Lake City: Howe Brothers, 1986), 22; and material from H. Adams in Philp, *Indian Self-Rule,* "Activism and Red Power—Lenada James, Ada Deer, Ramona Bennett, Gerald Wilkinson, Hank Adams," 228–42. See also Gary Orfield, *A Study of Termination Policy* (Denver: National Congress on the American Indian, 1965).

53. Ames and Fisher, 102; Shames, 8.

54. Quoted in Ames and Fisher, 104. See also Rachel Reese Sady, "The Menominee: Transition From Trusteeship," *Applied Anthropology* 6 (1947): 1–14.

55. Shames, 7–10.

56. Nancy Oestreich Lurie, "Historical Backgrounds," in Stuart Levine and

Nancy Oestreich Lurie, eds., *The American Indian Today* (Deland, Fla.: Everret/Edwards, 1965), 43.

57. Lurie, "Historical Backgrounds," 43.

58. Deloria and Lytle, 18–19.

59. Ritzenthaler and Sellers, "Indians in an Urban Situation," typescript in Oneida Indian Folder 1956–3/1960, pp. 1–10, Illinois-Wisconsin Friends Committee for American Indian Papers, SHSW; Lurie, *Mountain Wolf Woman*, 480–81.

60. William H. Hodge deals with many of these themes in his four biographies of Wisconsin Indians (see Hodge, 144–84).

61. Lurie, *Mountain Wolf Woman*; Francis Paul Prucha, *The Indians in American Society from the Revolutionary War to the Present* (Berkeley: University of California Press, 1985), 71.

62. Quoted in Prucha, *The Indians in American Society*, 74. See also Deloria and Lytle, 195–99.

CHAPTER 8. EPILOGUE: READING THE PAST

1. Marshall Sahlins is perhaps the foremost proponent of these views. See his *Islands of History* (Chicago: University of Chicago Press, 1985).

2. Alfonso Ortiz, *The Tewa World: Space, Time, Being, and Becoming in a Pueblo Society* (Chicago: University of Chicago Press, 1969).

3. Hodge, 95–192.

4. Sahlins, 136–56.

Bibliography

ARCHIVAL SOURCES

CHS: Chicago Historical Society, Chicago.
  Kane, Elias Kent. Papers.
National Archives, Washington, D.C.
  Records of the Michigan Superintendency of Indian Affairs, 1814–51.
SHSW: State Historical Society of Wisconsin, Madison.
  Adams, J. Papers.
  Boilvin Papers.
  Boyd, George. Papers.
  Brunson Papers.
  Campbell, S. W. Papers.
  "Chippewa Indian Statement of the Treaties between the Chippewa and the
      United States from 1825 to 1864 from the Chippewa Standpoint."
      SC-0/40, 1–2.
  Ely, Edmund. Papers.
  Forsyth, Thomas. Papers.
  Green Bay Papers.
  Green Bay–Prairie du Chien Papers.
  Grignon, Lawe, Porlier Papers.
  Haney, John. Papers.
  Illinois-Wisconsin Friends Committee for American Indians Papers.
  Marsh, Cutting. Papers.
  Senderl, Simon. Papers.
  Street, Joseph M. Papers.
  Tanner, H. B. Papers.
  Vilas, William F. Papers.
  Wheeler, Leonard. Papers.

NEWSPAPERS

Great Lakes Indian Community Voice
Menominee News

Bibliography

Menominee Tribal News
News from Indian Country (Hayward, Wis.)
Shawano Evening Leader
Weekly News Letter of the Menominee Tribe

BOOKS, ARTICLES, AND DISSERATIONS

Adams, Arthur T., ed. *The Explorations of Pierre Esprit Radisson.* Minneapolis: Ross and Haines, 1961.

Albers, Patricia, and Jeanne Kay. "Sharing the Land: A Study in American Indian Territoriality." In Thomas E. Ross and Tyrel G. Moore, eds., *A Cultural Geography of North American Indians,* 47–91. Boulder: Westview Press, 1987.

Allen, James. "Journal and Letters of Lieutenant James Allen." In Henry Rowe Schoolcraft, *Schoolcraft's Expedition to Lake Itasca. The Discovery of the Source of the Mississippi,* ed. Philip P. Mason, 163–241. East Lansing: Michigan State University Press, 1958.

Allen, Robert. "His Majesty's Indian Allies: Native People, the British Crown and the War of 1812." *Michigan Historical Review* 14, no. 2 (Fall 1988): 1–24.

Ames, David W., and Burton R. Fisher. "The Menominee Termination Crisis: Barriers in the Way of a Rapid Cultural Transition." *Human Organization* 18 (Fall 1959): 101–11.

Anderson, Gary C. *Kinsmen of Another Kind: Dakota-White Relations in the Upper Mississippi Valley, 1650–1862.* Lincoln: University of Nebraska Press, 1984.

Armstrong, Benjamin G. *Early Life among the Indians,* ed. Thomas P. Wentworth. Ashland, Wis.: A. W. Bowron, 1892.

Atwater, Caleb. *Remarks Made on a Tour to Prairie de Chien; Thence to Washington City, in 1829. By Calb Atwater, Late Commissioner Employed by the United States to Negotiate with the Indians of the Upper Mississippi for the Purchase of Mineral Country . . .* Columbus, Ohio: I. A. Whiting, 1831.

Axtell, James, ed. *The Indian Peoples of Eastern America: A Documentary History of the Sexes.* New York: Oxford University Press, 1981.

Baraga, Rev. Frederich. *Chippewa Indians as Recorded by Rev. Frederick Baraga in 1847.* New York–Washington: Studia Slovenica, 1976.

Baraga, Rev. Frederich. *A Theoretical and Practical Grammar of the Otchipwe Language, Spoken by the Chippewa Indians; Which Is Also Spoken by the Algonquin, Ottawa, and Potawatami Indians, with Little Difference. For the Use of Missionaries and Other Persons Living among the Above Named Tribes.* Detroit: J. Fox, 1850.

Baraga, Rev. Frederich, ed. *A Dictionary of the Otchipwe Language, Explained in English.* Cincinnati: Joseph E. Hemann, 1853.

Barnouw, Victor. *Acculturation and Personality among the Wisconsin*

Chippewa. American Anthropological Association, Memoir 72. Menasha, Wis.: American Anthropological Association, 1950.

Barnouw, Victor. "A Chippewa Mide Priest's Description of the Medicine Dance." *Wisconsin Archeologist* 41 (1960): 77–97.

Barnouw, Victor. "The Phantasy World of a Chippewa Woman." *Psychiatry* 12 (1949): 67–76.

Barnouw, Victor. "A Psychological Interpretation of a Chippewa Origin Legend." *Journal of American Folklore* 68 (1955): 73–85, 211–23, and 341–55.

Barnouw, Victor. "Reminiscences of a Chippewa Mide Priest." *Wisconsin Archeologist* 35 (1954): 83–112.

Barnouw, Victor. *Wisconsin Chippewa Myths and Tales*. Madison: University of Wisconsin Press, 1977.

Barrett, Samuel A. "The Dream Dance of the Chippewa and Menominee Indians of Northern Wisconsin." *Bulletin of the Public Museum of the City of Milwaukee* 1 (1911): 251–406.

Bauxar, J. Joseph. "History of the Illinois Area." In Bruce G. Trigger, ed., *Handbook of North American Indians*, Vol. 15: *Northeast*, 594–601. William C. Sturtevant, general editor. Washington, D.C.: Smithsonian Institution Press, 1978.

Beaver, R. Pierce. "American Missionary Efforts to Influence Government Indian Policy." *Journal of Church and State* 5 (May 1963): 77–94.

Beaver, R. Pierce. *Church, State and the American Indians: Two and a Half Centuries of Partnership in Missions between Protestant Churches and Government*. St. Louis: Concordia Publishing House, 1966.

Beaver, R. Pierce. "Church, State, and the Nation." *Journal of Church and State* 4 (May 1962): 11–30.

Berkhofer, Robert F., Jr. "Barrier to Settlement: British Indian Policy in the Old Northwest, 1783–1794." In David M. Ellis, ed., *The Frontier in American Development: Essays in Honor of Paul Wallace Gates*, 249–76. Ithaca: Cornell University Press, 1969.

Berkhofer, Robert F., Jr. "Faith and Factionalism among the Senecas: Theory and Ethnohistory." *Ethnohistory* 12, no. 2 (1965): 99–112.

Berkhofer, Robert F., Jr. "The Political Context of a New Indian History." *Pacific Historical Review* 40, no. 3 (August 1971): 357–82.

Berkhofer, Robert F., Jr. *The White Man's Indian: Images of the American Indian from Columbus to the Present*. New York: Alfred A. Knopf, 1978.

Biddle, James W. "Recollections of Green Bay in 1816–17." In *Wisconsin Historical Collections*, Vol. 1, 49–63. 1855; rpt., Madison: State Historical Society of Wisconsin, 1903.

Billington, Ray Allen. *Westward Expansion: A History of the American Frontier*. New York: Macmillan, 1960.

Blair, Emma H., ed. *The Indian Tribes of the Upper Mississippi Valley and Region of the Great Lakes, as Described by Nicolas Perrot, French Comman-*

dant in the Northwest; Bacqueville de la Potherie, French Royal Commissioner to Canada; Morrell Marston, American Army Officer; and Thomas Forsyth, United States Agent at Fort Armstrong, Vols. 1 and 2. Cleveland: Arthur H. Clark, 1911–12.

Blessing, Fred K. "Discovery of a Chippewa Peyote Cult in Minnesota." *Minnesota Archaeologist* 23 (June 1961): 1–8.

Bloom, John Porter, ed. *The Territorial Papers of the United States*. Vol. 27: *The Territory of Wisconsin*. Washington, D.C.: National Archives, 1969.

Bloomfield, Leonard. *Menomini Texts*. Publications of the American Ethnological Society, Vol. 12. New York: G. E. Stechert, 1928.

Boatman, John F. *My Elders Taught Me: Aspects of Western Great Lakes American Indian Philosophy*. Lanham, Md.: University Press of America, 1982.

Boatman, John F. *Wisconsin American Indian History and Culture: A Survey of Selected Aspects*. Milwaukee: University of Wisconsin Press–Milwaukee, 1993.

Brasser, T. J. "Mahican." In Bruce G. Trigger, ed., *Handbook of North American Indians*, Vol. 15: *Northeast*, 198–212. William C. Sturtevant, general editor. Washington, D.C.: Smithsonian Institution Press, 1978.

Brown, Theodore T. "Plant Games and Toys of Chippewa Children." *Wisconsin Archeologist* 9 (1930): 185–86.

Braided Lives and Anthropology of Multicultural American Writings. St. Paul: Minnesota Humanities Committee, 1991.

Busiahu, Thomas R. *Chippewa Treaty Harvest of Natural Resources Wisconsin 1983–1990*. Odanah, Wis.: Great Lakes Indian Fish and Wildlife Commission, 1991.

Butterfield, C. W. *History of the Discovery of the Northwest by John Nicolet in 1634 with a Sketch of His Life*. Cincinnati: Robert Clark, 1881.

Calkins, Hiram. "Indian Nomenclature of Northern Wisconsin, with a Sketch of the Manners and Customs of the Chippewa." In *Wisconsin Historical Collections*, Vol. 1, 119–26. Madison: State Historical Society of Wisconsin, 1855.

Callender, Charles. "Fox." In Bruce G. Trigger, ed., *Handbook of North American Indians*, Vol. 15: *Northeast*, 636–47. William C. Sturtevant, general editor. Washington, D.C.: Smithsonian Institution Press, 1978.

Callender, Charles. "Great Lakes–Riverine Sociopolitical Organization." In Bruce G. Trigger, ed., *Handbook of North American Indians*, Vol. 15: *Northeast*, 610–21. William C. Sturtevant, general editor. Washington, D.C.: Smithsonian Institution Press, 1978.

Callender, Charles. "Illinois." In Bruce G. Trigger, ed., *Handbook of North American Indians*, Vol. 15: *Northeast*, 673–80. William C. Sturtevant, general editor. Washington, D.C.: Smithsonian Institution Press, 1978.

Callender, Charles, Richard K. Pope, and Susan M. Pope. "Kickapoo." In Bruce G. Trigger, ed., *Handbook of North American Indians*, Vol. 15: *Northeast*,

656–67. William C. Sturtevant, general editor. Washington, D.C.: Smithsonian Institution Press, 1978.

Callender, Charles. "Miami." In Bruce G. Trigger, ed., *Handbook of North American Indians,* Vol. 15: *Northeast, 681–89.* William C. Sturtevant, general editor. Washington, D.C.: Smithsonian Institution Press, 1978.

Callender, Charles. "Sauk." In Bruce G. Trigger, ed., *Handbook of North American Indians,* Vol. 15: *Northeast, 648–55.* William C. Sturtevant, general editor. Washington, D.C.: Smithsonian Institution Press, 1978.

Calloway, Colin G. *Crown and Calumet: British-Indian Relations, 1783–1815.* Norman: University of Oklahoma Press, 1987.

Calloway, Colin G. "Suspicion and Self-Interest: The British-Indian Alliance and the Peace of Paris." *The Historian* 48 (1985–86): 41–60.

Campisi, Jack. "Oneida." In Bruce G. Trigger, ed., *Handbook of North American Indians,* Vol. 15: *Northeast, 481–90.* William C. Sturtevant, general editor. Washington, D.C.: Smithsonian Institution Press, 1978.

Campisi, Jack. "The Oneida Treaty Period, 1783–1838." In Jack Campisi and Laurence M. Hauptman, eds., *The Oneida Indian Experience: Two Perspectives.* 48–64. Syracuse: Syracuse University Press, 1988.

Campisi, Jack, and Laurence M. Hauptman, eds. *The Oneida Indian Experience: Two Perspectives.* Syracuse: Syracuse University Press, 1988.

Carmichael, Ann G. "Infection, Hidden Hunger, and History." *Journal of Interdisciplinary History* 14, no. 2 (Autumn 1983): 259–64.

Carver, Jonathan. *The Journals of Jonathan Carver and Related Documents,* ed. John Parker et al. St. Paul: Minnesota Historical Society Press, 1976.

Caudill, William. "Psychological Characteristics of Acculturated Wisconsin Ojibwa Children." *American Anthropologist* 51 (July–September 1949): 409–27.

Chalou, George. "The Red Pawns Go to War: British-American Indian Relations, 1810–1815." Ph.D. diss., Indiana University, 1971.

Chapin, John. "Sketch of Cutting Marsh." *Wisconsin Historical Collections,* Vol. 15, 25–38. Madison: State Historical Society of Wisconsin, 1900.

Clements, William L., ed. "Rogers's Michillimackinac Journal." In American Antiquarian Society *Proceedings,* n.s. 28, no. 2 (1919): 258–73.

Clifton, James. "Potawatomi." In Bruce G. Trigger, ed., *Handbook of North American Indians,* Vol. 15: *Northeast, 725–42.* William C. Sturtevant, general editor. Washington, D.C.: Smithsonian Institution Press, 1978.

Clifton, James. *The Prairie People: Continuity and Change in Potawatomi Culture, 1665–1965.* Lawrence: Regents Press of Kansas, 1977.

Clifton, James. "Wisconsin Death March: Explaining the Extremes in the Old Northwest Indian Removal." *Transactions of the Wisconsin Academy of Sciences, Arts and Letters.* 75 (1987): 1–39.

Cohen, Felix S. *Handbook of Federal Indian Law, with Reference Tables and Index.* 1942; rpt., Albuquerque: University of New Mexico Press, 1972.

Bibliography

Coleman, Michael C. "Not Race, but Grace: Presbyterian Missionaries and the American Indian, 1837–1893." *Journal of American History* 67 (June 1975): 41–60.

Coleman, Sister Bernard, Ellen Frogner, and Estelle Eich. *Ojibwa Myths and Legends.* Minneapolis: Ross and Haines, 1962.

Collier, John. *From Every Zenith.* Denver: Sage Books, 1963.

Collier, John. *The Indians of the Americas.* New York: W. W. Norton, 1947.

Colton, Calvin. *A Tour of the American Lakes, and among the Indians of the North-West Territory in 1830: Disclosing the Character and Prospects of the Indian Race . . .* 2 vols. London: F. Wetley and A. H. Davis, 1833.

Conkey, Laura E., Ethel Boissevain, and Ives Goddard. "Indians of Southern New England and Long Island: Late Period." In Bruce G. Trigger, ed., *Handbook of North American Indians,* Vol. 15: *Northeast,* 177–89. William C. Sturtevant, general editor. Washington, D.C.: Smithsonian Institution Press, 1978.

Connor, Thomas. "The Diary of Thomas Connor." In Charles M. Gates, ed., *Five Fur Traders in the Northwest,* 249–78. St. Paul: Minnesota Historical Society, 1965.

Cope, Alfred. "Mission to the Menominee: A Quaker's Green Bay Diary." *Wisconsin Magazine of History* 49, no. 4 (Summer 1966): 302–23; 50, no. 1 (Autumn 1966): 18–42; 50, no. 2 (Winter 1967): 120–44; 50, no. 3 (Spring 1967): 211–41.

Copway, George. *The Traditional History and Characteristic Sketches of the Ojibway Nation. By G. Copway, or Kah-ge-ga-gah-bowh, Chief of the Ojibway Nation.* Boston: B. F. Mussey and Co., 1851.

Cronon, William. *Changes in the Land: Indians, Colonists, and the Ecology of New England.* New York: Hill and Wang, 1983.

Crosby, Alfred W. *Ecological Imperialism. The Biological Expansion of Europe, 900–1900.* Cambridge: Cambridge University Press, 1986.

Cruikshank, Ernest Alexander. "Robert Dickson, the Indian Trader." In *Wisconsin Historical Collections,* Vol. 12, 133–53. Madison: State Historical Society of Wisconsin, 1892.

Curot, Michel. "A Wisconsin Fur-Trader's Journal, 1803–04." *Wisconsin Historical Collections* 20 (1911): 396–471.

Current, Richard. *Wisconsin: A Bicentennial History.* New York: W. W. Norton, 1977.

Danziger, Edmund Jefferson, Jr. *The Chippewas of Lake Superior.* Norman: University of Oklahoma Press, 1978.

Davidson, John Nelson. "Mission on Chequamegon Bay." In *Wisconsin Historical Collections,* Vol. 12, 434–52. Madison: State Historical Society of Wisconsin, 1892.

Davis, David Brion. *Antebellum American Culture: An Interpretive Anthology.* Lexington, Mass.: D. C. Heath, 1979.

Deloria, Vine, and Clifford M. Lytle. *American Indians, American Justice.* Austin; University of Texas Press, 1983.

Densmore, Francis. *Chippewa Customs.* 1929; rpt., St. Paul: Minnesota Historical Society Press, 1979.

Dewdney, Selwyn. *The Sacred Scrolls of the Southern Ojibway.* Toronto: University of Toronto Press, 1975.

Diamond, Stanley, ed. *Culture and History: Essays in Honor of Paul Radin.* New York: Columbia University Press, 1960.

"Dickson and Grignon Papers—1812–1815." In *Wisconsin Historical Collections,* Vol. 11, 271–315. Madison: State Historical Society of Wisconsin, 1888.

Diedrich, Mark, comp. *Ojibway Oratory: Great Moments in the Recorded Speech of the Chippewa, 1659–1889.* Rochester, Minn.: Coyote Books, 1990.

Diedrich, Mark, comp. *Winnebago Oratory: Great Moments in the Recorded Speech of the Hochungra, 1742–1887.* Rochester, Minn.: Coyote Books, 1991.

Dobyns, Henry F. *Their Number Become Thinned: Native American Population Dynamics in Eastern North America.* Knoxville: University of Tennessee Press, 1983.

Doty, James D. "Northern Wisconsin in 1820." In *Wisconsin Historical Collections,* Vol. 7, 195–206. Madison: State Historical Society of Wisconsin, 1876.

Draper, Lyman C. "Additional Notes on Eleazer Williams." In *Wisconsin Historical Collections,* Vol. 8, 353–69. 1879; rpt., Madison: State Historical Society of Wisconsin, 1908.

Ducatel, J. J. "A Fortnight among the Chippewas of Lake Superior." In *the Indian Miscellany . . . ,* ed. William Wallace Beach, 361–75. Albany: J. Munsell, 1877.

Eastman, Mary H. *Dahcotah; or, Life and Legends of the Sioux around Fort Snelling.* New York: John Wiley, 1849.

Eaton, S. Boyd, and Melvin Konner. "Paleolithic Nutrition: Consideration of Its Natural and Current Implications." *New England Journal of Medicine* 312, no. 5 (January 31, 1985): 283–89.

Eccles, W. J. "A Belated View of Harold Adams Innis, *The Fur Trade of Canada.*" *Canadian Historical Review* 60 (1979): 419–41.

Edmunds, R. David. *The Potawatomis, Keepers of the Fire.* Norman: University of Oklahoma Press, 1978.

Edmunds, R. David. *The Shawnee Prophet.* Lincoln: University of Nebraska Press, 1983.

Edmunds, R. David, ed. *American Indian Leaders: Studies in Diversity.* Lincoln: University of Nebraska Press, 1980.

Eggan, Fred. *The American Indian.* Chicago: Aldine Publishing Co., 1966.

Ellis, Albert G. "Fifty-four Years' Recollections of Men and Events in Wisconsin." In *Wisconsin Historical Collections,* Vol. 7, 207–68. 1876; rpt., Madison: State Historical Society of Wisconsin, 1908.

Ellis, Albert G. "Recollections of Rev. Eleazer Williams." In *Wisconsin Historical Collections,* Vol. 8, 322–52. 1879; rpt., Madison: State Historical Society of Wisconsin, 1908.

Ellis, Albert G. "Some Accounts of the Advent of the New York Indians into Wisconsin." In *Wisconsin Historical Collections,* Vol. 2, 415–49. Madison: State Historical Society of Wisconsin, 1856.

Ellis, David M., ed. *The Frontier in American Development: Essays in Honor of Paul Wallace Gates.* Ithaca: Cornell University Press, 1969.

Erikson, Kai T. *Everything in Its Path: Destruction of Community in the Buffalo Creek Flood.* New York: Simon and Schuster, 1972.

Fay, George E., comp. *Treaties between the Menominee Indians and the United States of America, 1817–1859.* Miscellaneous Series, No. 3. University of Wisconsin–Oshkosh, Museum of Anthropology, 1965.

Feest, Johanna E., and Christian F. Feest. "Ottawa." In Bruce G. Trigger, ed., *Handbook of North American Indians,* Vol. 15: *Northeast,* 772–86. William C. Sturtevant, general editor. Washingon, D. C.: Smithsonian Institution Press, 1978.

Fixico, Donald L., ed. *An Anthology of Western Great Lakes Indian History.* Milwaukee: American Indian Studies Program, University of Wisconsin–Milwaukee, 1987.

Freilich, Morris. "Cultural Persistence among the Modern Iroquois." *Anthropos* 53, nos. 3–4 (1958): 473–83.

Friedl, Ernestine. "An Attempt at Directed Culture Change; Leadership among the Chippewa, 1640–1948." Ph.D. diss., Columbia University, New York, 1950.

Friedl, Ernestine. "Persistence in Chippewa Culture and Personality." *American Anthropologist* 58 (October 1956): 814–25.

Fries, Robert F. *Empire in Pine: The Study of Lumbering in Wisconsin, 1830–1900.* Madison: State Historical Society of Wisconsin, 1951.

Funmaker, Walter Willard. "The Winnebago Black Bear Subclan: A Defended Culture." Ph.D. diss., University of Minnesota, 1986.

Galbraith, John S. "British-American Competition in the Border Fur Trade of the 1820s." *Minnesota History* 36 (September 1959): 241–49.

Gates, Charles M., ed. *Five Fur Traders in the Northwest.* St. Paul: Minnesota Historical Society, 1965.

Gibbon, Guy E. "A Brief History of Oneota Research in Wisconsin." *Wisconsin Magazine of History* 53 (1970): 278–93.

Gibbon, Guy E. "Cultural Dynamics and the Development of the Oneota Life Way in Wisconsin." *American Antiquity* 37 (1972) 166–85.

Gibbon, Guy E. "The Mississippi Tradition: Oneota Culture." *Wisconsin Archeologist* 67, nos. 3–4 (1986): 314–64.

Gillin, John. "Acquired Drives in Culture Contact." *American Anthropologist* 44 (October–December 1942): 545–54.

Gilman, Rhoda R. "The Fur Trade in the Upper Mississippi Valley, 1630–1850." *Wisconsin Magazine of History* 58 (Autumn 1974–75): 3–18.

Goddard, Ives. "Delaware." In Bruce G. Trigger, ed., *Handbook of North American Indians,* Vol. 15: *Northeast,* 213–39. William C. Sturtevant, general editor. Washington, D.C.: Smithsonian Institution Press, 1978.

Goddard, Ives. "Mascouten." In Bruce G. Trigger, ed., *Handbook of North American Indians,* Vol. 15: *Northeast,* 668–72. William C. Sturtevant, general editor. Washington, D.C.: Smithsonian Institution Press, 1978.

Goddard, James Stanley. "Journal of a Voyage, 1766–67," ed. Carolyn Gilman. In Jonathan Carver, *The Journals of Jonathan Carver and Related Documents,* ed. John Parker et al., 180–91. St. Paul: Minnesota Historical Society Press, 1976.

Goldstein, Lynne G. *Prehistoric Indians of Wisconsin.* Milwaukee: Milwaukee Public Museum, 1985.

Gorrell, James. "Lieutenant James Gorrell's Journal of 1762." In *Wisconsin Historical Collections,* Vol. 1, 24–48. 1855; rpt., Madison: State Historical Society of Wisconsin, 1903.

Griffin, James B. *Archaeology of Eastern United States.* Chicago: University of Chicago Press, 1952.

Grignon, Augustin. "Seventy-two Years' Recollections of Wisconsin." In *Wisconsin Historical Collections,* Vol. 3, 195–295. 1857; rpt., Madison: State Historical Society of Wisconsin, 1904.

A Guide to Understanding Chippewa Treaty Rights. Odanah, Wis.: Great Lakes Indian Fish and Wildlife Commission, 1991.

Haas, Theodore H. "The Legal Aspects of Indian Affairs from 1887 to 1957." *Annals of the American Academy of Political and Social Science* 311 (May 1957): 12–22.

Haeger, John D. "A Time of Change: Green Bay, 1815–1834." *Wisconsin Magazine of History* 54 (1970–71): 285–98.

Hagen, William T. *Indian Police and Judges: Experiments in Acculturation and Control.* New Haven: Yale University Press, 1966.

Hagen, William T. "Justifying Dispossession of the Indians: The Land Utilization Argument." In Christopher Vecsey and Robert W. Venables, eds., *American Indian Environments: Ecological Issues in Native American History,* 65–80. Syracuse: Syracuse University Press, 1980.

Hagen, William T. *The Sac and Fox Indians.* Norman: University of Oklahoma Press, 1958.

Hall, Robert L. *The Archaeology of Carcajou Point, with an Interpretation of the Development of Oneota Culture in Wisconsin.* 2 vols. Madison: University of Wisconsin Press, 1962.

Hall, Sherman. "Ojibwas." *Missionary Herald* 45 (1849): 14–15.

Hall, Sherman. "Prospects of the Ojibwa Mission." *Missionary Herald* 43 (1847): 161–62.

Hallowell, A. Irving. *The Role of Conjuring in Saulteaux Society.* New York: Octagon Books, 1971.

Hallowell, A. Irving. *Culture and Experience.* Philadelphia Anthropological Society, Vol. 4. Philadelphia: University of Pennsylvania Press, 1955.

Heckewelder, John. *History, Manners, and Customs of the Indian Nations Who Once Inhabited Pennsylvania and the Neighboring States.* 1876; rpt., New York: Arno Press, 1971.

Henry, Alexander. *Travels and Adventures in Canada and the Indian Territories between the Years 1760 and 1776.* 1921; rpt., Ann Arbor: University Microfilms, Inc., 1966.

Hertzberg, Hazel W. *The Search for an American Indian Identity: Modern Pan-Indian Movements.* Syracuse: Syracuse University Press, 1971.

Herzberg, Stephen J. "The Menominee Indians: From Treaty to Termination." *Wisconsin Magazine of History* 60 (Summer 1977): 267–329.

Hickerson, Harold. *Chippewa Indians.* Vol. 4: *Ethnohistory of Chippewa in Central Minnesota.* comp. and ed. David Agee Horr. 9–253. American Indian Ethnohistory, Northeastern Indians. New York: Garland Press, 1974.

Hickerson, Harold. *The Chippewa and Their Neighbors: A Study in Ethnohistory.* New York: Holt, Rinehart and Winston, 1970.

Hickerson, Harold. *Chippewa Indians.* Vol. 3: *Ethnohistory of Chippewa of Lake Superior.* comp. and ed. David Agee Horr. 13–180. American Indian Ethnohistory, Northeastern Indians. New York: Garland Publishing Co., 1974.

Hickerson, Harold. *Chippewa Indians.* Vol. 2: *Ethnohistory of Mississippi Bands and Pillager and Winnibigoshish Bands of Chippewa.* comp. and ed. David Agee Horr. American Indian Ethnohistory, Northeastern Indians. New York: Garland Publishing Co., 1974.

Hickerson, Harold. "The Chippewa of the Upper Great Lakes: A Study in Sociopolitical Change." In Eleanor B. Leacock and Nancy Oestreich Lurie, eds., *North American Indians in Historical Perspective,* 169–99. New York: Random House, 1971.

Hickerson, Harold. "The Feast of the Dead among the Seventeenth Century Algonkians of the Upper Great Lakes." *American Anthropologist* 62 (1960): 81–107.

Hickerson, Harold. *The Southwestern Chippewa: An Ethnohistorical Study.* American Anthropological Association Memoir 92. Menasha, Wis., 1962.

Hodge, Fredrick Webb, ed. *Handbook of American Indians North of Mexico.* 2 vols. Smithsonian Institution, Bureau of American Ethnology, Bulletin 30. Washington, D.C.: GPO, 1907–8.

Hodge, William H. "The Indians of Wisconsin." In *State of Wisconsin 1975 Blue Book,* 95–193. Madison: Department of Administration, 1975.

Bibliography

Hoffman, Walter J. "The Menomini Indians." In *14th Annual Report of the Bureau of American Ethnology for the Years 1892–1893*. Part 1. Washington, D.C.: GPO, 1896.

Hoffman, Walter J. "The Midēwiwin or 'Grand Medicine Society' of the Ojibwa." In *7th Annual Report of the Bureau of American Ethnology for the Years 1885–1886*, 143–300. Washington, D.C.: Bureau of American Ethnology, 1891.

Hollatz, Tom. *Louis No. 1: The Life and Legend of Louis St. Germaine.* Neshkoro, Wis.: Laranmark Press, 1984.

Horsman, Reginald. "British Indian Policy in the Northwest, 1807–1812." *Mississippi Valley Historical Review* 45, no. 1 (June 1958): 51–66.

Horsman, Reginald. *Expansion and American Indian Policy, 1783–1812.* East Lansing: Michigan State University Press, 1967.

Horsman, Reginald. "Wisconsin and the War of 1812." *Wisconsin Magazine of History* 46 (Autumn 1962): 3–15.

Horsman, Reginald. "The Wisconsin Oneidas in the Preallotment Years." In Jack Campisi and Laurence M. Hauptman, eds., *The Oneida Indian Experience: Two Perspectives*, 65–82. Syracuse: Syracuse University Press, 1988.

Hubbard, Gurdon Saltonstall. *The Autobiography of Gurdon Saltonstall Hubbard.* Chicago: R. R. Donnelly and Sons, 1911.

Hurst, James Willard. *Law and Economic Growth.* Madison: University of Wisconsin Press, 1984.

Jackson, Donald, ed. *Black Hawk, an Autobiography.* Urbana: University of Illinois Press, 1964.

Jackson, Donald, ed. *The Journals of Zebulon Montgomery Pike: With Letters and Related Documents*, Vol. 1. Norman: University of Oklahoma Press, 1966.

Jacobs, Wilbur R. *Dispossessing the American Indian.* New York: Charles Scribner's Sons, 1972.

Jacobs, Wilbur R. *Wilderness Politics and Indian Gifts: The Northern Colonial Frontier, 1748–1763.* Lincoln: University of Nebraska Press, 1966.

Johnson, Elden. "The Ojibwa." In Robert F. Spencer, Jesse D. Jennings, et al., *The Native Americans*, 398–401. New York: Harper and Row, 1965.

Johnston, Basil. *Ojibway Heritage: The Ceremonies, Rituals, Songs, Dances Prayers and Legends of the Ojibway.* Toronto: McClelland and Stewart Ltd., 1979.

Joint Hearings before the Subcommittees of the Committees on Interior and Insular Affairs. "Termination of Federal Supervision over Certain Tribes of Indians," Pt. 6, 83d Cong., 2d sess., March 10–12, 1954.

Jones, J. A. *Winnebago Ethnology.* comp. and ed. David Agee Horr, 27–223. American Indian Ethnohistory, North Central and Northeastern Indians. New York: Garland Publishing Co., 1974.

Jones, Rev. Peter. *History of the Ojebway Indians; with Especial Reference to Their Conversion to Christianity*. Freeport, N.Y.: Books for Libraries, 1970.

Jones, William. "Fox Texts." *Publications of the American Ethnological Society*, Vol. 1. Leiden, The Netherlands, 1907.

Kay, Jeanne. "John Lawe: Green Bay Trader." *Wisconsin Magazine of History* 64 (Autumn 1980): 3–27.

Kay, Jeanne. "The Land of La Baye: The Ecological Impact of the Green Bay Fur Trade, 1634–1836." Ph.D. diss., University of Wisconsin, Madison, 1977.

Kay, Jeanne. "Native Americans in the Fur Trade and Wildlife Depletion." *Environmental Review* 9 (Summer 1985): 118–30.

Kay, Jeanne. "Wisconsin Indian Hunting Patterns 1634–1836." *Annals of the Association of American Geographers* 69, no. 3 (September 1979): 402–18.

Keating, William H. *Narrative of an Expedition to the Source of St. Peter's River, Lake Winnepeek, Lake of the Woods, etc. etc., Performed in the Year of 1823, by Order of the Hon. J. C. Calhoun, Secretary of War, under the Command of Stephen H. Long, Major U.S.T.E.* 2 vols. Philadelphia: H. C. Carey and I. Lea, 1824.

Keesing, Felix M. *The Menomini Indians of Wisconsin: A Study of Three Centuries of Cultural Contact and Change.* 1939; rpt., Madison: University of Wisconsin Press, 1987.

Keller, Robert H. "An Economic History of Indian Treaties in the Great Lakes Region." *American Indian Journal* 4 (February 1978): 2–20.

Kelley, Lawrence C. "John Collier and the Indian New Deal: An Assessment." In Jane F. Smith and Robert M. Kvasnicka, eds., *Indian-White Relations: A Persistent Paradox,* 227–41. Washington, D.C.: Howard University Press, 1976.

Kellogg, Louise Phelps. *The British Regime in Wisconsin.* Madison: State Historical Society of Wisconsin, 1935.

Kellogg, Louise Phelps. "The Fox Indians during the French Regime." In *Proceedings of the State Historical Society of Wisconsin for 1907,* 142–88. Madison, 1908.

Kellogg, Louise Phelps. *The French Regime in Wisconsin and the Northwest.* Madison: State Historical Society of Wisconsin, 1925.

Kellogg, Louise Phelps. "The Removal of the Winnebago." *Transactions of the Wisconsin Academy of Sciences, Arts and Letters* 21 (1924): 23–29.

Kellogg, Louise Phelps, ed. *Early Narratives of the Northwest, 1634–1699.* New York: Charles Scribner's Sons, 1917.

Kemper, Jackson. "Journal of an Episcopalian Missionary's Tour to Green Bay, 1834." *Wisconsin Historical Collections,* Vol. 14, 394–449. Madison: State Historical Society of Wisconsin, 1898.

Kidd, K. E. "A Radiocarbon Date on a Midewiwin Scroll from Burntside Lake, Ontario." *Ontario Archaeology* 35 (1981): 41–43.

Kimball, Solon T., and James B. Watson, eds. *Crossing Cultural Boundaries:*

The Anthropological Experience. San Francisco: Chandler Publishing Co., 1972.

Kinietz, W. Vernon. *The Indians of the Western Great Lakes: 1615–1760.* Ann Arbor: University of Michigan Press, 1965.

Kinzie, Mrs. John H. *Wau-Bun, the "Early Days" in the North West.* New York: Derby and Jackson, 1856.

Kohl, Johann Georg. *Kitchi-Gami: Life among the Lake Superior Ojibway.* St. Paul: Minnesota Historical Society Press, 1985.

Kuhm, Herbert W. "Indian Place Names in Wisconsin." *Wisconsin Archeologist* 33 (1952): 1–57.

Kvasnicka, Robert M., and Herman J. Viola, eds. *The Commissioners of Indian Affairs, 1824–1977.* Lincoln: University of Nebraska Press, 1979.

Landes, Ruth. *The Mystic Lake Sioux: Sociology of the Mdewakantonwan Santee.* Madison: University of Wisconsin Press, 1968.

Landes, Ruth. *Ojibwa Religion and the Midewiwin.* Madison: University of Wisconsin Press, 1968.

Landes, Ruth. *Ojibwa Sociology.* Columbia University Contributions to Anthropology 29. New York: Columbia University Press, 1937.

Landes, Ruth. *The Ojibwa Woman.* Columbia University Contribution to Anthropology 31. New York: Columbia University Press, 1938.

Lapham, I. A. *The Antiquities of Wisconsin, as Surveyed and Described.* New York: AMS Press and Peabody Museum of Archaeology and Ethnology, 1973.

La Ronde, John T. de. "Personal Narrative." *Wisconsin Historical Collections,* Vol. 7, 345–65. 1876; rpt., Madison: State Historical Society of Wisconsin, 1908.

"Lawe and Grignon Papers, 1794–1821." In *Wisconsin Historical Collections,* Vol. 10, 90–141. Madison: State Historical Society of Wisconsin, 1883–85.

Lawson, Publius V. "The Potawatomi." *Wisconsin Archeologist* 19 (April 1920): 41–116.

Leacock, Eleanor B., and Nancy O. Lurie, eds. *North American Indians in Historical Perspective.* New York: Random House, 1971.

Leeds, Anthony. "Ecological Determinants of Chieftainship among the Yaruro Indians of Venezuela." In Andrew P. Vayda, ed., *Environment and Cultural Behavior: Ecological Studies in Cultural Anthropology,* 377–94. Published for the American Museum of Natural History. Garden City, N.Y.: Natural History Museum, 1969.

Levine, Stuart, and Nancy O. Lurie, eds. *The American Indian Today.* Deland, Fla.: Everett/Edwards, 1965.

Lipps, Eva. *Die Reiserate der Ojibwa-Indianer Wirtschaft und Recht eines Erntevolkes.* Berlin: Akademic Verlag, 1956.

Lurie, Nancy Oestreich. "An American Indian Renascence?" In Stuart Levine and Nancy Oestreich Lurie, eds., *The American Indian Today*, 25–50. Deland, Fla.: Everett/Edwards, 1965.

Lurie, Nancy Oestreich. "Historical Backgrounds." In Stuart Levine and Nancy Oestreich Lurie, eds., *The American Indian Today*, 25–45. Deland, Fla.: Everett/Edwards, 1965.

Lurie, Nancy Oestreich. "In Search of Chaetar: New Findings on Black Hawk's Surrender." *Wisconsin Magazine of History* 71, no. 3 (Spring 1988): 353–64.

Lurie, Nancy Oestreich. *North American Indian Lives*. Milwaukee: Milwaukee Public Museum, 1985.

Lurie, Nancy Oestreich. "Two Dollars." In Solon T. Kimball and James B. Watson, eds., *Crossing Cultural Boundaries: The Anthropological Experience*, 158–61. San Francisco: Chandler Publishing Co., 1972.

Lurie, Nancy O. "The Voice of the American Indian: Report on the American Indian Chicago Conference." *Current Anthropology* 2 (1961): 478–500.

Lurie, Nancy Oestreich. "Winnebago." In Bruce G. Trigger, ed., *Handbook of North American Indians*, Vol. 15: *Northeast*, 690–707. William C. Sturtevant, general editor. Washington, D.C.: Smithsonian Institution Press, 1978.

Lurie, Nancy Oestreich. "Winnebago Protohistory." In Stanley Diamond, ed., *Culture and History: Essays in Honor of Paul Radin*, 790–808. New York: Columbia University Press, 1960.

Lurie, Nancy Oestreich. *Wisconsin Indians*. Madison: State Historical Society of Wisconsin, 1980.

Lurie, Nancy Oestreich, ed. *Mountain Wolf Woman: The Autobiography of a Winnebago Indian*. Ann Arbor: University of Michigan Press, 1961.

Lyford, Carie A. *The Crafts of the Ojibwa*. Washington, D.C.: U.S. Office of Education, 1942.

McKenney, Thomas L. *Sketches of a Tour to the Lakes*. 1827; rpt., Minneapolis: Ross and Haines, 1959.

MacLeod, D. Peter. "Microbes and Muskets: Smallpox and the Participation of the Amerindian Allies of New France in the Seven Years' War." *Ethnohistory* 39 (Winter 1992): 42–64.

McNickle, D'Arcy. *Native American Tribalism: Indian Survivals and Renewals*. New York: Oxford University Press, 1973.

Magnaghi, Russell M. "Red Slavery in the Great Lakes Country during the French and British Regimes." *Old Northwest* 12, no. 2 (Summer 1986): 201–17.

Malhiot, François Victor. "A Wisconsin Fur-Trader's Journal, 1804–05." In *Wisconsin Historical Collections*, Vol. 19, 163–233. Madison: State Historical Society of Wisconsin, 1910.

Marble, H. P. "The Field Matron in Indian Work." In *Report of the Thirty-*

Fourth Annual Lake Mohonk Conference on the Indian and Other Dependent Peoples, 106–7. N.p., 1916.

Marryat, Frederick. "An English Officer's Description of Wisconsin in 1837." In *Wisconsin Historical Collections,* Vol. 14, 137–54. Madison: State Historical Society of Wisconsin, 1898.

Mason, Carol I. *Introduction to Wisconsin Indians: Prehistory to Statehood.* Salem, Wis.: Sheffield Publishing Co., 1987.

"Menominee Restoration Act. December 22, 1973." *United States Statutes at Large* 87: 770–73.

Meriam, Lewis, et al. *The Problem of Indian Administration.* Institute for Goverment Research, Studies in Administration. Baltimore: Johns Hopkins University Press, 1928.

Meyer, Melissa. "Tradition and the Market: The Social Relations of the White Earth Anishinaabeg, 1889–1920." Ph.D. diss. University of Minnesota, 1985.

Miller, Helen Miner, Nadine Day Sieber, and Nancy Oestreich Lurie. *The Wisconsin Winnebago People: Historical Background of the Wisconsin Winnebago Indian People.* Rev. ed. N.p.: Wisconsin Winnebago Business Committee, 1967.

Mooney, James. "The Ghost Dance Religion and the Sioux Outbreak of 1890." In *14th Annual Report of the Bureau of American Ethnology for the Years 1892–1893,* Part 1, 653–1136. Washington, D.C.: Bureau of American Ethnology, 1896.

Morse, Jedediah. *A Report to the Secretary of War of the United States on Indian Affairs.* New Haven: Converse, 1822.

Morse, Richard E. "The Chippewas of Lake Superior." In *Wisconsin Historical Collections,* Vol. 3, 338–69. Madison: State Historical Society of Wisconsin, 1856.

Morstad, Alexander E. *The Reverend Erik Olsen Morstad: His Missionary Work among the Wisconsin Pottawatomie Indians.* Clearwater, Fla.: Eldnar Press, 1971.

Nesbit, Robert C. *The History of Wisconsin.* Vol. 3: *Urbanization and Industrialization, 1873–1893.* Madison: State Historical Society of Wisconsin, 1985.

Nesbit, Robert C. *Wisconsin: A History.* Madison: State Historical Society of Wisconsin, 1973.

Neveu, Gustave de. "A Menominee Indian Payment in 1838." *Wisconsin Historical Society Proceedings 1910,* Vol. 58 (Madison, 1911): 153–6 .

Nichols, Roger L. *Black Hawk and the Warrior's Path.* Arlington Heights, Ill.: Harlan Davidson, 1992.

Oestreich [Lurie], Nancy. "Cultural Change among the Wisconsin Winnebago." *Wisconsin Archeologist* 25, no. 4 (1944): 124–25.

Oestreich [Lurie], Nancy. "Trends of Change in Patterns of Chil Care and

Training among the Wisconsin Winnebago." *Wisconsin Archeologist* 29, n.s. (September–December 1948): 40–140.

"Ojibwas." *Missionary Herald* 47 (1851): 100–101.

Orfield, Gary. *A Study of Termination Policy.* Denver: National Congress of American Indians, 1965.

Orfield, Gary. "The War on Menominee Poverty." *Wisconsin Indian Research Journal* 1 (October 1965): 54–63.

Ortiz, Alfonso. *The Tewa World: Space, Time, Being, and Becoming in a Pueblo Society.* Chicago: University of Chicago Press, 1969.

Ourada, Patricia. *The Menominee Indians: A History.* Norman: University of Oklahoma Press, 1979.

Peckham, Howard H. *Pontiac and the Indian Uprising.* Chicago: University of Chicago Press, 1961.

Pelto, Gretel H., and Pertti J. Pelto. "Diet and Delocalization: Dietary Changes since 1750." *Journal of Interdisciplinary History* 14, no. 2 (Autumn 1983): 507–28.

Peroff, Nicholas C. *Menominee Drums: Tribal Termination and Restoration, 1954–1974.* Norman: University of Oklahoma Press, 1982.

Peterson, Jacqueline L. "The People In Between: Indian-White Marriage and the Genesis of a Métis Society in the Great Lakes Regions, 1680–1830." Ph.D. diss., University of Illinois at Chicago, 1981.

Philp, Kenneth R. *Indian Self-Rule: First-hand Accounts of Indian-White Relations from Roosevelt to Reagan.* Salt Lake City: Howe Brothers, 1986.

Philp, Kenneth R. "John Collier, 1933–45." In Robert M. Kvasnicka and Herman J. Viola, eds., *The Commissioners of Indian Affairs, 1824–1977,* 273–82. Lincoln: University of Nebraska Press, 1979.

Philp, Kenneth R. "John Collier and the Indians of the Americas: The Dream and the Reality." *Prologue* 11 (Spring 1979): 5–21.

Philp, Kenneth R. *John Collier's Crusade for Indian Reform, 1920–1954.* Tucson: University of Arizona Press, 1977.

Pitzel, Rev. John H. *Lights and Shades of Missionary Life: Containing Travels, Sketches, Incidents and Missionary Efforts during Nine Years Spent in the Region of Lake Superior.* Cincinnati: Crauston and Stows, 1857.

Pond, Peter. "The Narrative of Peter Pond." In Charles M. Gates, ed., *Five Fur Traders of the Northwest,* 18–59. St. Paul: Minnesota Historical Society Press, 1965.

Porlier, Louis B. "Narrative by Louis B. Porlier." In *Wisconsin Historical Collections,* Vol. 15, 439–47. Madison: State Historical Society of Wisconsin, 1900.

"Prairie du Chien Documents, 1814–15": 'Capt. Thomas Anderson to Lieut. Col. R. McDouall, 18 October 1814.' In *Wisconsin Historical Collections,* Vol. 9, 262–81. Madison: State Historical Society of Wisconsin, 1882.

Prucha, Francis Paul. *American Indian Policy in the Formative Years: The Indian Trade and Intercourse Acts, 1790–1834.* Cambridge, Mass.: Harvard University Press, 1962.

Prucha, Francis Paul. *The Great Father: The United States Government and the American Indian,* Vol. 1. Lincoln: University of Nebraska Press, 1984.

Prucha, Francis Paul. *The Indians in American Society from the Revolutionary War to the Present.* Berkeley: University of California Press, 1985.

Prucha, Francis Paul, and Donald F. Carmony, eds. "A Memorandum of Lewis Cass Concerning a System for the Regulation of Indian Affairs." *Wisconsin Magazine of History* 52 (Autumn 1968): 35–50.

Quimby, George Irving. *Indian Culture and European Trade Goods: The Archaeology of the Historic Period in the Western Great Lakes Region.* Madison: University of Wisconsin Press, 1966.

Quimby, George Irving. *Indian Life in the Upper Great Lakes: 11,000 B.C. to A.D. 1800.* Chicago: University of Chicago Press, 1960.

Quinten, B. T. "Oklahoma Tribes, the Great Depression, and the Indian Bureau." In Bernard Sternsher, ed., *Hitting Home: The Great Depression in Town and Country,* 200–216. Chicago: Quadrangle Books, 1970.

Radin, Paul. *The Autobiography of a Winnebago Indian.* 1920; rpt., New York: Dover, 1963.

Radin, Paul. "The Influence of the Whites on Winnebago Culture." In *Proceedings of the State Historical Society of Wisconsin 1913,* Vol. 61, 137–45. Madison, 1914.

Radin, Paul. *The Trickster: A Study in American Indian Mythology.* New York: Schocken Books, 1972.

Radin, Paul. *The Winnebago Tribe.* 1923; rpt., Lincoln: University of Nebraska Press, 1970.

Radisson, Pierre Esprit. *The Explorations of Radisson,* ed. Arthur T. Adams. Rpt., Minneapolis: Ross and Haines, 1967.

Ray, Verne F. *The Menominee Tribe of Indians, 1940–1970.* Escanaba, Mich.: Photo Offset Printing Company, 1971.

Reagan, Albert B. "Picture Writings of the Chippewa Indians." *Wisconsin Archeologist* 6 (1927): 80–83.

"The Relationship of Nutrition, Disease, and Social Conditions: A Graphical Presentation." *Journal of Interdisciplinary History* 14, no. 2 (Autumn 1983): 503–6.

Rethinking Columbus. Milwaukee: Milwaukee Public Schools–Rethinking Schools, Ltd., n.d.

Ritzenthaler, Robert E. "Chippewa Preoccupation with Health; Changes in a Traditional Attitude Resulting from Modern Health Problems." *Bulletin of the Public Museum of the City of Milwaukee* 19, no. 4 (December 1953): 175–257.

Ritzenthaler, Robert E. "The Menominee Indian Sawmill: A Successful Community Project." *Wisconsin Archeologist* 32 (June): 69–74.

Ritzenthaler, Robert E. "The Oneida Indians of Wisconsin." *Bulletin of the Public Museum of the City of Milwaukee* 19, no. 1 (November 1950): 1–52.

Ritzenthaler, Robert E. "The Potawatomi Indians of Wisconsin." *Bulletin of the Public Museum of the City of Milwaukee* 19, no. 3 (1953): 105–74.

Ritzenthaler, Robert E. "Southwestern Chippewa." In Bruce G. Trigger, ed., *Handbook of North American Indians,* Vol. 15: *Northeast,* 743–59. William C. Sturtevant, general editor. Washington, D.C.: Smithsonian Institution Press, 1978.

Ritzenthaler, Robert E., and Pat Ritzenthaler. *The Woodland Indians of the Western Great Lakes.* American Museum Science Book B 21. Garden City, N.Y.: Published for the American Museum of Natural History by the Natural History Press, 1970.

Rogers, E. S. "Southeastern Ojibwa." In Bruce G. Trigger, ed., *Handbook of North American Indians,* Vol. 15: *Northeast,* 760–71. William C. Sturtevant, general editor. Washington, D.C.: Smithsonian Institution Press, 1978.

Rosenthal, Elizabeth Clark. "Culture and the American Indian." In Stuart Levine and Nancy Oestreich Lurie, eds., *The American Indian Today,* 47–52. Deland, Fla.: Everett/Edwards, 1965.

Ross, Thomas E., and Tyrel G. Moore, eds. *A Cultural Geography of North American Indians.* Boulder: Westview Press, 1987.

Roufs, Timothy G., comp. *Index to the Works Listed in the Working Bibliography of Chippewa/Ojibwa/Anishinabe and Selected Related Works.* Duluth: University of Minnesota Great Lakes Superior Basin Studies Center, 1983.

Roufs, Timothy G., comp. *Working Bibliography of Chippewa/Ojibwa/Anishinabe and Selected Related Works.* Duluth: University of Minnesota Lake Superior Basin Studies Center, 1981, 1982.

Roufs, Timothy, ed. *Information Relating to Chippewa Peoples from the Handbook of American Indians North of Mexico.* Duluth: University of Minnesota Lake Superior Basin Studies Center, 1984.

Sady, Rachel Reese. "The Menominee: Transition from Trusteeship." *Applied Anthropology* 6 (Spring): 1–14.

Sahlins, Marshall. *Islands of History.* Chicago: University of Chicago Press, 1985.

Sapolsky, Robert M. *Why Zebras Don't Get Ulcers.* New York: W.H. Freeman, 1994.

Satz, Ronald. *American Indian Policy in the Jacksonian Era.* Lincoln: University of Nebraska Press, 1975.

Satz, Ronald. "Chippewa Treaty Rights: The Reserved Rights of Wisconsin's Chippewa Indians in Historical Perspective." *Transactions of the Wisconsin Academy of Sciences, Arts and Letters* 79, no. 1 (1991).

Schafer, Joseph. *The Winnebago-Horicon Basin: A Type Study in Western History.* Madison: State Historical Society of Wisconsin, 1937.

Schoolcraft, Henry Rowe. *Narrative Journal of Travels through the Northwestern Regions of the United States Extending from Detroit through the Great Lakes to the Sources of the Mississippi River in the Year 1820,* ed. Mentor L. Williams. East Lansing: Michigan State University Press, 1953.

Schoolcraft, Henry Rowe. *Schoolcraft's Expedition to Lake Itasca, the Discovery of the Source of the Mississippi,* ed. Philip P. Mason. East Lansing: Michigan State University Press, 1958.

Shames, Deborah, ed. *Freedom with Reservation: The Menominee Struggle to Save Their Land and People.* Madison: National Committee to Save the Menominee People and Forests, 1972.

Silverberg, James. "The Kickapoo Indians: First One Hundred Years of White Contact." *Wisconsin Archeologist* 38, no. 3 (1957): 71–85.

Skinner, Alanson. "A Comparative Sketch of the Menomini." *American Anthropologist,* n.s., 13 (1911): 551–65.

Skinner, Alanson B. *Material Culture of the Menomini.* New York: Museum of the American Indian, 1921.

Slotkin, James S. *The Menomini Powwow: A Study in Cultural Decay.* Milwaukee Public Museum Publication in Anthropology. Milwaukee: Milwaukee Public Museum, 1957.

Smith, Alice. *The History of Wisconsin.* Vol 1: *From Exploration to Statehood.* Madison: State Historical Society of Wisconsin, 1973.

Smith, Dwight L. "Mutual Dependency and Mutual Distrust: Indian-White Relations in British America, 1701–1763." In Philip Weeks, ed., *The American Indian Experience: A Profile, 1524 to the Present,* 49–65. Arlington Heights: Forum Press, 1988.

Smith, Huron H. "Ethnobotany of the Forest Potawatomi Indians." *Bulletin of the Public Museum of the City of Milwaukee* 7, no. 1 (May 9, 1933).

Smith, Huron H. *Ethnobotany of the Menomini Indians.* New York: Greenwood, 1970.

Smith, James G. E. *Leadership among the Southeastern Ojibwa.* National Museum of Canada Publications in Ethnology, No. 7. Ottawa: National Museums of Canada, 1973.

Smith, Jane F., and Robert M. Kvasnicka, eds. *Indian-White Relations: A Persistent Paradox.* Washington, D.C.: Howard University Press, 1976.

Smith, William Rudolph. *Incidents of a Journey from Pennsylvania to Wisconsin Territory, in 1837.* Chicago: Wright Howes, 1927.

[Snelling, William J.]. "Early Days at Prairie du Chien and Winnebago Outbreak of 1827." In *Wisconsin Historical Collections,* Vol 5, 123–53. 1868; rpt., Madison: State Historical Society of Wisconsin, 1907.

Sniffen, Matthew K. "The Need of Protecting the Indians' Interests." In *Report* of the Twenty-eighth Annual Meeting of the Lake Mohonk Conference, 17–23. N.p., 1910.

Sosin, Jack M. *Whitehall and the Wilderness: The Middle West in British Colonial Policy, 1760–1775*. Lincoln: University of Nebraska Press, 1971.

Spector, Janet Doris. "Winnebago Indians, 1634–1829: An Archaeological and Ethnohistorical Investigation." Ph.D. diss., University of Wisconsin, 1974.

Spencer, Robert F., and Jesse D. Jennings, eds. *The Native Americans*. New York: Harper and Row, 1965.

Spindler, George D. "Identity, Militancy, and Cultural Congruence: The Menominee and Kainai." *Annals of the American Academy of Political and Social Science* 436 (March): 73–85.

Spindler, George D. *Sociocultural and Psychological Processes in Menomini Acculturation*. Berkeley: University of California Press, 1955.

Spindler, George, and Louise Spindler. *Dreamers without Power: The Menomini Indians*. New York: Holt, Rinehart and Winston, 1971.

Spindler, Louise. "Menominee." In Bruce G. Trigger, ed., *Handbook of North American Indians*, Vol. 15: *Northeast*, 708–24. William C. Sturtevant, general editor. Washington, D.C.: Smithsonian Institution Press, 1978.

Stambaugh, Samuel. "Report on the Quality and Condition of Wisconsin Territory, 1831." In *Wisconsin Historical Collections*, Vol. 15, 399–438. Madison: State Historical Society of Wisconsin, 1900.

State of Wisconsin 1975 Blue Book. Madison: Department of Administration, 1975.

Sternsher, Bernard, ed. *Hitting Home: The Great Depression in Town and Country*. Chicago: Quadrangle Books, 1970.

Stevens, Wayne E. *The Northwest Fur Trade, 1703–1800*. Urbana: University of Illinois Press, 1928.

"Stockbridge Indians." *Missionary Herald* 45 (1849): 15.

Stokes, Bill. "Social Call in the Land of the Ojibwas." *Milwaukee Journal*, May 6, 1973, 20.

Stone, Lyle M., and Donald Chaput. "History of the Upper Great Lakes Area." In Bruce G. Trigger, ed., *Handbook of North American Indians*, Vol. 15: *Northeast*, 602–9. William C. Sturtevant, general editor. Washington, D.C.: Smithsonian Institution Press, 1978.

Stott, D. H. "Cultural and Natural Checks on Population Growth." In Andrew P. Vayda, ed., *Environment and Cultural Behavior: Ecological Studies in Cultural Anthropology*, 90–120. Published for the American Museum of Natural History. Garden City, N.Y.: Natural History Press, 1969.

Tanner, Helen Hornbeck. *The Ojibwas: A Critical Bibliography*. Chicago: The Newberry Library, 1976.

Tanner, Helen Hornbeck, Adele Hast, Jacqueline Peterson, and Robert J. Surtees, eds. *Atlas of Great Lakes Indian History*. Norman: University of Oklahoma Press, 1987.

Tanner, John. *A Narrative of the Captivity and Adventures of John Tanner,* ed. Edwin James. Minneapolis: Ross and Haines, 1956.

Taylor, Graham D. "Anthropologists, Reformers, and the Indian New Deal." *Prologue* 7 (Fall 1975): 151–62.

Taylor, Graham D. *The New Deal and American Indian Tribalism: The Administration of the Indian Reorganization Act, 1934–45.* Lincoln: University of Nebraska Press, 1980.

Taylor, Graham D. "The Tribal Alternative to Bureaucracy: The Indian's New Deal, 1933–1945." *Journal of the West* 13 (January 1974): 128–42.

Terkel, Studs. *Division Street: America.* "Benny Bearskin, 45," 134–42. New York: Avon Books, 1967.

Thompson, David. *David Thompson's Narrative 1784–1812,* ed. R. Glover. Toronto: The Champlain Society, 1962.

Thwaites, Reuben Gold. "The Fur Trade in Wisconsin, 1815–1817." In *Wisconsin Historical Collections,* Vol. 19, 375–488. Madison: State Historical Society of Wisconsin, 1910.

Thwaites, Reuben Gold, ed. "The British Regime in Wisconsin." In *Wisconsin Historical Collections,* Vol. 18, xi–468. Madison: State Historical Society of Wisconsin, 1908.

Thwaites, Reuben Gold, ed. "The French Regime in Wisconsin, 1634–1727," Part 1. In *Wisconsin Historical Collections,* Vol. 16, 1–477. Madison: State Historical Society of Wisconsin, 1902.

Thwaites, Reuben Gold, ed. "The French Regime in Wisconsin, 1727–1748," Part 2. In *Wisconsin Historical Collections,* Vol. 17, 1–518. Madison: State Historical Society of Wisconsin, 1906.

Thwaites, Reuben Gold, ed. *The Jesuit Relations and Allied Documents: Travels and Explorations of the Jesuit Missionaries in New France 1610–1791.* 73 vols. Cleveland: Burrows Bros., 1896–1901.

Thwaites, Reuben Gold, ed. "The Wisconsin Winnebagoes: An Interview with Moses Paquette." In *Wisconsin Historical Collections,* Vol. 12, 399–433. Madison: State Historical Society of Wisconsin, 1892.

Titus, W. A. "A Brief Account of the Stockbridge." *Wisconsin Magazine of History* 30 (1946–47): 423–32.

Titus, W. A. "Historic Spots in Wisconsin. Brothertown: A Wisconsin Story with a New England Background." *Wisconsin Magazine of History* 21 (September–June 1937–38): 293–300.

Titus, Willard H. "Observations on the Menominee Indians." *Wisconsin Magazine of History* 14 (September–June 1930–31): 93–105, 121–32.

Tooker, Elisabeth. "Wyandot." In Bruce G. Trigger, ed., *Handbook of North American Indians,* Vol. 15: *Northeast,* 398–406. William C. Sturtevant, general editor. Washington, D.C.: Smithsonian Institution Press, 1978.

Trask, Kerry A. "Settlement in a Half-Savage Land: Life and Loss in the Metis Community of La Baye." *Michigan Historical Review* 15 (Spring 1989): 1–27.

Trigger, Bruce G. *The Children of Aataentsic: A History of the Huron People to 1660,* Vol. 1. Montreal: McGill-Queen's University Press, 1976.

Trigger, Bruce G. "Cultural Unity and Diversity." In Bruce G. Trigger, ed., *Handbook of North American Indians,* Vol. 15: *Northeast,* 798–804. William C. Sturtevant, general editor. Washington, D.C.: Smithsonian Institution Press, 1978.

Trigger, Bruce G. *The Huron: Farmers of the North.* New York: Holt, Rinehart and Winston, 1969.

Trigger, Bruce G. *Natives and Newcomers: Canada's "Heroic Age" Reconsidered.* Kingston and Montreal: McGill-Queen's University Press, 1985.

Trigger, Bruce G., ed. *Handbook of North American Indians.* Vol. 15: *Northeast.* William C. Sturtevant, general editor. Washington, D.C.: Smithsonian Institution, 1978.

Turner, Andrew Jackson. "The History of Fort Winnebago." In *Wisconsin Historical Collections,* Vol. 14, 65–102. Madison: State Historical Society of Wisconsin, 1898.

Turner, Frederick Jackson. *The Character and Influence of the Indian Trade in Wisconsin: A Study of the Trading Post as an Institution.* 1891; rpt., Norman: University of Oklahoma Press, 1977.

Usabel, Frances de, and Jane A. Roeber, comps. *American Indian Resources Manual for Public Libraries.* Madison: Wisconsin Department of Public Instruction, 1992.

Van Thiel, David H., Judith Gavaler, and Roger Lester. "Ethanol Inhibition of Vitamin A Metabolism in the Testes: Possible Mechanism for Sterility in Alcoholics." *Science* 186 (December 6, 1974): 941–42.

Vayda, Andrew P., ed. *Environment and Cultural Behavior: Ecological Studies in Cultural Anthropology.* Published for the American Museum of Natural History. Garden City, N.Y.: Natural History Press, 1969.

Vecsey, Christopher. *Traditional Ojibwa Religion and Its Historical Changes.* Philadelphia: American Philosophical Society, 1983.

Vecsey, Christopher, and Robert W. Venables, eds. *American Indian Environments: Ecological Issues in Native American History.* Syracuse: Syracuse University Press, 1980.

Vennum, Thomas J., Jr. *The Ojibwa Dance Drum: Its History and Construction.* Smithsonian Folklife Studies, No. 2. Washington, D.C.: Smithsonian Institution, 1982.

Vennum, Thomas J., Jr. *Wild Rice and the Ojibway People.* St. Paul: Minnesota Historical Society, 1988.

Viola, Herman. *Thomas L. McKenney: Architect of America's Early Indian Policy, 1816–1830.* Chicago: Swallow Press, 1974.

Vizenor, Gerald. *The People Named the Chippewa: Narrative Histories.* Minneapolis: University of Minnesota Press, 1984.

Vizenor, Gerald. *Wordarrows: Indians and Whites in the New Fur Trade*. Minneapolis: University of Minnesota Press, 1978.

Wallace, Anthony F. C. *The Death and Rebirth of the Seneca*. New York: Alfred A. Knopf, 1969.

Wallace, Anthony F. C. *Prelude to Disaster: The Course of Indian-White Relations Which Led to the Black Hawk War of 1832*. Springfield: Illinois State Historical Library, 1970.

Wallace, W. S. "The Beginnings of British Rule in Canada." *Canadian Historical Review* 6 (1925): 209–11.

Walters, Ronald. *American Reformers, 1815–1860*. New York: Hill and Wang, 1978.

Warren, William Whipple. *History of the Ojibways, Based upon Tradition and Oral Statements*. St. Paul: Minnesota Historical Society Press, 1984.

Washburn, Wilcomb E. *The American Indian and the United States: A Documentary History*, Vol. 3. New York: Random House, 1973.

Washburn, Wilcomb E. *The Assault on Indian Tribalism: The General Allotment Law (Dawes Act) of 1887*. Philadelphia: J. P. Lippencott, 1975.

Weeks, Philip, ed. *The American Indian Experience: A Profile, 1524 to the Present*. Arlington Heights: Forum Press, 1988.

White, Richard. *The Middle Ground: Indians, Empires, and Republics in the Great Lakes Region, 1650–1815*. New York: Cambridge University Press, 1991.

Whitney, Ellen M., ed. *The Black Hawk War, 1831–1832*. 3 vols. Collections of the Illinois State Historical Library, Vols. 35–37. Springfield: Illinois State Historical Library, 1970–75.

Wilson, Clyde H. "A New Interpretation of the Wild Rice District of Wisconsin." *American Anthropologist* 58, no. 6 (1956): 1059–64.

"Winnebago Hostilities." In *Wisconsin Historical Collections*, Vol. 20, 139–44. Madison: State Historical Society of Wisconsin, 1911.

Zanger, Martin. "Conflicting Concepts of Justice: A Winnebago Murder Trial on the Illinois Frontier." *Journal of the Illinois State Historical Society* 73 (1980): 263–76.

Zanger, Martin. "Red Bird." In R. David Edmunds, ed., *American Indian Leaders: Studies in Diversity*, 64–87. Lincoln: University of Nebraska Press, 1980.

Index

Acculturation, 148, 162; under federal policies, 152, 203, 204, 207; of the Menominee, 159–60, 161–62; through military service, 159, 188–89

Adoptions, effect on group identity, 96

Agent, Indian: power on Ojibwa reservations, 166–67, 170; role in Menominee society, 163–64; and tribal government, 207

Agriculture, 14, 16, 71; American and immigrant, 134–35, 154, 156; among the Sauk, 88; Fox patterns, 76, 88; Menominee, 25–26, 156; Ojibwa attempts at, 196; Winnebago, 39, 56, 89, 206

AIM (American Indian Movement), 6

A'kwine'mi (Menominee chief), 159

Alcoholism, 84–85, 90, 137, 139, 141; liqour as trade item, 83, 97–98; violence due to, 98, 141

Alexian Brothers novitiate, 6

Algonquian peoples, 64–69, 71; cultural patterns, 23–37. *See also* Fox; Kickapoo; Mascouten; Menominee; Miami; Ojibwa; Potawatomi; Sauk

Alliances: between British and Indians, 136–37; between French and Indians, 48–52; between Indian peoples, 57, 58, 65, 85, 86, 96. *See also* individual peoples

Allotments: on Oneida reservation, 164–65; refused by Menominee, 203

Allouez, Claude, 14, 17, 18, 61; observations of Indians, 56, 59, 74

Amata (Menominee chief), 140

American Fur Company, 134, 138, 139, 239n30

American Indian Chicago Conference (1961), 4, 210

American Indian Movement (AIM), 6

American Revolution, effect on British-Indian relations, 83–85

Amherst, Lord Jeffrey, 79, 83

Andre, Louis, 61

Annuity payments, 134, 142, 159, 165; used for liqour, 141, 148; used for trader goods, 139, 141

Archiquette, John (Oneida), 164

Army, U.S.: attempts to police Wisconsin Territory, 126, 128; removal of Winnebago to Nebraska, 171; Wisconsin Indians' service, 159, 197–98, *illus.* 188–90

Ashland, Wis., 168

Assiniboin, 67

Assemblies, colonial, Indian policies, 81, 83

Astor, John Jacob, 134

Atkinson, Henry, 132

Bad River reservation, 195

Balfour, Captain, 78

Band system: adopted by the Menominee, 63; among the Fox, 75–76; in Ojibwa culture, 31, 93, 98

Bark, uses made by Indians, 18, 25, 27

Baskets, sales to tourists, 196, *illus.* 183

Bear Clan: role in Menominee culture, 23–24, 26, 159; role in Winnebago culture, 24, 40–41

277

Index